That Ye May Teach the Children

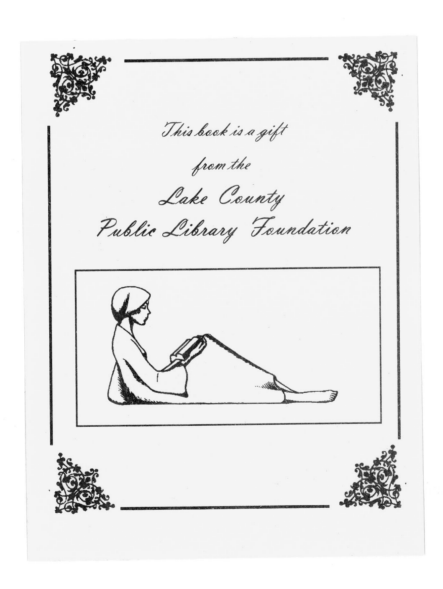

That Ye May Teach The Children

A Bible Outline with Questions for Parents and Teachers

by
Joan Koelle Snipes

cover art and illustrations by
Kristin Joy Pratt Serafini

Bible Teaching Press
Shepherdstown, West Virginia
2001

Bible Teaching Press
2016 Willowdale Drive
Shepherdstown, WV 25443
(304) 876-1332
snipes@principia.edu

Copyright © 2001 by Joan Koelle Snipes

Second Edition, revised, 2001

ISBN   0-9674009-1-0

Illustrations by Kristin Joy Pratt Serafini
Book and cover design by Michael Höhne

Title of the First Edition, copyrighted in 1999:
Bible Study for Children: An Outline with Questions for Parents and Teachers

Printed in the United States of America

To my Sunday School students

"…continue thou in the things which thou hast learned and hast been assured of, knowing of whom thou hast learned them; And that from a child thou hast known the holy scriptures, which are able to make thee wise unto salvation through faith which is in Christ Jesus.

All scripture is given by inspiration of God, and is profitable for doctrine, for reproof, for correction, for instruction in righteousness: That the man of God may be perfect, throughly furnished unto all good works."

II Timothy 3:14-17

Table of Contents

Old
Testament

New
Testament

Vocabulary
Questions

Review
Questions

Worksheets

Worksheets

Bibliography

Index

List of Maps and Illustrations

Notes

That Ye May Teach the Children

Acknowledgments

I owe thanks to many, many people for their help and inspiration in my journey to learn more about the Bible. They include, above all, my many Sunday School pupils. I think gratefully and happily of every student I have ever had, but want to mention Jeff Luzadder, a pupil in my Sunday School class in Reston, Virginia. I remember him with fondness and gratitude, for he motivated me to be extra prepared each Sunday.

Among those who have shed light on the Bible for me are: Arline Walker Evans, Dr. Elaine Follis, Lorine Richmond Wheaton, Joseph M. Caldwell, B. Cobbey Crisler, Kathryn L. Merrill, Dr. Elizabeth Carey, Dr. Frank C. Darling, Pamela L. Bradford, Honey Dobyns, Gail Haslam, and dozens of authors of books and periodical articles about the Bible.

Several people read and commented on drafts of this book. I am grateful to all of them for taking the time to do this. The book is much improved thanks to their input. They include: Dr. Christopher Scott Langton, Beverly Jean Scott, Linda Swanson, Anne Elizabeth Kidder, Dr. Russell D. Robinson, Ann F. S. Cummings, Susan Koelle Olsen, Penny D. Seay, Kristy L. Christian, Nancy Charlton, Olene Carroll, and James Cook Snipes.

The second edition of this book is much improved thanks to the splendid efforts of my copy editor, Enicia Fisher.

Special thanks go to my parents, Paul Warren Koelle and Betty Tomlinson Koelle, whose example of daily Bible study laid the foundation for my love of the Bible. I'm also grateful to my two daughters, Amy and Kimberly, for answering hundreds of questions about the Bible.

For his incredible support and help on this project, my final thanks go to my husband, Robert T. Snipes.

Preface

The purpose of this book is to give parents and Sunday School teachers immediately useful ideas for teaching children about the Bible. This book presents an outline of the Bible and questions corresponding to the better-known stories and passages. The title of the book, a quote from Leviticus, summarizes the book's purpose: "that ye may teach the children" (see Leviticus 10:11). The underlying premise is that parents and Sunday School teachers can teach the fundamentals of the Bible by reading or telling the stories and then asking questions (although the questions presented herein are by no means an exhaustive treatment of the Bible). I have considerable experience using these questions as a teaching tool; the system is both child-tested and time-tested.

To make the questions easily retrievable, I have arranged them into a simple outline that follows the order of the sixty-six books of the Bible from Genesis to Revelation. The King James Version of the Bible is quoted most often, though I have often consulted other English translations of the Bible.

The questions are written for a wide range of ages. I have used some of these questions with a class of two-year-olds and some with high school students. Most are aimed at about the fourth to sixth grade level, though they can be adapted to children much younger or older. These questions are meant to be a springboard for many other questions that teachers and students will ask about the Bible.

This book is not intended to be formulaic. Each parent or Sunday School teacher needs to pray and prepare individually for teaching children at home or church. This book is simply my sharing of a rather simple idea that has worked for me. It has been my experience that the question and answer format allows for a lively class with many interactions, which is preferable to a lecture style presentation. Questions should go both ways, with pupils asking their own questions as well. The questions in this book are intended not only as a springboard for deeper discussions in Sunday School class, but for deeper study of the Bible. My hope is that others will find this system of using the outline of the Bible and selected questions helpful and inspiring.

Evolution of this book

The idea to write this book came as a result of my Sunday School teaching experience. During my growing up years, I had some sincere, loving, well intentioned, and, occasionally, inspired Sunday School teachers. However, as a young adult with a desire to serve my church, I discovered that I actually knew very little about the Bible or how to teach effectively its contents to young people. I also observed that I was not the only member of my church with this problem. So, I delved into the Bible and reference books for guidance.

Among the first helpful books I read were a series of three paperbacks entitled *Guide for Bible Teaching* by Ann Putcamp. The author suggested questions to use with Sunday School classes of various ages. I used those questions as examples of others I might write on my own. Soon, I was writing questions every week for use in my Sunday School class. Writing a good question, be it a simple comprehension question, a multiple-choice question, or a more thought-provoking question, proved to be a time-consuming process. Some questions were better than others. I eliminated questions that were poorly worded, ambiguous, or trivial. And I began saving the good questions.

I wrote each question on a four-by-six index card and put the answer, along with citations and related information, on the back of the card. One of my earliest classes included a group of bright four-year-olds who did not yet read but were rapidly acquiring reading readiness skills. I used larger cards for this class and printed simple questions on the cards with colored markers. Using this method of asking questions had a number of unexpected benefits. For one thing, the children sometimes weren't able to distinguish when I was asking them a question and expected an answer and when I was just sharing information. But once I used the cards, they knew when a question was directed at them. Also, by occasionally pointing to the words of the question, the children learned to sight-read easy words, such as God and love. Using the question cards enabled the children to identify the key points I was trying to teach.

Eventually, I had a large stack of cards that I intended to reuse on other occasions with my Sunday School class. At that point I was faced with the need to develop a way to retrieve questions on a particular topic. This is how the outline to the Bible evolved. On each card, I wrote the Roman numeral, letters, and numbers that corresponded with the Bible outline. The outline numbers enabled me to file and retrieve the index cards in a box. I wrote the questions first, as a general rule, and then expanded my simple outline to include them.

This book does not include the answers for the questions. However, there are citations for most questions and most outline headings. The answers may be found in the Bible. Both teacher and child should turn to the Bible passages for answers. This book is intended for the teacher's use before entering the Sunday School. It should not be taken into class, because the emphasis should always be on the Bible texts themselves.

I have changed and expanded my outline numerous times over the years. It began as a single-page document. The process of outlining the whole Bible has been challenging, enriching, and inspiring. Although highlights of the entire Bible are included, I have gone into much more depth in some areas than in others. Two areas where I have a great many questions include the Ten Commandments and the Sermon on the Mount (including the Beatitudes and our Lord's Prayer.)

Although this work includes at least one question on every book of the Bible, it is not a balanced treatment of all aspects of the Bible. I have emphasized stories and passages which traditionally appeal to children. There is also an emphasis on the history of the Hebrew people. I have had to omit some of my favorite Bible passages (Isaiah 54, for example) because they do not lend themselves to the type of basic comprehension questions presented here. Well-known stories, such as David and Goliath and Daniel in the lions' den, necessarily lay the foundation for Bible literacy.

As I developed my own outline of the Bible, I found two books of particular help: Russell Robinson's *Teaching the Scriptures: A Study Guide for Bible Students and Teachers* and *An Outline of the Bible: Book by Book* by Benson Y. Landis. They gave me the necessary information to design my own Bible outline. Both books are still in print, reasonably priced, relatively short, and written by lay students of the Bible. Together with a good Bible dictionary, these resources offer solid information that is easily understood by someone without much previous background.

My background

Since 1974 I have been a Sunday School teacher in various branches of The First Church of Christ, Scientist. I have also taught several years in a community ecumenical Vacation Bible School in Shepherdstown, West Virginia. Most of my Bible teaching experience has been with children of elementary school age. I've also used the outline and questions in this book to teach the Bible to my own two daughters, Amy and Kim, who are now college students.

I earned a Bachelor of Arts degree from Principia College in Elsah, Illinois, where I double majored in elementary education and English. I have taught children in public and private schools and Head Start.

Joan Koelle Snipes
Shepherdstown, West Virginia
Second edition, December, 2000

Chronology

Sunday School teachers should begin giving children a sense of the Bible's chronology at a young age. This can begin with simple questions comparing major biblical figures such as Moses and Jesus and asking who lived first. There are many helpful timelines and chronological Bibles available. The following timeline utilizes dates provided in *The One Year Chronological Bible, New International Version*.

ca.	2160 BCE	Abraham's call.
ca.	2060 BCE	Isaac's birth.
ca.	1898 BCE	Joseph sold into slavery.
ca.	1446 BCE	The Exodus from Egypt.
ca.	1445 BCE	God gives Moses the Ten Commandments.
ca.	1367 BCE	Othniel becomes the first of Israel's fourteen judges.
ca.	1105 BCE	Samuel's birth.
ca.	1050 BCE	Saul becomes Israel's first king.
ca.	1010 BCE	David becomes king.
ca.	971 BCE	Solomon becomes king.
ca.	959 BCE	The first temple in Jerusalem is completed.
ca.	930 BCE	The kingdom splits into two parts: Israel and Judah.
ca.	740 BCE	Isaiah's ministry begins.
ca.	722 BCE	The Northern Kingdom (Israel) falls to Assyria.
ca.	701 BCE	Sennacherib, king of Assyria, fails to conquer Jerusalem.
ca.	627 BCE	Jeremiah's ministry begins.
ca.	609 BCE	Josiah, king of Judah, killed in battle at Megiddo.
ca.	605 BCE	Daniel exiled to Babylon.
ca.	605 BCE	Nebuchadnezzar ascended throne in Babylon.
ca.	586 BCE	Judah falls to Babylonia (Chaldea); temple destroyed.
ca.	539 BCE	The fall of Babylonia to Cyrus of Persia.
ca.	538 BCE	The edict of Cyrus permits first exiles to return to Jerusalem.
ca.	516 BCE	The second temple in Jerusalem is completed and dedicated.
ca.	479 BCE	Esther becomes queen of Persia.
ca.	458 BCE	Ezra returns to Jerusalem from exile. (This date is debated.)
ca.	445 BCE	Nehemiah returns to Jerusalem; rebuilds wall.
ca.	433 BCE	Malachi's ministry begins.
ca.	6 BCE	Jesus' birth.
ca.	26 CE	John baptizes Jesus.
ca.	33 CE	Jesus' resurrection and ascension.
ca.	33 CE	Pentecost.
ca.	34 CE	Paul's conversion.

For more detailed chronologies, see *The New Westminster Dictionary of the Bible*, pages 162–175, or *An Outline of the Bible, Book by Book*, pp.176–178. The abbreviation ca. means "about or approximately."

Introduction

The following introductory pages are intended to give Sunday School teachers and parents some guidance in using this book. My hope is that a new teacher, equipped with this book, will immediately have some practical, helpful tools to employ for that very first class. However, the focus of this book is not teaching methods or a comprehensive treatment of how to teach Sunday School. Rather, I am sharing one method of teaching the Bible that has worked for me. Teachers should note that there are a wide array of options available to them, in the areas of teaching methods, techniques, and resources.

Content of this book

Questions in this book are divided into six major sections:

    I **Introductory Questions**
    II **Old Testament**
    III **New Testament**
    IV **Vocabulary Questions**
    V **Review Questions for Old and New Testaments**
    VI **Bible Study Worksheets**

The questions in Section I constitute a simple introduction to the Bible in outline form. Knowing something of the Bible's design, authorship, chronology, and historical setting gives children a framework on which to hang the many stories and Bible facts they will learn.

Old Testament

The next section of questions covers the Old Testament, book by book. Some of the Bible stories appear more than once. Some scholars refer to the duplication of a story as a "doublet." Sometimes, biblical authors used different sources and a very early editor wove the two versions together into one written account. This practice accounts for some of the small contradictions in Old Testament stories. Many of the stories in the Chronicles are repeats of stories told in Kings. Scholars believe the accounts in Kings were written first. The Chronicler retold the stories, with an emphasis on the Southern Kingdom's point of view. Occasionally, a story appears three times, as is the case with Hezekiah, a king of Judah. Besides appearing in Kings and Chronicles, Hezekiah's story is also told in the book of Isaiah. (See *Who Wrote the Bible?*, Friedman, p. 22.)

New Testament

Although most of the questions in this book follow a book by book organization, the questions concerning the Gospel stories from Matthew, Mark, Luke, and John are combined. The questions generally follow a "Harmony of the Gospels," outlined in *The New Westminster Dictionary of the Bible*, pp. 342–349. One of the reasons I elected this approach with the Gospels was so I could group the parables and the healings performed by Jesus. However, with high school aged students, I think it is helpful to consider the four Gospels separately, so that students can grasp the particular flavor of each of the four writers.

Although one section of this book focuses on the Acts, Paul's life and ministry merits an additional, separate section. Each of the fifteen epistles are listed separately in the New Testament outline, and there is at least one question about each of those epistles. The New Testament section concludes with questions about Revelation, the last book of the Bible.

Vocabulary Questions

The fourth section of this book contains an alphabetical list of questions focused on vocabulary. Every Sunday School session should contain at least a couple of questions related to vocabulary. There are many words that are initially unfamiliar to children, and it is well to increase their familiarity with the meanings of Bible words, in the context of stories, every week. The vocabulary section of this book is not at all comprehensive but gives a sampling of words children will need to learn as their Bible knowledge increases.

There are several ways you can approach vocabulary questions. Sometimes, as a child reads the Bible story aloud, I simply tell him the meanings of strange words as we go along. This method has the advantage of keeping attention on the narrative, without getting the child bogged down in turning to a Bible dictionary repeatedly. When those same strange words appear in subsequent questions during class time, the child will most likely remember the meaning. Sometimes, however, it is good practice to look up words in either a regular dictionary or a Bible dictionary. Although Barbara Smith's *Young People's Bible Dictionary* is designed specifically for children, many words in the vocabulary section of this book are not defined in her book. Teachers should always be sure a particular word is in the dictionary before having a child turn to it. Not finding a word consumes valuable class time and can be frustrating to a young child.

Another difficulty with the use of dictionaries is the sometimes long, complicated defi-

nitions given for a word. Teachers might want to prepare a list of new vocabulary encountered in the Bible stories they are teaching, and simply have simple definitions written out for each of those words. A collection of new vocabulary words could be kept at Sunday School in a box with index cards arranged alphabetically.

Review Questions for Old and New Testaments

A section of Review Questions follows the Vocabulary section. Children benefit from reviewing some stories almost every week. I try to allow plenty of time for review, and I find that this period of our class time together is generally the children's favorite. Children enjoy showing what they remember and getting a chance to share what they have learned over a period of time. I try to make the review sessions rather fast-paced. We don't dwell long on any one character, story, or time period. Regular review reinforces the stories and builds the children's confidence about what they know. If a child stumbles on a question, have another child quickly tell the relevant story. Or, review the highlights of that story yourself. Or, just skip that question and go on to one that is easier. Sometimes, if no one remembers an answer, I tell the class the answer and promise that they will see that question again — either before class is over or the following week. Consistent review sessions will enable the child to effortlessly memorize the names of major Bible people and associate their names with important stories and passages. For instance, regularly asking questions about Moses and the Ten Commandments helps the children link the two.

Bible Study Worksheets

The last section of this book consists of Bible study worksheets, which were designed as homework assignments. They are usually fairly simple, and students should be able to do a worksheet in about fifteen minutes. I recommend using worksheets only to review material that has already been covered in class. In other words, before a child attempts the worksheet about Jacob, he should already be familiar with all the stories covered in that worksheet. When I teach Sunday School, we usually only have time to read and discuss two or three stories per class period. Therefore, even with a focus on Jacob, it would probably take at least two weeks before I would assign the Jacob worksheet for homework. When I begin teaching a new group of students, it is usually at least a month before I give the first homework assignment. Once I begin giving homework, I do not necessarily assign a worksheet every week.

The worksheets are arranged in the same order as the outline for this book. They begin with Introductory Information about the Bible, the Old Testament, the New Testament, Vocabulary, and Review. There are two basic types of worksheets. The first type covers one individual and asks a series of questions about that person. The second type of worksheet includes a set of review questions grouped thematically. This type usually has the answers at the bottom of the page.

There are five worksheets that correspond to Introductory Information about the Bible. The titles of those worksheets are: Bible Design, Bible Themes, Literary Styles in the Bible, Famous Quotations, and Chronology. Only the worksheet titled Bible Design is appropriate for younger classes. The other four are for more advanced students and would logically follow many of the worksheets which center on a particular individual and ask more in-depth questions. One of the most difficult worksheets is Chronology. Students normally do the Chronology worksheet after all forty-three of the other worksheets are completed. Ideally, the child should

already be familiar with a Bible timeline when he tackles the Chronology worksheet.

The largest group of worksheets focuses on the Old Testament. I generally start with Abraham and Sarah, followed by Jacob and Joseph. Those stories are all found in Genesis and provide a solid foundation for future Bible study. There are nineteen worksheets with an Old Testament emphasis. After doing the three worksheets about the patriarchs, I would recommend doing a New Testament worksheet next. The Christmas Story is a logical first choice. I think it is wise to keep a balance between the Old and New Testaments when assigning the worksheets. Staying with the Old Testament until all the topics are completed would require too many consecutive weeks.

There are twelve worksheets focusing on New Testament topics. Some of the individuals mentioned are somewhat minor, compared to major figures such as Jesus, Abraham, Moses, David, and Paul. I recommend that as a general rule, a teacher cover the most important people and stories first, followed by the lesser known individuals.

The next two worksheets have to do with vocabulary: Biblical Vocabulary and Vocabulary Match. Again, the child should have encountered at least a few of these words during class sessions before they are given the worksheets. I recommend spacing these worksheets. A child will probably not enjoy doing vocabulary homework two weeks in a row.

Finally, there is a section of review worksheets. They include these titles: Prayer, Kings, Mothers, Women of the Bible, Who Said This?, and Z Words. Perhaps the easiest and most logical first choice for a review worksheet is the one entitled Prayer. Who Said This? requires the student to look up a series of quotes and is relatively easy for good readers.

The worksheets may be reproduced and used in any order by the teacher. Although the worksheets with one or two word answers at the bottom of the page tend to be the easier ones, they usually cover five to eight Bible stories and should be used for review.

Ideas for using the questions in Sunday School teaching

Many of the comprehension questions in this book center on small details within the Bible stories. By looking carefully at the Bible verses, the children build a broad understanding from a simple beginning. Learning the details of a story often makes that story more alive for the children. The first step in Bible study is a simple comprehension of the vocabulary, plot, and characters.

Questions, particularly in areas of emphasis, are deliberately repetitive, asking the same thing in a new way. This varying of the questions is important to prevent boredom. It is certainly not intended that every question be used with every retelling of a particular story. Sometimes it happens that just one or two questions on a given passage are all that is necessary during one Sunday School session. The questions in this book are generally written to stand alone, and this means that they can be pulled out of the outline's order and asked as a review question without revision.

Using a question-and-answer teaching method with children has worked well for me. It is important to keep in mind, however, that knowing the "right answers" is not the goal. The goal is gaining familiarity with the Bible, "the Book of books."

The questions in this book may be used in a variety of ways. The first step in the teaching process is to read or tell a passage or story to the children. For the youngest children, stories such as Noah's ark, Daniel in the lions' den, or the Good Samaritan parable are excellent first choices. Immediately follow the narrative with questions.

The children generally read aloud a card with the printed question on it, and then answer it. If they have trouble, other children are asked to help. In younger classes, a limited number of question cards are used over and over again. This gives the children the opportunity to master a few basic stories or verses and their correlative questions. The repetition enables the children to learn the answers during a class period or two. If the children are too young to read, I select simple, short questions and read them aloud to the class, pointing at the card (or, sometimes, each word on the card.)

At first, the children may have difficulty answering even the easiest comprehension question. Once they understand the teacher's expectations, however, the children will learn to listen carefully, both for the main ideas of the story and for details. With practice, the children will be able to demonstrate their comprehension of vocabulary, chronology, and the story's spiritual significance by answering simple questions. Children love to recite the facts of a story. Soon they are able to tell the story themselves. Once they have mastered the plot and characters of two or three Bible stories, the questions for those stories may be combined and used as a review tool.

Before teaching a Sunday School class, I make a short outline of material I plan to cover. Then, I pull from the card file questions that correspond to the given stories or passages for that day's lesson. Having the questions written on cards enables the children to read the questions aloud, allowing them to have the floor during class time more often. The written questions also serve as a signal that this is an important point — one the child is likely to see again sometime. Also, when things get bogged down in class (when I'm spending too long on one point), I can sense the need for a change and simply move on to the next question, without having to give much thought to what should come next.

I have found it most effective to use a combination of *new* stories and *review* stories or passages during each class period. Children need to review the basics over and over again, both to recall a given passage and to provide a foundation for new insights on the material. The introduction of new material keeps the class dynamic. Reviewing familiar material, the children can demonstrate their mastery of a topic.

In a 45-minute Bible teaching session, I try to divide the time into sections. The first of these is a time to tell or read stories and passages. The next section is the time for questions and answers, with periods of extended discussion occurring naturally. In other words, the teacher can expand on a point raised in a question and try to lead the group into a discussion. Once finished, the class can move on to the next question. Finally, once the questions on the stories or passages featured that Sunday are finished, reviewing material from previous weeks is a good way to end the class.

Using the cards with questions on them in a Sunday School class in a competitive way usually is not a good idea. The weight of a right or wrong answer becomes too great, and wondering who answered the most questions correctly becomes an unnecessary distraction. What has worked best for me is to give each child a question/card in turn. The child gets to hold the card, whether he or she can answer correctly alone or not. By the end of a class period, each child has had the opportunity to focus on the same number of questions as every other child. Thus, when you have a newcomer in a class with some regular attendees, that newcomer has as many cards to hold as does anyone else. I try to give the easier questions to the newcomers, even if this means altering the order of who

gets the next question. The children understand and easily adapt.

Although most of the questions have one factual answer, some have the possibility of several different correct answers. Often interpretive questions elicit a wide variety of correct answers.

Using the Illustrations

The illustrations in this book may be used in several different ways. For young children, these line drawings by Kristin Pratt Serafini may be copied and used for coloring. For all ages, the illustrations can be copied and used as a tool for teaching chronology. For example, teachers can point to the picture of Joseph in his coat of many colours and the one of baby Jesus with Mary and Joseph and ask, Who lived first? As children gain an understanding of who lived first, teachers may ask them to sort a group of five pictures chronologically, arranging them in order from left to right.

English Versions of the Bible and Bible Resources

Any student of the Bible has to make decisions about what to read among the vast amount of material available regarding the Bible. Among the first of these decisions is which Bibles to use. There are numerous versions and translations of the English Bible available, including condensed, chronological, reference, study, retold, paraphrased, illustrated, online, and children's. Most Bible students use more than one type of Bible.

One source with a helpful, annotated list of Bibles and study aids is Robinson's *Teaching the Scriptures*, pages 119–136. Blair's *Abingdon Bible Handbook* gives a full description and history of many English versions in use today on pages 38–56.

Students of the Bible need a few basic tools, including a Bible dictionary and a concordance. Beyond that, there are numerous books offering insight and background on the Bible. A visit to the library (public, college, or church) is one good way to learn what is available. Most books have bibliographies which will point to other sources. *The Cambridge Companion to the Bible* has four lengthy bibliographical essays, for example.

With young children I have enjoyed using some retold and simplified story books with illustrations. Usually, however, I prefer telling the Bible story in my own words or having the older children read directly from the Bible itself. In my view, gaining familiarity with the actual text of the Bible is one of the purposes of Sunday School.

Citations

In most cases, if a child cannot answer a question, this book makes it easy for teacher and student to turn to the appropriate place in the Bible to find the answer. Citations for Bible stories are included for most questions. If there are no citations listed, as in the case of some of the review questions, teacher and child should consult a Bible concordance in book form (for example, *Cruden's*) or on a computer.

Very occasionally in this book, there will be a question without a citation because the child is expected to find the answer or verse without aid. These rare questions are for the more advanced student who is very familiar with the Scriptures. Generally speaking, I require very little memorization. I do point the students in my classes to Exodus 20 and Matthew 5 frequently and expect that they will know how to locate the Ten commandments and the Beatitudes without prompting after a few sessions.

The design of the Bible

The outline of this book follows the order of English Bibles. For this reason, it is impor-

tant to consider how the sixty-six books of the Bible came to be organized the way they are.

The Bible is not just one book written by one author. It is more like a library of books. It was written over a period of many years by a number of different writers. Writing styles in the Bible vary considerably. One can find history, poetry, short stories, laws, prophecy, drama, letters, genealogy, biography, theology, essays, songs, revelation, sermons, and parables. The Hebrew Bible is arranged in three parts: the Law or Torah, the Prophets, and the Writings or Hagiographa.

In his book *How Came the Bible?*, Edgar J. Goodspeed notes that "Deuteronomy was the first presentation of the Hebrew law in anything resembling a book, and this book became the kernel of the Old Testament" (p. 24). He adds: "Wherever the Jews wandered, they organized synagogues and read and studied the Law. It became their supreme treasure" (p. 26). Eventually, the Law was translated from Hebrew into Greek. At this point, the Law was divided into five rolls and given the names we know them by today — Genesis, Exodus, Leviticus, Numbers, and Deuteronomy. These five books are also referred to as the Pentateuch.

Hebrew literature that ultimately constituted Old Testament canon "grew up by degrees and was carefully preserved" (see "canon" in *The New Westminster Dictionary of the Bible*, p. 143). Writings by the Prophets were next added to the Old Testament. In the Hebrew canon, the Prophets are divided into the Former (Joshua, Judges, I and II Samuel, I and II Kings) and the Latter (Isaiah, Jeremiah, Ezekiel, and the Twelve or "minor prophets," which follow directly after Ezekiel and have the same order as in the English Bible).

According to Blair's *Abingdon Bible Handbook*, "In Jewish circles at the time of Jesus much literature not in the Law and the

Prophets also was read, including the eleven books now in 'the Writings'" (p. 30). The Writings (listed in the traditional Jewish arrangement) include these books: Psalms, Proverbs, Job, Song of Songs, Ruth, Lamentations, Ecclesiastes, Esther, Daniel, Ezra, Nehemiah, I and II Chronicles.

The canon of the Old Testament in the English Bible contains the same books as the Hebrew Bible. The main differences are the order, how they are counted, and how they are categorized or divided.

The English Bible is made up of two Testaments, the Old and the New. The Old Testament is further divisible into four parts: The Law (also called the Pentateuch or Books of Moses), the Books of History, the Books of Poetry and Wisdom Literature, and the Books of Prophecy. *That Ye May Teach the Children* uses these four divisions to help children see the relationship of the thirty-nine books of the Old Testament. Having children learn the names of all thirty-nine books in order is desirable, but rarely accomplished. Therefore, learning the four major categories of each Testament is a more reachable goal.

Teachers should be cautious about presenting this arrangement as the only acceptable one. Although helpful to beginning students of the Bible, it can be misleading. For example, a number of the Books of Prophecy were written in poetry. Proverbs is a collection of maxims or wise sayings and is not technically poetry. Designating the first five books as the Books of Moses makes the designation parallel with the Books of History, but is not accurate since Moses himself wrote little or none of the books. Still, I have concluded that categorizing the Old Testament books is helpful to children. For more information on the arrangement of the books of the Bible, please consult one of the many reference books which address this issue more fully.

The **Old Testament** consists of thirty-nine books divided as follows:

   the Law, also called the Books of Moses or the Pentateuch (five: Genesis through Deuteronomy)

   the Books of History (twelve: Joshua through Esther)

   the Books of Poetry and Wisdom Literature (five: Job through the Song of Solomon)

   the Books of Prophecy (seventeen: Isaiah through Malachi)

The **New Testament** consists of twenty-seven books divided as follows:

   Gospels (four: Matthew, Mark, Luke and John)

   history (one: The Acts of the Apostles, a sequel to Luke)

   epistles or letters (twenty-one: Romans through Jude)

   Revelation or Apocalypse (one: Revelation, the last book of the Bible)

Who wrote the Bible?

With very young students I spend very little time on the topic of the Bible's authorship. I explain that many different people wrote the Bible over a long period of time. When I ask the question, "Who wrote the Bible?" I am simply checking to see that the children understand this simple point. Young children accept the explanation that we don't know the names of many of the Bible writers.

Older students might enjoy exploring the subject of the Bible's authorship in more detail. One source I have found helpful is Richard E. Friedman's book, *Who Wrote the Bible?*, which is available in paperback.

Scripture quotations, spellings, capitalization and abbreviations

Unless otherwise noted, Scripture quotations are from the King James Version of the Bible. The spellings of personal names, geographical place names, and various other words are those used in the King James Version of the Bible. I have usually retained the spelling and capitalization of words used in the King James Version of the Bible to enable users of my book to quickly find words in a Bible concordance. These spellings are frequently the British spelling or a less used spelling, and they include such words as: colour, neighbour and recompence.

CE, meaning "of the common era," and BCE, meaning "before the common era," are equivalent to A.D. and B.C.

A note about the Gospel of Mark

Bible scholars question whether the last twelve verses of Mark were an original part of this Gospel. The Revised Standard Version prints these verses (*Mark 16:9–20*) in small, italic type as a marginal note. Thus, questions in this volume relating to these Mark citations are enclosed in parentheses.

I. Introductory Questions

A. Design

? What is the Bible?

? The Bible is a big book made up of many smaller books. How many of these smaller books are in the Bible?

? The English Bible is divided into two parts. What are these two parts called?

? How many testaments are in the Holy Bible?

? How many books are in the Old Testament?

? The Old Testament books in English Bibles may be arranged in four categories:
- the Law (also called the Books of Moses)
- the Books of History
- the Books of Poetry and Wisdom Literature
- the Books of Prophecy

Please name the first five books of the Bible, which are known as the Law.

? Each of the four sections of the Old Testament is composed of several books.
- There are five Books of Moses (or the Law.)
- There are twelve Books of History.
- There are five Books of Poetry and Wisdom Literature.
- There are seventeen Books of Prophecy.

Please name at least one book from each of the four sections. (Teachers should note that much of Old Testament prophecy is also poetry, so these four categories are simply a beginning point for further discussion of the Old Testament books in English Bibles.)

? Job, Psalms, Proverbs, Ecclesiastes, and Song of Solomon make up a category of Old Testament books in English Bibles. Are they
- the Law (or Books of Moses),
- the Books of History,
- the Books of Poetry and Wisdom Literature, or
- the Books of Prophecy?

? Which five Old Testament books are known as the books of the major prophets?
Abingdon Bible Handbook, Blair, pp. 146–149

? How many books of the Old Testament make up the section in English Bibles known as the books of the minor prophets? *Abingdon Bible Handbook,* Blair, p. 148

? Please name the twelve Old Testament books of the minor prophets. *Abingdon Bible Handbook,* Blair, pp. 146–149

? Are the following Old Testament books from the Books of Poetry and Wisdom Literature or the Books of Prophecy?
- Isaiah
- Jeremiah
- Lamentations
- Ezekiel
- Daniel

? Which of the following books of the Bible is shortest?
- Psalms
- Revelation
- Obadiah
- Nehemiah

? Please name two Old Testament books that are written in the literary form of short stories. These short stories emphasize the idea that God is the Father of people everywhere. *Teaching the Scriptures,* Robinson, p. 2

? The many authors of the Bible used a variety of literary styles. Please tell whether the following books are written in prose or poetry.
- Ruth
- Psalms
- Song of Solomon
- Jonah

? The New Testament may be divided into four sections:
- Gospels (four books)
- history (one book)
- epistles or letters (twenty-one books)
- the Apocalypse (one book)

Please name one book from each section.

? How many books are in the New Testament?

? The first four books of the New Testament (Matthew, Mark, Luke, and John) are called the Gospels. Which book of the Bible follows the four Gospels?

? Which book tells about the activities of the apostles after Jesus' resurrection and ascension?

? The majority of New Testament books (21 of the 27) are called epistles. Most of the epistles were originally letters, though some are sermons or essays, such as Hebrews. Paul probably wrote seven to ten of the epistles. Please name five epistles.

? The longest epistle to a church comes immediately after the book of Acts. Please name it. *Abingdon Bible Handbook*, Blair, pp. 252–253

? The last book of the New Testament is an apocalyptic book written by John. Please name it.

? How many letters to Timothy are included in the New Testament?

? How many letters to Titus are included in the New Testament?

B. Authorship and Preservation

? Who wrote the Bible?

? The Bible was written over a period of ten to twenty centuries. How long is a century? *Teaching the Scriptures*, Robinson, p. 1

? About how long did it take for the Bible to be written?
- 10–100 years
- 1000–2000 years
- 4000–6000 years

? True or false? The Bible was written over a period of 1000–2000 years.

? The books of the Bible were originally written in Hebrew and Greek on clay tablets, skins, or papyrus. Which Testament was mainly written in Hebrew? Which Testament was mainly written in Greek? *Teaching the Scriptures*, Robinson, pp. 1–2

? The Old Testament books were originally written in Hebrew. In what language were the New Testament books written?

? The New Testament books were originally written in Greek. In what language were the Old Testament books written?

? In what languages was the Bible written originally? *Teaching the Scriptures, Robinson*, p. 1

? Do Bible scholars know the names of every person who wrote a part of the Bible? *Who Wrote the Bible?*, Friedman

? Please name an individual who wrote parts of the New Testament.

? A Christian Gentile physician who travelled with Paul is identified with the third Gospel. Although no one knows whether this physician actually wrote the Gospel that carries his name, he is mentioned by name twice in New Testament epistles. Please name him.
Colossians 4:14; II Timothy 4:11

? Matthew is a Gospel. I Timothy is an epistle. Tell whether the following New Testament books are epistles or Gospels:
- Romans
- Mark
- Ephesians
- Luke
- Philippians
- I Corinthians

? Some of the New Testament epistles were originally letters sent to church congregations. Some of the epistles were written to individuals. Please tell whether the follow epistles were written to a church or to an individual:
- Titus
- Romans
- Philemon
- I Timothy
- Philippians
- Galatians

? Which of the following Bible translations was completed in 1611?
- The Vulgate – written in Latin
- King James Version – written in English
- Septuagint – written in Greek

? What English king appointed forty-seven scholars to prepare a new English translation of the Bible in 1604?

? James Stuart was the king of England when the Authorized Version of the Bible was written. He was a Protestant. Who was James Stuart's mother?

? Whose long reign in England did King James follow?

? Was King James of England raised as a Protestant or a Catholic?

? There have been many different translations of the Bible. Occasionally it is helpful to read another translation to better understand a passage. Please give the King James Version text for: "How blest are those who know their need of God; the kingdom of Heaven is theirs." *Matthew 5:3 The New English Bible*

? True or false? Words written in italics in the King James Version of the Bible are words that have been added by the translators and do not appear in the original manuscript.

? Many years before Christ Jesus was born, some Greek speaking Jews who lived in Alexandria, Egypt translated the Old Testament from Hebrew into Greek. This very important Bible translation was called the Septuagint. It was followed by a translation of the Scriptures into Latin by Jerome. What was this early Latin Bible translation called?

? The Latin Vulgate was "the first great translation of the whole Bible." Who did this translation? *The Concise Columbia Encyclopedia,* Levey and Greenhall, p. 86; *The New Westminster Dictionary of the Bible,* pp. 976, 977

? In about 1450 CE, a man named Johannes Gutenberg invented printing with movable type. The first book printed by Gutenberg using his new invention was the Bible. In which country did this take place? *Teaching the Scriptures,* Robinson, pp. 2, 109

? True or false? Before printing was invented, it took a scribe one year to copy a Bible.

? What was the first book ever printed?

? When was the Bible first printed?

? Why was the invention of printing with movable type in 1450 by Gutenberg important to Christianity?

C. Chronology

? Are these stories from the Old Testament or the New Testament?
- Daniel in the lions' den
- David and Goliath
- Jesus born in Bethlehem
- Paul survives a shipwreck near an island
- Noah's ark

? Are these people from the Old Testament or the New Testament?
- Joseph, who receives a coat of many colours.
- Gideon and three hundred of his countrymen, who defeat the Midianites.
- Peter and John, who heal a crippled beggar.

? Who lived first — Moses or Jesus?

?   Are these stories from the Old Testament or the New Testament?
- Cornelius, a non-Jew, is baptized.
- Abraham and Lot set out for Canaan.
- Paul's friends help him escape from Damascus by lowering him from the city wall at night in a basket.

?   Are these people from the Old Testament or the New Testament?
- Nehemiah, who rebuilt the walls of Jerusalem during the Persian Empire
- Paul, whose missionary journeys spread Christianity
- Solomon, who was a powerful king of Israel

?   True or false? There are many interesting stories about Jesus Christ in the Old Testament.

?   Hebrew history is divided into various periods when the children of Israel were under foreign rule. Nehemiah lived under Persian rule, and Paul lived under Roman rule. Which came first — Persian or Roman rule?

?   The history of the Hebrew people was greatly influenced by the various empires that rose and waned over the centuries. Arrange these empires in their correct chronological order:
- Greek Empire
- Babylonian Empire
- Persian Empire

?   Please name a Bible character who lived under Roman rule.

?   Please match:

1. sojourn in Egypt	a. David
2. independent rule	b. Paul
3. under Persian rule	c. Joseph (Old Testament)
4. under Roman rule	d. Nehemiah

?   In the following list of pairs, please tell who lived first:
- Abraham or David
- Moses or David
- Joshua or Hezekiah
- Paul or Isaac
- Daniel or Jacob
- Solomon or Noah
- Isaac or Jeremiah
- Nehemiah or Jacob

?   King Solomon directed the building of the first temple in Jerusalem about 1000 BCE. Who destroyed this temple?

? Who lived first?
- Jacob or Elisha
- Solomon or Abraham
- Daniel or Joseph (Israel's son)
- Joshua or Nehemiah

? Nebuchadnezzar's Babylonian army destroyed Jerusalem and forced most of the Hebrew people of Judah to leave their land and live in exile. Please name a Jewish youth who was carried off to Babylon and received special permission to eat simple foods instead of the king's meat. *Daniel 1:3–20*

? The temple built in Jerusalem during Solomon's reign was plundered and burned by the Babylonians. Was another temple ever built in Jerusalem? *II Kings 25:8–17; The New Westminster Dictionary of the Bible*, pp. 929–934

? Zerubbabel was the leader of a large group of Jews who returned to Jerusalem from Babylonian exile. He was largely responsible for the reconstruction of a temple on the same site where the temple stood in Solomon's time. Please name two prophets who were contemporaries of Zerubbabel. *Zechariah 4:8, 9; Getting Better Acquainted with your Bible*, Shotwell, pp. 134–135

? It was during the reign of Cyrus the Great of Persia that Jewish exiles began to return to Palestine from their captivity in Babylon. Jerusalem was refortified and reconstruction began on the second temple. The book of Ezra mentions a leader named Sheshbazzar (about whom nothing is otherwise known) who returned with the first group of exiles. What leader is most identified with the rebuilding of the second temple? *The Cambridge Companion to the Bible*, pp. 148–157

? Please list the following Bible characters in the correct chronological order:
- Simon Peter
- Elijah
- Isaac
- Joshua

? Please list the following Bible characters in the correct chronological order:
- Samuel
- Daniel
- Moses
- Jacob (renamed Israel)
- Abraham
- Christ Jesus

D. Historical Setting (See Figure 1)

? During the time of Abraham (also called Abram), what did the people of Babylonia worship? *The New Westminster Dictionary of the Bible*, "Abraham," pp. 8–11

? In Ur, a city of Babylonia, the people worshipped many gods. This is known as polytheism. A moon-god named Nannar was the most important God in Ur. What Bible character left Ur of the Chaldees and moved to Canaan? *Genesis 11:27–31; 12:1–4; 17:1–5; The New Westminster Dictionary of the Bible*, "Abraham," pp. 8–11

? The Old Testament includes much history of the Hebrew people. Many different geographical areas serve as the background for these historical stories. Which biblical figure rose from slavery to great power under Pharaoh in Egypt? *Genesis 30:22–24; chs. 37, 39 to 50*

? After their Exodus from Egypt, the Hebrew people wandered in the wilderness forty years. After the Hebrew's invasion of Canaan, various judges, then kings, led the people. Did the kingdom established under Saul remain independent in Bible times?

? Please give another name by which the Hebrew people were called.

? In Bible times many cities had walls around them. Two well-known Bible stories mention walled cities: Jericho, whose walls fell down, and Jerusalem, whose walls were rebuilt by Nehemiah and other Hebrews. Why did people build walls around their cities?

? Please name the city which became the religious center of the Hebrew people about the time of David. *The Cambridge Companion to the Bible*, p. 120

? Which sacred city was the capital of the United Kingdom of Israel and Judah?

? Please name the capital of the Southern Kingdom of Judah.

? Jerusalem was the capital of the Southern Kingdom of Judah. What city became the capital of the Northern Kingdom of Israel? *The Cambridge Companion to the Bible*, p. 201

? Who were the Samaritans? *The Cambridge Companion to the Bible*, p. 201

? After the fall of the Northern Kingdom of Israel, its capital, Samaria, was resettled by Assyrian captives. These new Samaritans gradually adopted a modified form of the Jewish religion and worshipped at a temple on Mt. Gerizim. An enmity between the people of Samaria and the people of Judah developed. Please tell a Bible story that concerns a Samaritan. *Luke 10:25–37; 17:11–19; John 4:1–42*

? True or false? The land of the Bible is only desert, where there is just enough water to grow grass here and there.

? For Jews in Bible times and today, what day of the week is the Sabbath?

? Please explain the differences between the fall of Israel, the Northern Kingdom, and the fall of Judah, the Southern Kingdom.

? The temple in Jerusalem was rebuilt during the reign of a Persian king named Darius. Please name the man who was largely responsible for the completion of this second temple. *The New Westminster Dictionary of the Bible*, pp. 735–737; 1022–1023

? During which empire did Nehemiah live?
  - Persian, ca. 539 – 333 BCE
  - Greek, ca. 333 – 165 BCE
  - Roman, ca. 63 BCE – 395 CE

? Of the following Bible characters, who spent time in Egypt?
  - Joseph, son of Jacob
  - Moses
  - Jesus

? Who was the first emperor (27 BCE to 14 CE) of the Roman Empire? *Teaching the Scriptures,* p. 46; *The New Westminster Dictionary of the Bible,* p. 131

? The first sole emperor of the Roman Empire was Caesar Augustus. The language widely used throughout this enormous empire, including Judea, was Greek. The Romans were responsible for building a huge number of roads and bridges that connected the parts of the empire. Please name someone from the Bible who lived during the time of the Roman Empire. *The New Westminster Dictionary of the Bible,* "Rome," pp. 810–811

? At the time Jesus lived, "Aramaic was the official language of the empire." Jesus and his disciples spoke Aramaic, which had been the common language in Palestine for many decades. What language was spoken by the Jewish community during its "golden age" under the leadership of David and Solomon? *Discovering the Biblical World,* Frank, p. 150

? The Roman Empire covered most of the civilized world for several centuries, including the time when Christ Jesus lived. Although Aramaic was the language spoken by Jesus and most other people living in Palestine, another language began to be widely used for commerce in the empire during this time. What was that language? *The New Westminster Dictionary of the Bible,* "Rome," pp. 810811; *Teaching the Scriptures,* Robinson, p. 46; *Discovering the Biblical World,* Frank, p. 150

Figure 1: Map of the Bible lands

That Ye May Teach the Children

II. Old Testament

A. The Law (also called the Books of Moses or the Pentateuch)

1. Genesis

a) Opening account of creation *Genesis, chs. 1:1 to 2:3*

? Where in the Bible can you find these words: "In the beginning God created the heaven and the earth"?

? On which of the six days of creation did God create light? *Genesis 1:3–5*

? "God created man in his own image, in the image of God created he him; male and female created he them." In what book of the Bible can you find these words?

? Please finish this verse: "And God saw everything that he had made, and, behold, _____ _____ _____ _____." *Genesis 1:31*

? The story of creation is short. It is told in chapter one of Genesis, plus the next three verses in chapter two. How many days did it take God to finish "the heavens and the earth ... and all the host of them"?

? What was created on each of the six creation days? *Genesis 1:1–31*

? A prose poem in Genesis tells what God created on each of six days:
- first day: light
- second day: firmament ("God called the firmament heaven.")
- third day: waters, dry land, grass, herb, fruit
- fourth day: two great lights, stars
- fifth day: moving creature, winged fowl
- sixth day: living creature, man "in his own image…male and female"

How many times do these words appear: "God saw that it was good"? *Genesis 1:4, 10, 12, 18, 21, 25; Teaching the Scriptures, Robinson, p. 9*

? What did God do on the seventh day of creation? *Genesis 2:2, 3*

? "And God saw everything that he had made, and, behold, it was very good." Are these words from the opening account of creation in Genesis or from the story of Adam and Eve?

b) Adam and Eve *Genesis 2:3 to 4:2*

? "But there went up a mist from the earth, and watered the whole face of the ground." These words from are from the beginning of a well-known Bible story. What is that story? *Genesis 2:6*

? According to the second chapter of Genesis, "the Lord God formed man of the dust of the ground." What was this man named? *Genesis 2:7, 19*

? Where did Adam and Eve live? *Genesis 2:8*

? Where in the Bible do we read: "the Lord God formed man of the dust of the ground and breathed into his nostrils the breath of life"? *Genesis 2:7*

? Who tempted Eve to eat the forbidden fruit from the tree of the knowledge of good and evil? *Genesis 3:1–6*

? In the story of Adam and Eve, what animal "was more subtil than any beast of the field which the Lord God had made"? *Genesis 3:1*

? Adam and Eve had children. Please name their first two sons. *Genesis 4:1,2*

? Did the same person write the story of creation found in chapter one of Genesis and the story of Adam and Eve?

? True or false? Pison, Gihon, Hiddekel, and Euphrates are four biblical cities mentioned in Genesis. *Genesis 2:8–14*

? Four rivers "went out of Eden." Please name them. *Genesis 2:8–14*

c) Cain and Abel *Genesis 4:1–16*

? In Genesis we read that "Abel was a keeper of sheep, but Cain was a tiller of the ground." How were Cain and Abel related? *Genesis 4:1–16*

? What happened to Abel, the second son of Adam and Eve, according to the book of Genesis? *Genesis 4:8*

? Why did Cain kill Abel, his brother? *Genesis 4:1–16*

Figure 2: Noah's ark

d) The generations of Adam *Genesis, chs. 4, 5*

? Please name the third son born to Adam and Eve after Cain slew Abel. *Genesis 4:25*

? The great prophet Elijah was taken up into heaven by a whirlwind. Elisha witnessed the event. Elijah was not, however, the first person in Bible history who never died. Who was translated years before Elijah? *Genesis 5:18–24; Hebrews 11:5*

? True or false? Methuselah, the son of Enoch, lived to be 969 years old. *Genesis 5:27*

e) Noah *Genesis 6:5 to 9:29* (See Figure 2)

? What did Noah build to protect his family and the animals from the flood? *Genesis 6:13–14*

? How did Noah know how to build the ark? *Genesis 6:14–16*

? What did God tell Noah to bring with him into the ark? *Genesis 6:18–21*

? Shem, Ham, and Japheth were brothers. Please name their father. *Genesis 5:32*

? What were the names of Noah's three sons? *Genesis 6:10*

? While Noah and his family were safe inside the ark, "the rain was upon the earth forty days and forty nights." As the "waters returned from off the earth," the ark rested "upon the mountains of Ararat." What two birds did Noah send out the window "to see if the waters were abated…"? *Genesis 8:4–8*

? God said, "I do set my bow in the cloud, and it shall be for a token of a covenant between me and the earth." To whom was God speaking? *Genesis 9:13*

? How many years did Noah live after the flood? *Genesis 9:28*

f) The tower of Babel *Genesis 11:1–9*

? On a plain in the land of Shinar, the people said, "let us build us a city and a tower, whose top may reach unto heaven…." Please name this ancient city. *Genesis 11:1–9*

? How many languages were spoken in the world after the flood? *Genesis 11:1*

? What happened at the place which came to be called Babel? *Genesis 11:1–9*

Figure 3: Abraham and Sarah

g) Abraham and Sarah *Genesis 11:27–32; chs. 12 to 24; Nehemiah 9:7*

(1) Abram and Sarai leave Ur for Haran *Genesis 11:31*

? Which Bible character was brought forth out of Ur of the Chaldees and given a new name? *Nehemiah 9:7; Genesis 11:31; 17:5*

? A man from Ur of the Chaldees named Abram moved with Terah and Lot to Haran. Abram's wife, who was barren, also went with them. Please name her. *Genesis 11:29–31*

(2) Depart Haran for Canaan *Genesis 12:1–5*

? At the age of 75, Abram "departed out of Haran" with "Sarai his wife, and Lot his brother's son." Where did they go, according to the Lord's command? *Genesis 12:5*

? When Abram "departed out of Haran" in Mesopotamia at the age of seventy-five, he was obediently doing "as the Lord had spoken unto him." Who went with him to Canaan? *Genesis 12:1–5*

(3) To Egypt; famine *Genesis 12:9, 10*

? Why did Abram leave Canaan temporarily and journey south into Egypt? *Genesis 12:9, 10*

(4) Return to Bethel; Lot and Abraham separate *Genesis 13:1–18*

? Please name the man who parted from Lot and said to him: "Let there be no strife, I pray thee, between me and thee, and between my herdmen and thy herdmen; for we be brethren." *Genesis 13:8*

(5) Rescues Lot and pays tribute to Melchizedek *Genesis 14:18–22*

? Who among the patriarchs did Melchizedek, "priest of the most high God," bless? *Genesis 14:18–20*

(6) Ishmael born to Hagar *Genesis 16:1–16*

? Abraham had two sons: Ishmael and Isaac. Sarah was Isaac's mother. Who was Ishmael's mother? *Genesis 16:1, 2, 16*

? Hagar, Sarah's maid, was Abraham's secondary wife. Having a secondary wife was a "common custom in patriarchal times." Please name Hagar's son. *Genesis 16:1–16; All of the Women of the Bible, Deen, p. 12*

(7) Covenant with God   *Genesis 17:1–27 (see also: Genesis 12:13; 13:17; 15:18)*

? With whom did God establish this covenant: "And I will establish my covenant between me and thee and thy seed after thee...for an everlasting covenant, to be a God unto thee, and to thy seed after thee"? *Genesis 17:1–7*

? What was Abraham's name before the Lord appeared unto him and said, "I will make my covenant between me and thee"? *Genesis 17:1–9*

? A covenant is an agreement or compact between two or more parties. The book of Genesis gives several versions of God's covenant with Abraham. Part of this covenant included giving Abraham and his descendants the land of Canaan. Where did Abraham and Sarah live before they moved to Canaan (also called the promised land or Palestine)? *Genesis 12:1–3; 13:17; 15:18; 17:1–27*

? About whom was God speaking when He said: "I will bless her, and she shall be a mother of nations"? *Genesis 17:15, 16*

? When Abraham was ninety-nine years old, God said He would bless Sarah and give Abraham a son of her. Why did Abraham fall upon his face and laugh? *Genesis 17:17*

(8) Sodom destroyed and Lot saved   *Genesis, chs. 18, 19*

? Who looked back at the destruction of Sodom and Gomorrah and "became a pillar of salt"? *Genesis 19:23–26*

(9) Isaac born; Ishmael sent away   *Genesis 21:1–21 (See Figure 3)*

? When Abraham was one hundred years old, he and Sarah had a baby son. What was this son's name? *Genesis 21:1–5*

? In Galatians, Paul mentions a story from Genesis about Abraham's son, Isaac, saying, "we, brethren, as Isaac was, are the children of promise." Please name Abraham's other son who was cast out with his mother, Hagar. *Galatians 4:2831; Genesis 21:2, 9–21*

? Who said to Hagar, the Egyptian maid: "Behold thou art with child, and shalt bear a son, and shalt call his name Ishmael..."? *Genesis 16:1–11*

? What happened to Abraham's bondwoman, Hagar, and their child, Ishmael, after she and the boy "departed and wandered in the wilderness of Beersheba"? *Genesis 21:9–21*

? Abraham sent Hagar and her son away. At first Hagar was discouraged and thought they would die for lack of water. Then, "God opened her eyes, and she saw a well of water." Please name Hagar's son. *Genesis 21:2, 9–21*

(10) Isaac and burnt offering *Genesis 22:1–19*

? Please name the Old Testament character that offered a ram for a burnt offering instead of his son, Isaac. *Genesis 22:13*

? What father and son had the following conversation:
Son: "Behold the fire and the wood: but where is the lamb for a burnt offering?"
Father: "My son, God will provide himself a lamb for a burnt offering."
Genesis 22:7, 8

(11) Isaac's marriage to Rebekah *Genesis 24:1–67* (See Figure 4)

? When the time came for Isaac to marry, Abraham sent his servant back to Mesopotamia to find a wife for him. Please name Isaac's wife. *Genesis 24:1–67*

? Rebekah meets Abraham's servant as she carries water from the well. He is looking for a wife for Isaac and is "attracted by her courtesy and kindness." Rebekah travels with Abraham's servant to Canaan and marries Isaac. By what means do Rebekah and her damsels travel? *Genesis 24:63, 64; All of the Women of the Bible*, Deen, p. 21

(12) Overview of Abraham and Sarah *Genesis 11:27–32; chs. 12 to 24; Nehemiah 9:7; Hebrews 11:8–10*

? Abraham's family tree includes his wife Sarah, their son Isaac, their grandson Jacob and their great-grandson Joseph. In what book of the Bible is the story of this family? *Genesis 21:3; 25:21–26; 30:22–24*

? Guess who? When he was a little boy, he lived in a city called Ur, where people worshipped idols. When he grew up, the real God told him to start a new nation. When he was very old, his name was changed. Please name him. *Genesis 11:27–31; 12:1–4; 17:1–5*

? In the honor roll of the faithful given in Hebrews, this man is described thus: "He looked for a city which hath foundations, whose builder and maker is God." Please name this Old Testament patriarch. *Hebrews 11:8–10*

h) Jacob *Genesis 25:19 to 35:29*

(1) Twins born to Isaac and Rebekah *Genesis 25:19–26*

? Who was Jacob's father? *Genesis 25:21–28*

? Who was Jacob's brother? *Genesis 25:21–28*

? Jacob and Esau were twin brothers. Their story is in the book of Genesis. Please name their parents. *Genesis 25:19–26*

Figure 4: Isaac and Rebekah meet each other

? Please name Isaac's wife, the mother of Esau and Jacob. *Genesis 25: 21–28*

? In Genesis, Esau is described as "a cunning hunter, a man of the field." Please name Esau's twin brother. *Genesis 25:24–27*

? Jacob and Esau were twins. Who was born first? *Genesis 25:24–26*

(2) Esau sells his birthright *Genesis 25:27–34*

? What Bible character sold his birthright to his brother, Jacob, for some red pottage of lentils? *Genesis 25:27–34*

(3) Blessing trick; Jacob flees *Genesis 27:1–45*

? Isaac and Rebekah were the parents of twin boys. The younger twin cheated his older brother of Isaac's blessing by disguising himself. Please name the brothers. *Genesis 27:1–45*

? Who helped Jacob deceive his father, Isaac, and cheat Esau out of his father's blessing? *Genesis 27:1–45*

? Jacob and his mother were able to deceive Isaac because "his eyes were dim, so that he could not see." What was their plan? *Genesis 27:1–45*

? In the story of Jacob and Esau, what does Jacob do while Esau goes to the field to hunt for venison to bring to their father, Isaac? *Genesis 27:1–45*

? Why did Jacob leave his home and go to live with his mother's brother, Laban? *Genesis 27:1 to 28:9*

(4) Bethel and the ladder to heaven *Genesis 28:10–22*

? What did Jacob call the place where he had a dream in which he saw angels going up and down a ladder? *Genesis 28:10–19*

(5) Marriages; eleven sons *Genesis 29:1–35; 30:1–24; 35:22–26*

? Who worked seven years for a wife and got her sister instead? *Genesis 29:16–30*

? Leah and Rachel were sisters from Haran in Mesopotamia. Which patriarch did they marry? *Genesis, chs. 29, 30*

? The Bible says that "Jacob loved Rachel." How, then, did Jacob come to marry Leah, Rachel's older sister, first? *Genesis 29:16–30*

? Please name Jacob's two wives. *Genesis 29:9–30*

? Jacob's two wives were Laban's daughters, Leah and Rachel. They each had a maidservant. The two maidservants became secondary wives and bore two sons each. Please name the maidservants. *Genesis 29:29; 30:3–13*

? Jacob had six sons and a daughter by his wife, Leah. Jacob had two sons by Zilpah, Leah's maid: Gad and Asher. Jacob had two sons by Bilhah, Rachel's maid: Dan and Naphtali. Who were Jacob's two sons by his wife, Rachel? *Genesis 30:22–24; 35:16–18*

? Please name the oldest of Leah's six sons, Jacob's firstborn. *Genesis 35:23*

(6) Jacob returns home *Genesis, ch. 32*

? Which Bible character said to God: "Deliver me, I pray thee, from the hand of my brother, from the hand of Esau; for I fear him, lest he will come and smite me...." *Genesis 32:11*

? When the Lord told Jacob to return to his homeland, Jacob obeyed. However, Jacob was afraid to see Esau again. Why? *Genesis, chs. 32, 33*

(7) Peniel and Jacob's name change *Genesis 32:24–30*

? What did Jacob name the place where he wrestled with "a man"? *Genesis 32:24–30*

? What is the new name given to Jacob at Peniel? *Genesis 32:24–30*

? "Let me go, for the day breaketh," said the angel. "I will not let thee go, except thou bless me," said the man. Which Old Testament character had this conversation with an angel at Peniel? *Genesis 32:24–30*

? Please tell what happened to Jacob (renamed Israel) at Peniel. *Genesis 32:24–30*

? What was the original name of the man after whom "the children of Israel" were named? *Genesis 32:24–30*

(8) Reunion with Esau *Genesis 33:1–12*

? Did Esau ever forgive his brother Jacob for cheating him? *Genesis 33:1–10*

? Jacob and Esau had not seen each other for many years. Jacob was worried about their reunion. What did Esau do when he first saw Jacob again? *Genesis 33:4*

(9) Jacob's twelfth son born; Rachel dies *Genesis 35:16–20*

? How many sons did Jacob have? *Genesis 35:22–26*

? Jacob had twelve sons. Which two sons of Jacob were the children of Rachel? *Genesis 30:25; 35:18*

? In which book of the Bible is the story of Jacob (later called Israel)?

? Who lived first — Jacob (renamed Israel) or Moses?

i) Joseph *Genesis 30:22–24; chs. 37; 39 to 50* (See Figure 5)

(1) Joseph at age 17; cast into pit *Genesis, ch. 37*

? Who was Joseph's father? *Genesis 37:2,3*

? What did Israel (Jacob) make for Joseph to show his great love for him? *Genesis 37:3*

? Why did Joseph's brothers hate him? *Genesis 37:2–11*

? Joseph's brothers dipped the coat of many colours in goat's blood and brought it to their father. What did Israel think had become of his son, Joseph? *Genesis 37:31–34*

(2) Served Potiphar for thirteen years *Genesis 39:1–20*

? Joseph was taken to Egypt and sold to the captain of the guard. Please name the Egyptian officer of Pharaoh who bought Joseph. *Genesis 37:36; 39:1*

? "Joseph was brought down to Egypt...." An officer of Pharaoh, captain of the guard, an Egyptian, bought Joseph. Please name this man, in whose sight Joseph "found grace." *Genesis 39:1–4*

? Who "cast her eyes upon Joseph" and said to him, "lie with me"? *Genesis 39:7*

? Why did Potiphar's wife lie to her husband about Joseph and cause Joseph to be put into prison? *Genesis 39:1–20*

(3) Imprisonment for two years *Genesis 39:21–23; 40:1–23; 41:1–36*

? Who was called out of prison to interpret a Pharaoh's dream? *Genesis 41:14–16*

? What was Joseph's interpretation of the Egyptian Pharaoh's dream? *Genesis 41:1–37*

(4) Oversees food storage in Egypt *Genesis 41:37–57*

? How did Pharaoh reward Joseph for his wisdom in interpreting his dream? *Genesis 41:37–41*

? Jacob (renamed Israel) had twelve sons. Joseph was the son of Jacob's beloved wife, Rachel. Please name Rachel's second son, youngest of Joseph's brethren. *Genesis 35:24*

Figure 5: Joseph in his coat of many colours.

(5) Brothers' trips to Egypt to buy corn *Genesis, chs. 42 to 45*

? Joseph tested his brothers' love for young Benjamin when he had his steward hide a silver cup in Benjamin's sack. How did the older brothers react when this alleged crime was discovered? *Genesis, chs. 44, 45*

(6) Family settles in Egypt *Genesis 46:1–30*

? Joseph was able to forgive his older brothers for throwing him into the pit. Despite his years in slavery and in prison, Joseph knew he had a special part in God's plan for the Hebrew people. What was Joseph's part in God's plan? *Genesis 45:5–7*

? Who am I? My brothers sold me into slavery, but I didn't hate them. I loved them! I even rescued them during a famine. *Genesis, ch. 37; 41:56, 57; 42:18, 25, 26*

? In what book of the Bible is the story of Joseph and his coat of many colours?

? Jacob (renamed Israel) blessed Ephraim and Manasseh. Were they the sons of Abraham, Jacob, or Joseph? *Genesis 48:1–5, 8–22*

2. Exodus

a) Moses *Exodus, chs. 2 to 40* (See Figure 6)

? What happened to the children of Israel in Egypt when "there arose up a new king over Egypt, which knew not Joseph"? *Exodus 1:8–14*

? Why did the new Pharaoh enslave the children of Israel? *Exodus 1:9–11*

? What did the king of Egypt order to be done to the Hebrew baby boys? *Exodus 1:16*

? What did the midwives do when the king commanded them to kill any newborn boys? *Exodus 1:17*

(1) In the ark of bulrushes *Exodus 2:1–10*

? Who was the baby found by Pharaoh's daughter in an ark of bulrushes floating in the river? *Exodus 2:1–10*

? Why did Moses' mother hide him three months and then put him in an ark of bulrushes by the river's brink? *Exodus 1:22; 2:1–10*

? Where did Pharaoh's daughter find the baby Moses in his ark of bulrushes? *Exodus 2:1–10*

? Who watched the baby Moses as he floated in the ark of bulrushes at the river? *Exodus 2:1–10*

? Guess who? I am the sister of Aaron and Moses. I watched Moses when he was a baby hidden in an ark of bulrushes. *Exodus 2:1–4; Numbers 26:59*

? Please name Moses' older sister who watched him from a distance when he floated in the ark at the edge of the river. *Exodus 2:1–4; Numbers 26:59*

? Pharaoh's daughter adopted Moses. Who nursed the child for her? *Exodus 2:110*

? Who adopted Moses? *Exodus 2:1–10*

? How did Moses' older sister help him when he was very young? *Exodus 2:1–10*

? Where was Moses born? *Exodus 2:1–10*

? Please tell the relationship of these three Bible characters:
  - Aaron
  - Miriam
  - Moses
  Numbers 26:59

? According to a sermon preached by Stephen, "Moses was learned in all the wisdom of the Egyptians." Do you suppose Moses' upbringing was similar to that of other Hebrew children? *Exodus 2:10; Acts 7:22*

? In which book of the Bible can you read the story of Moses in the ark of bulrushes? *Exodus 2:1–10*

? What is the term used for a king in Egypt? *Exodus 1:8–11*

(2) Kills Egyptian *Exodus 2:11–15*

? Why did Moses kill an Egyptian? *Exodus 2:11–15*

(3) Zipporah *Exodus 2:16–22*

? Moses was afraid after he killed the Egyptian. He left his home and became a shepherd for the priest of Midian, who had seven daughters. What was the name of the daughter who married Moses? *Exodus 2:21*

? Who was Moses' wife? *Exodus 2:16–22*

(4) Burning bush *Exodus 3:1–20*

? Who kept the flock of his father-in-law, Jethro, and led the flock to the mountain of God, Horeb? *Exodus 3:1*

? True or false? Moses was a shepherd for a while. *Exodus 3:1*

? Which biblical mountain is referred to as "the mountain of God"? *Exodus 3:1*

? What man saw a burning bush and then heard God call him "out of the midst of the bush"? *Exodus 3:1–4*

? Where was Moses when God said, "put off thy shoes from off thy feet, for the place whereon thou standest is holy ground"? *Exodus 3:1, 2, 5*

? Who made the lives of the children of Israel "bitter with hard bondage, in mortar, and in brick, and in all manner of service in the field"? *Exodus 1:14; 3:7–10*

? What message did God give Moses at the burning bush? *Exodus 3:1–20*

? What Bible character asked God this question: "Who am I, that I should go unto Pharaoh, and that I should bring forth the children of Israel out of Egypt?" *Exodus 3:11*

? Fill in the blank: "And God said unto _____, I AM THAT I AM ...." *Exodus 3:14*

? Whom did God direct to bring the children of Israel out of Egypt? *Exodus 3:10, 11*

(5) Rod to serpent and leprous hand *Exodus 4:1–18*

? Who told Moses to cast his rod on the ground? What did the rod become? *Exodus 4:1–5*

? God called to Moses out of the midst of a burning bush. When Moses cast down his rod, it became a serpent. Did God instruct Moses to pick the serpent up by the neck or the tail? *Exodus 4:4*

? When Moses picked up the serpent, as God commanded, what did the serpent then become? *Exodus 4:4*

(6) Aaron *Exodus 4:27–31*

? Moses' brother helped Moses lead the children of Israel out of Egypt. What was his name? *Exodus 4:28–31; 7:1,2*

(7) Plagues; the Exodus *Exodus, chs. 5 to 13*

? The Hebrews made bricks for the king of Egypt. After Moses and Aaron told Pharaoh that the Lord God of Israel said, "Let my people go," Pharaoh gave the taskmasters an order that made the people's work more difficult. What was the command that made the work even harder? *Exodus 5:6–7, 12–13*

?   Pharaoh and the Egyptians suffered a series of terrible plagues. These plagues included fish dying; too many frogs, lice, and flies; the death of all their cattle; hail storms; locusts; three days of darkness; and, finally, the death of all firstborn children. Why? *Exodus, chs. 7 to 12*

?   How many of the ten plagues in Egypt can you name? *Exodus 7:14 to 12:13*

?   What was the last and most awful plague, the one that finally persuaded Pharaoh to let the children of Israel go? *Exodus 12:29–31*

?   The children of Israel left Egypt about 1450 BCE. What do we call this event? *The One Year Chronological Bible, New International Version*, p. xxii

?   Led by Moses, the children of Israel were able to travel by day and by night. What did they follow by day "to lead them the way"? What gave them light at night? *Exodus 13:21*

?   What does the annual festival called passover commemorate? See *passover* in a Bible Dictionary.

(8) Crossing the Red Sea   *Exodus, ch. 14*

?   Who were pursuing the children of Israel when the Lord said unto Moses: "stretch out thine hand over the sea, and divide it: and the children of Israel shall go on dry ground through the midst of the sea"? *Exodus 14:10, 16*

?   Why did the Lord cause "the sea to go back by a strong east wind…and made the sea dry land"? *Exodus 14:21–23*

?   The Hebrew people went through the midst of the Red Sea on dry ground. When the waters returned, the sea covered the Egyptian chariots and horsemen. How many of the host of Pharaoh escaped the waters? *Exodus 14:28*

(9) Wandering in the wilderness   *Exodus, chs. 16 to 40*

?   Who were given bread from the Lord and called it *manna*? *Exodus 16:2, 3, 11–15*

?   What did the Israelites call the food that God provided for them in the wilderness? *Exodus 16:13–15*

?   "As it is written, He that had gathered much had nothing over; and he that had gathered little had no lack." What biblical event is Paul referring to in this verse from II Corinthians? *Exodus 16:18; II Corinthians 8:15*

?   Moses was able to help the children of Israel during a battle with Amalek by holding the rod of God high above his head. Who helped to hold up Moses' hands when they were heavy? *Exodus 17:8–13*

?   When Moses let down his hand, which held the rod of God, during a battle between Amalek and Joshua, Amalek prevailed. How did Aaron and Hur help Moses? *Exodus 17:8–13*

?   Jethro advised his son-in-law to set up a system of judges, using men of truth to be rulers of thousands, and rulers of hundreds, rulers of fifties, and rulers of tens. Who was Jethro's son-in-law? *Exodus 18:12–17, 19–23*

?   Where did Moses receive the Ten Commandments? *Exodus 19:20*

?   Were the children of Israel still slaves in Egypt when Moses received the Ten Commandments from God? *Exodus 19:1; 20:1–17*

?   For how long was Moses on Mt. Sinai when he received the Commandments? *Exodus 24:18*

?   Moses received from God detailed directions for constructing some things to be used in worship. What were they? *Exodus 25:10; 26:1; 27:1*

?   What jobs did God assign Aaron and his sons? *Exodus 28:1*

?   Moses was gone for a long time while he was receiving directions from God. The people were getting restless. What did Aaron do for them at their request? *Exodus 32:1–4*

?   When Moses came down from Mt. Sinai, his "anger waxed hot, and he cast the tables" with the Ten Commandments "out of his hands" and "brake them." Why? *Exodus 32:7, 8, 19*

?   What did Moses do when he came down from Mt. Sinai and saw what his people had done while he was gone? *Exodus 32:15–20*

?   Moses, in his wrath, broke the original tables of the Ten Commandments. Were they ever replaced? *Exodus 34:1*

b) The Ten Commandments   *Exodus, ch. 20; compare with Deuteronomy 5:2–22*
(See Figure 6)

?   Where in the Bible are the Ten Commandments?

?   Which commandment states: "Thou shalt have no other Gods before me"? *Exodus 20:3*

?   Which commandment tells us not to make any graven images? *Exodus 20:4–6*

?   Which commandment states: "Thou shalt not take the name of the Lord thy God in vain"? *Exodus 20:7*

Figure 6: Moses with the Ten Commandments

? Which commandment reminds us to remember the Sabbath day to keep it holy?
Exodus 20:8–11

? Which commandment tells us to honour our father and mother? *Exodus 20:12*

? Which commandment tells us not to kill? *Exodus 20:13*

? Which commandment states: "Thou shalt not commit adultery"? *Exodus 20:14*

? Which commandment states: "Thou shalt not steal"? *Exodus 20:15*

? Which commandment forbids us to bear false witness against our neighbour?
Exodus 20:16

? Which commandment teaches us not to covet any thing that is our neighbour's?
Exodus 20:17

? What is the first commandment? *Exodus 20:3*

? What is the second commandment? *Exodus 20:4–6*

? What is the third commandment? *Exodus 20:7*

? What is the fourth commandment? *Exodus 20:8–11*

? What is the fifth commandment? *Exodus 20:12*

? What is the sixth commandment? *Exodus 20:13*

? What is the seventh commandment? *Exodus 20:14*

? What is the eighth commandment? *Exodus 20:15*

? What is the ninth commandment? *Exodus 20:16*

? What is the tenth commandment? *Exodus 20:17*

? Give two examples of "other gods" a person might be tempted to have.

? Fill in the blanks: The first commandment states, "Thou shalt have no other gods
_____ _____." *Exodus 20:3*

? Of the following Old Testament characters, who risked his life while obeying the second commandment? *Daniel 3:1–30*
  - Solomon
  - Meshach
  - Isaac
  - Noah

? In the Old Testament, Hosea writes how the people "have made them molten images of their silver, and...they say of them, Let the men that sacrifice kiss the calves." What commandment were the children of Israel breaking? *Exodus 20:3; Hosea 13:2*

? Fill in the blank: The third commandment teaches us not to take the name of the Lord our God in _____ . *Exodus 20:7*

? Fill in the blanks: The fourth commandment teaches us to remember the _____ _____ to keep it holy. *Exodus 20:8–11*

? Fill in the blank: The fifth commandment teaches us to _____ our father and mother. *Exodus 20:12*

? Give an example of how we can "honour our father and mother." *Exodus 20:12*

? Say the sixth commandment, which teaches mankind not to murder. *Exodus 20:13*

? Fill in the blank: The eighth commandment is very short. It says, "Thou shalt not _____ ." *Exodus 20:15*

? In Old Testament times, what was the punishment for committing adultery? *Exodus 20:14; Leviticus 20:10*

? What is the term, mentioned in the Ten Commandments, for a "sexual relationship between a married man and a woman not his wife, or vice versa"? *Young People's Bible Dictionary*, Smith.

? Fill in the blank: The ninth commandment states "Thou shalt not bear false _____ against thy neighbour." *Exodus 20:16*

? Finish saying the commandment which directs us not to lie: "Thou shalt not bear...." *Exodus 20:16*

? Which commandment teaches us not to lie? *Exodus 20:16*

? Does slander break the ninth commandment"? *Exodus 20:16*

? What does the tenth commandment, "Thou shalt not covet," mean? *Exodus 20:17*

? In his relationship with Bathsheba, King David broke several of the Ten Commandments. Which ones? *II Samuel 11:2–27*

3. Leviticus

? What is the third book of the Bible (also called the third Book of Moses)?

? Which book of the Old Testament contains specific precepts for worship, which are to be followed by the priests, the Levites, and the people? *Getting Better Acquainted with Your Bible,* Shotwell, p. 13

? Which book of the Bible contains many laws regarding sacrifices and worship, such as: "ye shall bring a sheaf of the firstfruits of your harvest unto the priest"? *Leviticus 22:20–22; 23:10*

? Please read chapter 19 of Leviticus. Are these laws familiar to you? Why?

4. Numbers

a) Law of the Nazarite *Numbers 6:1–12*

? What vows did a man or woman take to become a Nazarite? *Numbers 6:1–12*

? A Nazarite in Bible times was someone specially consecrated to God. A Nazarite did not drink wine or strong drink, touch a dead body or cut his hair. Please name someone who was a Nazarite. *Numbers 6:1–6; Judges 13:2–24; The New Westminster Dictionary of the Bible,* p. 654

b) Blessing the people *Numbers 6:22–27*

? The Lord bless thee, and keep thee: The Lord make his face shine upon thee, and be gracious unto thee: The Lord lift up his countenance upon thee, and give thee peace." To whom did God speak this blessing? *Numbers 6:22–27*

? Please fill in the blanks on this blessing for the children of Israel from the Lord: "The Lord bless thee, and _____ thee: The Lord make his face _____ upon thee, and be gracious unto thee...." *Numbers 6:22–25*

c) Ark of the covenant *Numbers 10:33–36* (See Figure 7)

? What was the ark of the covenant? *Exodus 25:10–22; Numbers 10:33–36*

Figure 7: The priests carry the ark of the covenant to the promised land

d) Moses feels burdened *Numbers 11:11–17*

? Moses was feeling burdened by the responsibility of leading so many people by himself. How did God solve this problem? *Numbers 11:11–17*

e) Moses heals Miriam of leprosy *Numbers 12:1–15*

? Whom did Moses heal of leprosy? *Numbers 12:1–15*

? Please fill in the blank: Miriam spoke against Moses because of the Ethiopian woman he had married. Then Miriam became _____. *Numbers 12:10*

? For what was Miriam punished? *Numbers 12:1–15*

? God forgave Miriam for speaking against Moses and healed her of a resulting disease. What was the disease from which she was saved? *Numbers 12:1–15*

f) Caleb *Numbers, chs. 13, 14; Joshua 14:6–11*

? Who sent a group of men to "spy out the land of Canaan" for the children of Israel? *Numbers 13:1, 2, 17*

? Caleb and other men were sent to "spy out the land of Canaan" for the children of Israel. They found "men of a great stature" and walled cities in their land of "milk and honey." Who proposed that they go up at once and possess the land? *Numbers 13:17–20, 26–28, 30*

g) Aaron's rod *Numbers 17:1–18*

? Whose rod "brought forth buds, and bloomed blossoms, and yielded almonds"? *Numbers 17:8*

? The children of Israel encountered many difficulties during their long years in the wilderness (from 1450–1410 BCE). At one time they had no water for themselves or their cattle. What did the Lord direct Moses to do to provide them with water? *Numbers 20:7–11*

h) Balaam and Balak, king of Moab *Numbers, chs. 22 to 24; 31*

? In the Old Testament, who was promised "great honour" by the king of Moab if he would curse the children of Israel? *Numbers, chs. 22, 23*

? Three times Balak asked Balaam to curse the children of Israel. Balak was king of which country? *Numbers 22:10*

? Who had a donkey that could see "the angel of the Lord standing in the way"? *Numbers 22:23*

? Who spoke these words to Balaam? "What have I done unto thee, that thou hast smitten me these three times?" *Numbers 22:28*

? What did Balak, the king of Moab, ask Balaam to do? *Numbers 23:3–8, 11–23*

? Why did Balak, the king of Moab, want Balaam to curse the children of Israel? *Numbers 22:3, 6*

? Balak, the king of Moab, wanted Balaam to curse the children of Israel. Why did Balaam tell the king of Moab that he could not curse the Israelites? *Numbers 23:8, 11, 12*

? In the Old Testament, who asked this question: "How shall I curse, whom God hath not cursed?" *Numbers 23:5, 8*

? Balaam found that he could not curse the people whom God had blessed. But, later, Balaam "taught Balac [sic] to cast a stumblingblock before the children of Israel...." What was Balaam's fate? *Numbers 23:8; 31:8; Revelation 2:14*

? In which book of the Bible is the story of Balak, the king of Moab, and Balaam? *Numbers, chs. 22, 23*

? Who "slew with the sword" Balaam, the son of Beor? *Numbers 31:1–3, 8*

? Who am I? The author of II Peter refers to me as an example of those who have "forsaken the right way, and are gone astray." *II Peter 2:15, 16*

5. Deuteronomy

? "Fear not, neither be discouraged." These words are from the fifth book of the Law. Please name this book of the Bible. *Deuteronomy 1:21*

? Which book of the Bible follows Numbers?

? The fifth book of the Bible, Deuteronomy, contains the words of Moses as he restated the law for the benefit of new generations of the children of Israel who were about to enter the promised land. What is another name for this promised land? (Possible answers to this question include: Canaan, Israel, Palestine, Zion, Judea, and the Holy Land.) *Deuteronomy 1:7; Hebrews 11:7; The New Westminster Dictionary of the Bible, "Palestine"*

? In the book of Deuteronomy, Moses reminds the people of events during the journey to Canaan. How many years were the Israelites wandering in the wilderness? *Deuteronomy 2:7*

? Please read chapter five of Deuteronomy. What is this chapter about?

? The Ten Commandments may be found in two books in the Pentateuch. Please name them. *Exodus, ch. 20; Deuteronomy, ch. 5*

a) The great commandment *Deuteronomy 6:4–9*

? Fill in the blanks: "And thou shalt love the Lord thy _____ with all thine heart, and with all thy _____, and with all thy _____." *Deuteronomy 6:5*

? In chapter six of Deuteronomy we read, "thou shalt love the Lord thy God with all thine heart, and with all thy soul, and with all thy might." Who later repeats this commandment, changing only the word "might" to "mind"? *Matthew 22:35–38*

? In which book of the Bible are these words: "Hear, O Israel: The Lord our God is one Lord: And thou shalt love the Lord thy God with all thine heart, and with all thy soul, and with all thy might"? *Deuteronomy 6:4, 5*

? The opening words of the Jewish prayer, the Shema, (*shema* means "hear!") are from Deuteronomy 6:4–9. Please read theses verses aloud. *The Cambridge Companion to the Bible, pp. 93–94*

b) "God will raise up...a Prophet" *Deuteronomy 18:15–22*

? Who spoke this Old Testament prophecy about the coming of Christ Jesus: "The Lord thy God will raise thee up a Prophet from the midst of thee, of thy brethren, like unto me"? *Deuteronomy 5:1; 18:15; Acts 3:22; 7:37*

c) Moses' song *Deuteronomy 31:30; 32:1–12*

? Who said: "My doctrine shall drop as the rain, My speech shall distill as the dew, As the small rain upon the tender herb, And as the showers upon the grass: Because I will publish the name of the Lord: Ascribe ye greatness unto our God"? *Deuteronomy 31:30 to 32:3*

? Who said this about God? "He is the Rock, his work is perfect: for all his ways are judgment: a God of truth and without iniquity, just and right is he." *Deuteronomy 32:4*

d) The death of Moses *Deuteronomy 34:1–8*

? When Moses died at an advanced age, "his eye was not dim, nor his natural force abated." How old was Moses when he died? *Deuteronomy 34:7*

? Who is described in this passage from Deuteronomy? "_____was an hundred and twenty years old when he died: his eye was not dim, nor his natural force abated." *Deuteronomy 34:7*

B. Books of History

1. Joshua

? After the death of Moses, God instructed the new leader of the Israelites to take the people across the river Jordan into the land of Canaan. Who was the Hebrew leader chosen to go on with Moses' work? *Joshua 1:1, 2*

a) Rahab hides Israelite spies and is spared *Joshua, ch. 2; 6:22–25*

? The author of Hebrews notes that Rahab "perished not with them that believed not" when her city was destroyed. She gained fame by hiding some Israelite spies from the king. Please name Rahab's city. *Hebrews 11:31; Joshua, ch. 2; 6:22–25*

b) Children of Israel pass over Jordan *Joshua 3:12–17*

? When Moses led the children of Israel out of Egypt, they walked on "dry ground" through the Red Sea. Please name the river that Joshua and the children of Israel "passed over on dry ground." *Joshua 3:17*

c) Battle of Jericho *Joshua 6:1–16, 20, 27*

? Who was the leader of the Hebrew people when the walls of Jericho fell? *Joshua 6:1–20, 27*

? Please name two famous cities that had walls around them in Bible times. *Joshua 6:1–5; Nehemiah 1:1–3*

? Joshua and his soldiers marched in a circle around the walled city of Jericho once a day for six days and seven times on the seventh day. Then they shouted and the wall fell down flat. Who told them to do this? *Joshua 6:2–5*

? Seven priests bearing seven trumpets of rams' horns blew their trumpets at Joshua's command each time the children of Israel compassed Jericho. On the seventh day, what else did the people do to make the walls fall down? *Joshua 6:1, 16, 20*

? Please name the Hebrew leader who told the people with him at Jericho to "Shout; for the Lord hath given you the city." *Joshua 6:16*

d) The sun stood still *Joshua 10:12–13*

? "The sun stood still in the midst of heaven, and hasted not to go down about a whole day." In what book of the Bible do we read about this unusual event? *Joshua 10:12–13*

e) Division of the land among the twelve tribes *Joshua, chs. 13 to 22*

? Caleb was one of twelve men sent to spy out the land of Canaan. Thirty-eight years later, he took part in the conquest of Canaan. How old was Caleb when he said, "I am as strong this day as I was in the day Moses sent me" to "espy out the land"? *Joshua 14:7–14*

? After Joshua and the children of Israel renewed their covenant with God, Joshua died. How old was Joshua when he died? *Joshua 24:29*

2. Judges

? After Joshua died, the Israelites were led by a series of fourteen judges. The first judge ruled for forty years. What was his name? *Judges 3:9–11*

? Deborah, Gideon, Jephthah, Samson and Samuel were among the more noteworthy leaders during the two hundred-year period of the judges. Othniel, a military hero, was the first judge. Samuel was the last and greatest of the judges. Please briefly recount a Bible story about one of these judges.

? Jephthah, one of the judges, made a vow to the Lord: "If thou wilt give the Ammonites into my hand, then whoever comes forth from the doors of my house to meet me, when I return victorious from the Ammonites, shall be the Lord's and I will offer him up for a burnt offering." This promise proved to be a very foolish one. Who greeted Jephthah at his house? *Judges 11:30–35*

a) Deborah and Barak *Judges, chs. 4, 5*

? One of Israel's judges was a woman. What was her name? *Judges 4:4*

? Who was the patriotic and brave woman who went with Barak and encouraged him and the children of Israel to a victory over the Canaanite tribes? *Judges, chs. 4, 5*

b) Gideon *Judges, chs. 6 to 8; Hebrews 11:32*

? Gideon was the next judge after Deborah. He came along at a time when the Midianites were troubling the Israelites. An angel of the Lord told Gideon to save Israel from the Midianites. Gideon was obedient, and "the country was in quietness forty years" afterwards. In which book of the Bible can you read this story? *Judges 6:7–24; 8:22–28*

? In the book of Judges we read of God's provision for saving Israel from the Midianites. Please name the man called by the angel of the Lord to lead the Israelites against this enemy. *Judges 6:7–24*

? When Gideon prepared to attack the Midianites' camp, the Lord told him to reduce the number of people with him. In what two ways was the group's size to be reduced? *Judges, chs. 6 to 8*

? God told Gideon to deliver Israel from the hand of the Midianites. Twice Gideon tested God's promise to deliver Israel by Gideon's hand. To test God, Gideon laid a fleece of wool on the floor. What happened to the fleece of wool each time? *Judges 6:36–40*

? What did Gideon give to each of the 300 men in his army as they surrounded the camp of the Midianites? *Judges 7:16*

? What did Gideon's men shout after blowing their trumpets and breaking their pitchers? *Judges 7:18*

? Was Gideon successful in his task of saving Israel from wicked acts of the Midianites? *Judges 8:28*

? Every time one of the judges died, the Israelites went astray until a new judge was raised up. After Gideon died, his son, Abimelech set himself up unlawfully as king for three years. Please name two other judges, besides Gideon and Abimelech. *Judges 10:1–3*

c) Samson   *Judges, chs. 13 to 16; Hebrews 11:32–39*

? One of the fourteen judges who led the Hebrew people was a Nazarite, famous for his strength. Please name him. *Judges 13:24*

? The angel of the Lord appeared to this Nazarite's mother and said, "Behold, you are barren, but you shall conceive and bear a son." Please name her son. *Judges 13:2, 3, 5, 24; The Reader's Digest Bible, p. 127*

? The Bible does not give the name of Samson's mother, but records that she was Manoah's wife. She was barren until the angel of the Lord told her she would bear a son. What instructions did the angel give Samson's mother? *Judges 13:4, 5*

? Please name the man who judged Israel twenty years and was famous for his great strength. He loved Delilah, who betrayed him by having his hair shaved off and allowing the Philistines to seize him. *Judges 16:15–31*

? Which of the following judges was famous for his great physical strength: Gideon, Samson, or Samuel? *Judges 16:6*

Figure 8: Ruth brings grain to Naomi.

That Ye May Teach the Children

3. Ruth (See Figure 8)

? The book of Ruth is a beautiful short story about two women who were loved and protected by God. After the death of her husband, Ruth left her own country and went with her mother-in-law to Bethlehem. Please give the mother-in-law's name. *Ruth 1:8, 14, 16, 19*

? Why did Elimelech, Naomi, and their two sons leave Bethlehem-judah and go to sojourn in the country of Moab? *Ruth 1:1, 2*

? *Sojourn* means "to stay as a temporary resident." In which country did Elimelech, Naomi and their two sons *sojourn* during a time of famine in Judah? *Ruth 1:1, 2*

? Please name the country where Ruth grew up. *Ruth 1:4*

? The people of Moab worshipped different gods. They did not honor the one God of the Hebrew people. When Ruth left Moab, she also left behind the worship of many gods. Where was Ruth's new home? *Ruth 1:8–19*

? Who said this? "Entreat me not to leave thee, or to return from following after thee: for whither thou goest, I will go; and where thou lodgest, I will lodge: thy people shall be my people, and thy God my God...." *Ruth 1:16*

? A Moabitess named Ruth was married to one of Naomi's sons. After her husband died, Ruth went to Bethlehem with Naomi. Ruth said to Naomi, "Whither thou goest, I will go...thy people shall be my people, and thy God, my God." Did Ruth ever marry again? *Ruth 4:13*

? What well-known woman of the Bible was from Moab? *Ruth 1:4*

? Who left her own country and people to follow her mother-in-law? *Ruth 1:11–22*

? What was Ruth's plan for feeding herself and Naomi after they arrived in Bethlehem? *Ruth 2:1,2*

? The Bible tells how Ruth "gleaned in the field after the reapers." The reapers' work was to cut and gather the stalks of barley. What does it mean to *glean*? *Ruth 2:3*

? What bearing do verses 9 and 10 in chapter 19 of Leviticus have on the story of Ruth and Naomi?

? After Naomi and Ruth arrived in Bethlehem, Ruth gleaned corn in a field belonging to Boaz. Ruth later married Boaz. Did Ruth and Boaz ever have children? *Ruth 4:13–17*

? Obed was the son of Ruth and Boaz. Obed begat Jesse and Jesse begat David. David, of course, became the king of Israel. Please name David's son, the next king. *Matthew 1:5,6*

? Please name David's father, grandfather, and great grandparents as recorded in Ruth. *Ruth 4:17*

? True or false? Ruth appears in Matthew's genealogy of Christ Jesus. *Matthew 1:5*

? Which two books in the Old Testament are named for women?

4. I and II Samuel

a) Samuel as a child *I Samuel 1:1–28; 3:1–20*

(1) Birth *I Samuel 1:1–28*

? In the book of I Samuel is the story of Samuel's birth. Samuel's mother was "in bitterness of soul" and "wept sore" because she had no children. But she prayed unto the Lord and had a son. Please name Samuel's mother. *I Samuel 1:1–28*

? What was the name of the priest who spoke with Hannah after she prayed for a child? This man was also one of the Hebrew judges; he judged for forty years. *I Samuel 1:9–18*

? An Old Testament woman had no children and "was in bitterness of soul." As she prayed to God, "she spake in her heart." Because her lips moved without sound, the priest, Eli, thought she was drunk. Please name her. *I Samuel 1:1–28*

? What promise did Hannah make to God when she asked Him for a child? *I Samuel 1:11*

? Did Hannah keep her promise to God? *I Samuel 1:25–28*

? In response to her prayers, Hannah bore a son and named him Samuel. How many more children did Hannah bear after she gave birth to Samuel? *I Samuel 2:21*

(2) Hears God *I Samuel 3:1–20*

? What little boy in the Old Testament learned to listen to God after jumping out of bed and going to Eli, his teacher, three times? *I Samuel 3:1–10*

? When Samuel was a child living with Eli the priest, he heard someone calling him one night. Please tell this story. *I Samuel 3:1–20*

b) Samuel as leader; anoints King Saul *I Samuel 9:1 to 10:16*

? This Old Testament Hebrew was a priest, a prophet, and the last of the judges. Eli, the priest, raised him. He anointed Saul the first king of Israel and David, the second king. Please name him. *I Samuel 1:9–11, 20–28; 3:1–10; 16:1–13*

? While Samuel was judge, the Philistines, in a great battle, took something that was very precious to the Hebrews. What was it? *I Samuel 4:10–11*

? The Philistines had the ark of the covenant seven months. They did not want to keep it longer because bad things were happening to them. How did they decide to return it? *I Samuel 6:3–9*

? When Samuel was old, he appointed his sons as judges — but they were very bad judges. The people asked Samuel to give them a king. Samuel prayed to God, who told him to anoint Saul. How was Samuel to know the man who would be king? *I Samuel 9:15–17*

? True or false? Saul was Israel's first king. *I Samuel 9:15–17*

? Did Saul feel that he was the right person to be king? *I Samuel 9:19–21*

? Gideon, Samson, and Samuel are three well-known judges from Bible times. Please match each Judge to the correct description below:
   - He had long hair and great strength.
   - He had only 300 men in his army; he knew God's help was most important.
   - Eli, the priest, raised him. He was the last judge.

? True or false? The author of Hebrews notes that Gideon, Samson and Samuel "obtained a good report through faith...." *Hebrews 11:32, 39*

c) Saul and David (See Figure 9)

(1) Samuel secretly anoints David as Saul's successor *I Samuel 16:1–13*

? To whom did Samuel say, "You have rejected the word of the Lord, and the Lord hath rejected thee from being king over Israel"? *I Samuel 15:26*

? During Saul's reign, God told Samuel to anoint a new king from among whose sons? *I Samuel 16:1*

? How many sons did Jesse, the Bethlehemite, show Samuel at first? *I Samuel 16:10*

? Seven sons passed before Samuel, and the prophet said: "The Lord hath not chosen these." Where was David, the youngest son? *I Samuel 16:1–13*

? Who was the father of David? *II Samuel 23:1*

? Samuel did not see the one described by God among Jesse's seven sons, but who was away keeping the sheep? *I Samuel 16:11–13*

? Who was Jesse's youngest son, the one anointed by Samuel to be the new king?
I Samuel 16:11–13

? Which prophet anointed David, the son of Jesse, because David was to become the next king after Saul? *I Samuel 16:1–7,10–13*

? The prophet Samuel secretly anointed David, the son of Jesse. Where did this take place?
I Samuel 16:1–13

(2) Saul is healed when David plays a harp *I Samuel 16:14–23*

? An "evil spirit" troubled King Saul. Saul's servants suggested that they seek out "a cunning player on an harp" so that "he shall play with his hand," and Saul "shalt be well." Who played his harp for Saul? *I Samuel 16:23*

? Toward the end of his life, Saul was not a very happy man. He asked to have someone come to play music for him, thinking this might make him happier. Who was asked to play for him? *I Samuel 16:19, 23*

? Who was refreshed and well after "David took an harp, and played with his hand"?
I Samuel 16:23

(3) David battles Goliath *I Samuel 17:1–51*

? The Philistines were enemies of the Israelites, and they were especially dangerous because they had one soldier who was from Gath, a land of giants. What was his name?
I Samuel 17:4

? Who was a giant man in the Bible, whose height was "six cubits and a span"?
I Samuel 17:4

? Is the story of David and Goliath in the Old Testament or the New Testament?

? The Philistines wanted to have the battle decided by having Goliath fight one of the Israelite soldiers. How many days did Goliath challenge the Israelites, with no one volunteering to fight him? *I Samuel 17:16*

? How did David happen to be in the camp of the Israelite soldiers when Goliath issued his challenge? *I Samuel 17:17–23*

? Who said to David, "Thou art not able to go against this Philistine to fight with him: for thou art but a youth, and he a man of war from his youth"? *I Samuel 17:33*

? What did David say to convince King Saul that he was capable of fighting Goliath?
I Samuel 17:34–37

Figure 9: David sings psalms to his sheep

? What animals came to the flock while David was taking care of his father's sheep? *I Samuel 17:34–37*

? Who said, "The Lord that delivered me out of the paw of the lion, and out of the paw of the bear, he will deliver me out of the hand of the Philistine"? *I Samuel 17:37*

? When David was about to fight Goliath, who gave him his own armour and helmet of brass? *I Samuel 17:38, 39*

? Why did David decide not to wear armour when he went to battle Goliath? *I Samuel 17:39*

? What did David use to slay Goliath? *I Samuel 17:50*

? How many smooth stones did David choose from the brook before fighting Goliath? *I Samuel 17:40*

? True or false? David ran toward the army to meet and slay the Philistine, Goliath. *I Samuel 17:48*

? David exhibited courage when he fought Goliath. Please give two other qualities that David used in his battle with Goliath. *I Samuel 17:1–58*

? Please name the Philistine whom David, the shepherd-boy, killed with a sling and a stone. *I Samuel 17:4,48–50*

? True or false? Goliath was a Philistine. *I Samuel 17:4*

? True or false? David was descended from Ruth, the Moabitess. *Ruth 4:13–22*

? Which came first?
  • "David prevailed over the Philistine with a sling and with a stone, and smote the Philistine and slew him...."
  • The prophet Samuel anoints David, the son of Jesse, to become king after Saul.
  I Samuel 16:1–13; 17:50

? Who lived first, Moses or David?

(4) Saul envies David; Saul's daughter marries David *I Samuel 18:1–29*

? What caused King Saul to hate David after David had helped Saul by slaying Goliath and leading Saul's "men of war"? *I Samuel 18:5–9*

? Why was Saul jealous of David? *I Samuel 18:6–9*

? Who was David's first wife? *I Samuel 18:20–29*

? Which of the following became king of the Hebrew people after King Saul?
- David
- Jonathan, the son of Saul
- Solomon
- Herod the Great

II Samuel 2:4

(5) David escapes; Jonathan befriends him. *I Samuel, chs. 18 to 20*

? Saul, the first king of the United Kingdom of Israel and Judah, had four sons. The oldest became close friends with David. Please name this eldest son, known for his unselfishness and heroism. *I Samuel 13:22; 14:49; 31:1, 11–13; I Chronicles 10:2, 8–12*

? Who was David's best friend? *I Samuel 18:1–4; 20:16–17*

? Jonathan is best known for his friendship with David. The Bible says Jonathan loved David "as he loved his own soul." Jonathan was the oldest son of which king? *I Samuel 14:49; 20:17*

? How did Jonathan plan to warn David if his father, Saul, planned to harm David? *I Samuel 20:12–23*

? Which signal did Jonathan give David regarding Saul's plan? *I Samuel 20:35–42*

? Where did David go to be safe from King Saul? *I Samuel 22:1*

? Was David alone while he was hiding from King Saul? *I Samuel 22:1, 2*

? Did King Saul search for David? *I Samuel 23:14, 15*

(6) David spares Saul twice *I Samuel, chs. 24, 26*

? King Saul became increasingly jealous of David. He even tried to kill David with a javelin. Later, David has the opportunity to kill Saul. Does David kill Saul? *I Samuel 18:10, 11; chs. 20, 24, 26*

? On two occasions, David had a chance to kill Saul, but chose not to do so. Why? *I Samuel, chs. 24, 26*

(7) David seeks assistance from Nabal and Abigail *I Samuel, ch. 25*

? David and his followers had helped protect the property of the people in the neighborhood from bands of robbers. So David sent ten of his men to a wealthy man named Nabal. They asked Nabal to give them food and supplies. What did Nabal say? *I Samuel 25:10–12*

? How did David react to Nabal's refusal to give his men supplies? *I Samuel 25:13*

? After Nabal's refusal, who convinced David to be calm and have no bloodshed? *I Samuel 25:14–31*

? What happened to Abigail after Nabal died? *I Samuel 25:42*

? Abigail was one of David's wives. Before her marriage to David, Abigail was married to a very wealthy man named Nabal, who died suddenly. What kind, generous thing did Abigail do to help David and his followers? *I Samuel, ch. 25*

(8) Saul consults a woman at Endor to contact dead Samuel *I Samuel 28:3–20*

? Although King Saul was loyal to God throughout most of his reign, before his last battle with enemies he succumbed to temptation and consulted with a woman who had a "familiar spirit." This woman was reputed to have the power of calling up the dead. What did the woman tell Saul? *I Samuel 28:7–20*

? To whom did Saul go for help when he was afraid of the Philistines? *I Samuel 28:7*

? Please name the king who disguised himself and went to visit a woman with a "familiar spirit" at Endor. *I Samuel 28:7, 8*

(9) David laments, "How are the mighty fallen" *II Samuel 1:17, 19, 23–27*

? Saul was Israel's first king, and he reigned from about 1028–1013 BCE. How did Saul die during a battle with the Philistines? *I Samuel 31:4*

? Who besides King Saul died in a battle with the Philistines? *I Samuel 31:6*

? How did David feel when he learned of the deaths of King Saul and Jonathan? *II Samuel 1:17–27*

(10) David becomes king of Judah, then Israel *II Samuel 2:14; 5:15; I Chronicles, chs. 11 to 29*

? David was anointed king of the Southern Kingdom of Judah. How many years did he reign in Hebron before Judah and Israel were united? *II Samuel 2:11*

? Hebron is "one of the oldest towns in the world which is still inhabited, instead of being simply a ruin." It is about 20 miles from Jerusalem. Sarah died in Hebron. For seven and a half years, Hebron was the capital city of Judah. Who reigned during this period? *II Samuel 2:11; The New Westminster Dictionary of the Bible, pp. 374–375*

? David reigned first in Judah, the southern region, and then over all of Israel. How old was David when he began to reign over all Israel, and how long was his total reign? *II Samuel 5:4*

? King David had eight wives and many children. His best known wife was named Bathsheba. One of her sons became the next king of Israel after David. This same son is credited with having said many proverbs. Please name him. *I Kings 2:12*

? Joab, David's military commander, helped David unite the kingdoms of Israel and Judah and conquer land from neighboring countries. Joab, however, was guilty of several bad deeds, including the murders of Abner and Amasa. After David's death, Joab was put to death by the command of what king? *I Kings 2:134*

? How many wives did David have? *I Samuel 18:27; II Samuel 3:2–5; 12:24*

(11) David's affair with Bathsheba; rebuke by Nathan *II Samuel 2:14; 5:15; 12:1–9*

? Although David was generally faithful to God, once he sinned terribly and "displeased the Lord." First he coveted Bathsheba. Then he committed adultery and arranged for her husband, Uriah the Hittite, to be killed in battle. What commandments did David break? *II Samuel 11:2–4 (to first ;), 5, 6, 14, 15, 26, 27*

? David and Bathsheba's first child died in infancy. Their next child grew to adulthood and became the third king of the United Kingdom. Please name him. *II Samuel 12:24*

? Who was the Old Testament prophet who rebuked King David for his adultery with Bathsheba and his subsequent order to place her husband at the battlefront?
  - Elijah
  - Daniel
  - Nathan
  - Isaiah
  II Samuel 12:1–9

? Nathan showed great moral courage when he rebuked David for his adultery with Bathsheba and his subsequent plan to have Uriah killed in battle. Who was Nathan? *II Samuel 12:1–9*

? How did Nathan the prophet rebuke David for committing adultery and murder? *II Samuel 12:1–9*

? Nathan told King David a parable after David's misdeeds concerning Bathsheba and Uriah. Please tell the parable Nathan told David. *II Samuel 12:1–9*

(12) Absalom's conspiracy *II Samuel, chs. 15 to 18*

? David had a son named Absalom who did many things that displeased David. How did Absalom die? *II Samuel 18:9–15*

? Although Absalom was beautiful to look at and evidently had an attractive personality, he proved to be treacherous. Who was Absalom's father? *II Samuel, chs. 13 to 18*

? Why did Absalom work to win over the affections of the Hebrew people against his father, David? *II Samuel, ch. 15*

? Who am I? I plotted to overthrow my father, King David, and reign over Israel from Hebron. *II Samuel, chs. 13 to 18*

? Who was Absalom? *II Samuel 13:1; 14:25; 18:32–33*

? What happened to David's son, Absalom, on the day of the battle in the wood of Ephraim? *II Samuel 18:9–15*

? What did David say when he learned that Absalom had died? *II Samuel 18:33*

? Absalom was the son of the king of Israel. Despite Absalom's history of evil deeds, Absalom's father mourned his death, crying: "O my son Absalom, my son ...would God I had died for thee...." Who was Absalom's father? *II Samuel 18:3*

5. I and II Kings

a) Solomon, King David's son

? Who was Solomon's father? *I Kings 3:6, 7*

? Who was Solomon's mother? *I Kings 1:11*

? As David grew old and was not well, one of his sons, Adonijah, appointed himself David's successor. Some of David's friends told Bathsheba what Adonijah was doing, and she went to David. What did she ask David to do? *I Kings 1:15–17*

? Of David's sons, who succeeded him as king of the Hebrew people? *I Kings 1:28–31*

? Whom did David ask to anoint Solomon? *I Kings 1:34*

? How did Adonijah, Solomon's half brother, receive the news that Solomon was anointed king? *I Kings 1:50–53*

? Please name the first three kings of Israel. *I Samuel 10:17–26; II Samuel 2:4, I Kings 2:12*

? True or false? King Saul, King David, and King Solomon each reigned over the United Kingdom for forty years. *I Kings 2:11; 11:42*

(1) Solomon's prayer for wisdom *I Kings 3:5–15; I Chronicles 1:7–12*

? When the Lord said to Solomon, "Ask what I shall give thee," for what did Solomon ask? *I Kings 3:5–9*

? The Lord was pleased with Solomon's request. What did He give Solomon? *I Kings 3:10–14*

? What king asked for an understanding heart instead of riches — and received both? *I Kings 3:5, 9, 12, 13*

? Which of the following did Solomon ask God to give him?
- long life
- riches
- the life of his enemies
- an understanding heart

I Kings 3:9, 11

(2) Dividing the baby *I Kings 3:16–28*

? Two women came before Solomon to ask him to decide who was the true mother of a baby. How did Solomon decide who was the real mother? *I Kings 3:16–27*

? Did the people feel that King Solomon judged wisely in the case of two women both claiming to be the mother of a baby? *I Kings 3:28*

? Please name the wise king who said: "Divide the living child in two, and give half to the one, and half to the other." *I Kings 3:25*

(3) Building of the temple *II Samuel 24:21–25; I Kings, chs. 5 to 7*

? Who was the Hebrew leader to first construct a temple for worship in Jerusalem? *I Kings 5:1–5; 6:1, 14*

? King David envisioned building a temple for worship in Jerusalem. David purchased a threshing floor from Araunah for this purpose. However, it was David's son, Solomon, who actually had the temple built. What famous building is today located on this ancient site? *II Samuel 24:21–25; Discovering the Biblical World, Frank, pp. 84, 85*

? Who was the king of Israel who said to Hiram, king of Tyre: "I purpose to build an house unto the name of the Lord my God...?" *I Kings 5:5*

? What did Solomon ask his friend Hiram, king of Tyre, to do? *I Kings 5:2, 6–12*

? How long did the construction of Solomon's temple in Jerusalem take? *I Kings 6:38*

? Solomon held a feast of dedication when the ark of the covenant was put in the temple. What did the ark hold? *I Kings 8:9*

(4) Visit of the Queen of Sheba *I Kings 10:1–13; I Chronicles 9:1–12*

? What queen came to visit Solomon to see if all she had heard about Solomon was true? *I Kings: 10:1*

? Please fill in the blank: "when the queen of Sheba heard of the fame of _____ concerning the name of the Lord, she came to prove him with hard questions." *I Kings 10:1*

? Did Solomon continue in his old age to be as wise as he had been in his youth? *I Kings 11:4–6, 9, 10*

? For how many years was Solomon king of the United Kingdom? *I Kings 11:42*

b) Two kingdoms (Judah and Israel) and miscellaneous kings

(The chronology of kings is from *The New Westminster Dictionary of the Bible*, p. 540. During its more than 300 year history as a kingdom, Judah had twenty rulers. Nineteen were kings descended from David; one was a usurper named Athaliah. Israel had nineteen kings, beginning with Rehoboam, during its approximately 200 year history.)

(1) Kings of Judah, the Southern Kingdom

? After Solomon's death, Jeroboam became king of the northern section, Israel, and Rehoboam became king of the southern section, Judah. Of these kings, who was the son of Solomon — Jeroboam or Rehoboam? *I Kings 11:28, 43*

? Jeroboam, the son of Nebat, became the first king of Israel after the division. Rehoboam became the first king of Judah, the Southern Kingdom. Please name Rehoboam's father. *I Kings 11:43*

? After the United Kingdom of the Hebrew people was split into two parts, Jeroboam became king of Israel, the Northern Kingdom. He led the people back to idolatry. Was Jeroboam descended from David? *I Kings 11:26–40; 12:26–30; I Chronicles 13:8*

? After Solomon's death, the United Kingdom split into two parts. The Southern Kingdom was known as _____. The Northern Kingdom was called _____.

(a) Asa, third king of Judah *I Kings, chs. 15, 16; II Chronicles, chs. 14 to 16*

? The third king of Judah was loyal to God through most of his life. He abolished idols in Judah. Toward the end of his reign, he became diseased in his feet. The king sought help from physicians but not from God. Please name this king. *I Kings 15:23*

(b) Jehoshaphat, fourth king of Judah *I Kings, ch. 22; II Chronicles, chs. 17 to 21*

? Jehoshaphat was the fourth king of Judah. He reigned for twenty-five years and was one of the best, most pious kings of Judah. Who was Jehoshaphat's father? *I Kings 15:24*

? This fourth king of Judah reigned well and strengthened his kingdom. "He took away the high places...out of Judah." He sent Levites throughout Judah to teach Mosaic Law. Please name him. *I Kings 15:24; 22:1–50; II Chronicles, chs. 17 to 20*

(c) Ahaz, twelfth ruler of Judah *II Kings, ch. 16; II Chronicles, ch. 28; Micah 1:1; Isaiah 1:1*

? What prophet lived and taught in Judah during the reigns of these four kings: Uzziah, Jotham, Ahaz and Hezekiah? *Isaiah 1:1*

? Elijah was a prophet. David was a king. Were the following leaders of the Hebrew people prophets or kings?
- Elisha
- Ahaz
- Jehoshaphat
- Isaiah

(d) Hezekiah, thirteenth ruler of Judah *II Kings, chs. 18 to 20; II Chronicles, chs. 29 to 32; Isaiah, chs. 36 to 39; Hosea 1:1*

? The following four kings were the best this kingdom had after the division of the United Kingdom. Known as the "godly kings", they were Asa, Jehoshaphat, Hezekiah and Josiah. Did they reign in Judah or Israel? *The New Westminster Dictionary of the Bible, p. 540; Getting Better Acquainted with Your Bible, Shotwell, pp. 122–123*

? Whose army was smitten by a plague and unable to fight against Jerusalem during King Hezekiah's reign? *II Kings, chs. 18 to 20*

? When Sennacherib, king of Assyria, sent "a great host against Jerusalem," this king of Judah prayed, with the help of Isaiah. An angel of the Lord smote the Assyrians in their camp. Please name this king of Judah. *II Kings, chs. 18 to 20*

? The soldiers in Sennacherib's army died in their camp, without a battle, thanks to the prayers of Isaiah, Hezekiah and the people of Judah. After that unusual event, Sennacherib returned to the capital city of Assyria. Please name the capital city of Assyria. *Isaiah 37:37*

(e) Manasseh, fourteenth ruler of Judah *II Kings, ch. 21; II Chronicles, ch. 33*

? Manasseh "did that which was evil in the sight of the Lord, after the abominations of the heathen." This king of Judah was the son of Hezekiah, and he had a very long reign. How long did Manasseh reign? *II Kings 21:1*

? Which of the following was not a king of Judah, the Southern Kingdom?
- Hezekiah
- Manasseh
- Jeremiah
- Zedekiah

(f) Josiah, sixteenth ruler of Judah *II Kings, chs. 22, 23; II Chronicles, chs. 34, 35; Jeremiah 1:1–3*

? Please name the king who began to reign when he was eight years old and reigned thirty-one years in Jerusalem. "And like unto him was there no king before him, that turned to the Lord with all his heart, and with all his soul, and with all his might...." *II Kings 22:1; 23:25*

? The kingdom of Judah, comprised of the tribes of Judah and Benjamin, survived as a nation for almost one and a half centuries longer than the kingdom of Israel. This was due, in part, to the leadership of four "godly kings." Please name them. *I Kings 15:8–24; 22:2–50; II Kings 3:6–27, chs. 18 to 23; I Chronicles, chs. 14 to 21, 29 to 32; II Chronicles, chs. 34, 35; Isaiah, chs. 36 to 39; Jeremiah 26:17–19; Getting Better Acquainted with Your Bible, Shotwell, pp. 122–123*

? Please name the great prophet of Judah whose public life extended through all or part of the following five kings' reigns: Josiah, Jehoahaz, Jehoiakim, Jehoiachin and Zedekiah. *Jeremiah 1:1–10; The New Westminster Dictionary of the Bible, pp. 457, 540*

? The prophet Jeremiah writes that "the word of the Lord" came to him during the reigns of three kings of Judah. Please name the three kings Jeremiah mentions. *Jeremiah 1:1–3*

? The kingdom of Israel ended in 722 BCE when the Israelites were carried captive to Assyria. What happened to the Southern Kingdom of Judah in about 586 BCE? *II Kings 25:8–12*

(g) Zedekiah, twentieth and last ruler of Judah *II Kings, chs. 24, 25;*
II Chronicles 36:9–21; Jeremiah, chs. 37 to 39, 52

? Zedekiah was the last Hebrew king of Judah. In the last year of his reign, Jerusalem fell captive to Babylon. The city was burned and the walls leveled. Who was Babylon's king? *II Kings, chs. 24, 25; Jeremiah, ch. 52.*

? Of these kings of Judah, who imprisoned Jeremiah for his dire prophecies?
- Asa
- Hezekiah
- Josiah
- Zedekiah

Jeremiah 37:21; Getting Better Acquainted with Your Bible, Shotwell, p. 89

? Nebuchadnezzar and the Chaldeans practically destroyed Jerusalem, the capital of Judah, about 586 BCE. Many of the Hebrew people were deported to Babylon at that time. Who was king of Judah when Jerusalem fell to Nebuchadnezzar's army? *Jeremiah 37:1 to 38:28*

? A number of spiritually minded prophets spoke out about the self-indulgence and complacency in Israel and Judah that eventually led to their overthrow. Assyria invaded Israel. Who invaded Judah about 586 BCE? *Jeremiah 39:110*

c) Two prophets who become Israel's real leaders: Elijah and Elisha

(1) Elijah's great works (See Figure 10)

(a) Ahab, king of Israel, and his wife, Jezebel oppose Elijah
I Kings 16:30–33; 21:5–16

? In the Old Testament books of I and II Kings, most of the spiritually inspired stories have to do with great prophets. Please name them.

? Please name the Tishbite prophet who was "an hairy man" and wore "a girdle of leather about his loins." *II Kings 1:8*

? King Ahab and his wife Jezebel were the worst of all Israel's rulers. They built an altar to Baal and tried to lead the Israelites back to idolatry. What great prophet finally defeated them and did many great works, such as raising a widow's son from death? *I Kings 17:17–24*

? Jezebel was the wife of Ahab, king of the Northern Kingdom, Israel. She introduced the worship of Baal, a god of the Canaanites. What prophet opposed her? *I Kings 16:30–33; 19:1–12*

? Ahab, king of Israel, wanted a vineyard that was owned by Naboth, but Naboth would not consent to let him have it. How did Jezebel get the vineyard for Ahab? *I Kings 21:5–16*

Figure 10: The prophet Elijah talks with God.

That Ye May Teach the Children

(b) Fed by ravens; fed by widow of Zarephath   *I Kings 17:6–16*

? Please name the Hebrew prophet who was first fed by ravens and then fed by a poor widow woman of Zarephath.   *I Kings 17:1–16*

? When the Lord told Elijah to go to Zarephath, whom did He say would care for him?   *I Kings 17:10*

? What did the widow in Zarephath say when Elijah asked her for food?   *I Kings 17:12*

? What happened to the widow of Zarephath's barrel of meal and cruse of oil after she "did according to the saying of Elijah"?   *I Kings 17:16*

(c) Raises widow's son   *I Kings 17:1, 8–24*

? Who was the prophet who obeyed God and went to the home of a widow woman in Zarephath and healed her son when "there was no breath left in him"?   *I Kings 17:1, 8–24*

? Who healed the son of a widow woman in Zarephath?   *I Kings 17:17–24*

? True or false? Elijah raised a boy from death.   *I Kings 17:17–24*

? Why did the widow woman in Zarephath say to Elijah: "Now by this I know that thou art a man of God, and that the word of the Lord in thy mouth is truth"?   *I Kings 17:23, 24*

(d) Four hundred and fifty prophets of Baal   *I Kings 18:1, 17–40*

? In what book of the Bible is the well-known story of the "contest" between Elijah, the prophet of Jehovah, and the 450 prophets of Baal to see whose God answered by fire?   *I Kings 18:1, 17–26, 30–39*

? Elijah told Ahab that he and his family were the cause of Israel's troubles because they followed the god Baal. Where did Elijah propose meeting the prophets of Baal?   *I Kings 18:19, 20*

? Who was Ahab's wife and how did she feel about Elijah?   *I Kings 19:1, 2*

? Elijah slew the prophets of Baal after the contest on Mt. Carmel. Who, then, sent a messenger unto Elijah, saying, "So let the gods do to me...if I make not thy life as the life of one of them..."?   *I Kings 19:2*

(e) Escapes to wilderness; fed by an angel under a juniper tree   *I Kings 19:1–10*

? Elijah fled after Jezebel threatened to kill him. Where did he go?   *I Kings 19:4*

? Once Elijah became so discouraged that he wanted to die in the wilderness. Why was Elijah so unhappy?   *I Kings 19:1–10*

? Which Old Testament prophet sat down under a juniper tree and requested that he might die? *I Kings 19:1–10*

? Please tell how an angel helped Elijah in the wilderness. *I Kings 19:5–8*

? Who touched Elijah as he slept under a juniper tree in the wilderness and said: "Arise and eat"? *I Kings 19:5*

? After being fed by the angel of the Lord, how long did Elijah go "in the strength of that meat"? *I Kings 19:4–8*

? In Luke we read that Christ Jesus fasted forty days and forty nights. Jesus was not the first Bible character to do this, however. Can you name two Old Testament prophets who fasted forty days and forty nights? *Exodus 34:28; I Kings 19:8*

(f) The still small voice *I Kings 19:9–13*

? In the book of I Kings, a prophet experiences wind, earthquake, and fire. After the fire he hears "a still small voice." Please name the prophet. *I Kings 19:12, 13*

? Why did Elijah flee to Horeb, the mount of God? *I Kings 19:1–12*

? On Horeb, the mount of God, Elijah experienced wind, earthquake, and fire. Was God in any of these? What happened next? *I Kings 19:11–12*

(g) Divides waters of Jordan *II Kings 2:1–18*

? How did Elijah and Elisha cross the river Jordan? *II Kings 2:8*

? In Exodus we read that Moses led the children of Israel across the Red Sea on dry ground, because "the waters were divided" by the Lord. What two prophets divided the waters of the river Jordan and "went over on dry ground"? *II Kings 2:5–8, 14, 15*

? When it came time for Elijah to be taken up to heaven by a whirlwind, who went with him to Gilgal? *II Kings 2:1*

(h) Ascends to heaven by a whirlwind *II Kings 2:1–11*

? What prophet ascended into heaven by a whirlwind? *II Kings 2:11*

? Elijah was translated to heaven without dying. A chariot and horses of fire took him up in a whirlwind to heaven. Who was translated before Elijah? *Genesis 5:24*

? Who witnessed Elijah ascending into heaven by a whirlwind? *II Kings 2:1–11*

? Please name the river Elisha was near when he witnessed Elijah's ascension into heaven. *II Kings 2:11–14*

Figure 11: Elisha thanks God for bringing a boy back to life.

(i) Mentioned in the Gospels as Elias (Greek form of name) over twenty-five times

? How is Elijah's name spelled in the New Testament, which was translated from the Greek language? *Matthew 16:13, 14*

? Of the Old Testament prophets, who is mentioned frequently in the Gospels, where his name is spelled "Elias"? *Luke 4:24–26*

(2) Elisha's great works (See Figure 11)

(a) Succeeds Elijah *II Kings 2:9–15*

? Who was Elijah's disciple and successor? *II Kings 2:9–15*

(b) Increases widow's oil *II Kings 4:1–7*

? Why did Elisha tell a certain widow: "Go, borrow thee vessels abroad of all thy neighbours, even empty vessels; borrow not a few"? *II Kings 4:1–4*

? What famous prophet increased the widow's oil and saved her two sons from becoming bondmen to their creditor? This prophet told the widow to borrow empty vessels from her neighbours and to fill them with the pot of oil in her house. *II Kings 4:1–7*

(c) Heals son of the Shunammite woman *II Kings 4:8–37*

? When Elisha went to Shunem, "a great woman ... constrained him to eat bread." So, "as oft as he passed by he turned in thither to eat bread." This woman and her husband even fixed a guestroom for Elisha. How did Elisha repay her hospitality? *II Kings 4:8–37*

? Gehazi, Elisha's servant, told Elisha that the Shunammite woman "hath no child, and her husband is old." Elisha prophesied that she would bear a son. Was the prophecy fulfilled? *II Kings 4:8–17*

? A "great woman" and her husband lived in a town of Canaan. When Elisha came to town, she invited him to "eat bread." In return, Elisha prayed, and she bore a son. Please name the town where this "great woman" lived. *II Kings 4:8*

? The young son of a Shunammite woman became ill one day when "he went out to his father to the reapers." Then he died. So his mother went to "the man of God" for help. Please name the Old Testament prophet who raised this boy from death. *II Kings 4:17–37*

? When the Shunammite woman's son died, she laid him on Elisha's bed, shut the door, and went to get "the man of God." How did she answer Gehazi's question: "Is it well with the child?" *II Kings 4:17–37*

(d) Neutralizes pottage *II Kings 4:38–44*

? Elisha and the sons of the prophets tasted some pottage and cried out: "O thou man of god, there is death in the pot." What did Elisha do with the pottage? *II Kings 4:38–44*

(e) Heals Naaman *II Kings, ch. 5*

? Naaman, a captain in Syria, was a brave, honorable man. Unfortunately, he had a terrible disease called leprosy. Naaman finally dipped himself seven times in the river Jordan, according to Elisha's command, and was healed. In what book of the Bible can you read this story? *II Kings 5:1–15 (to second :)*

? Naaman's wife had a little maid. This girl knew Naaman was a leper, so she said unto her mistress that the prophet Elisha would recover Naaman of his leprosy. What country was this maid from? *II Kings 5:1–15 (to second :)*

? Who healed Naaman of leprosy? *II Kings 5:1–15 (to second :)*

? When Elisha healed Naaman, the Syrian captain, of leprosy, he knew Naaman needed to learn humility. Therefore, Elisha sent a messenger instructing Naaman to wash in a river seven times. Which river was Naaman to go to, and why did he not want to obey? *II Kings 5:1–4, 9–15 (to second :)*

? Who convinced Naaman to follow Elisha's instructions and wash in Jordan seven times? *II Kings 5:13–15 (to second :)*

? Was Naaman an Israelite like Elisha? *II Kings 5:1*

? What did Naaman learn about God from this experience? *II Kings 5:15*

(f) Causes axe head to float *II Kings 6:1–7*

? Elisha and the sons of the prophets were too crowded where they were living, so they agreed to go to Jordan to make a better place to dwell. One man was using a borrowed axe when the axe head fell in the water. He was afraid because it did not belong to him. How did Elisha help him? *II Kings 6:6,7*

(g) Opens servant's eyes at Dothan *II Kings 6:8–18*

? During the time of Elisha, the prophet, "the king of Syria warred against Israel." How did the Israelites know what the Syrians were going to do? *II Kings 6:8–12*

? Elisha's city was compassed with horses and chariots. Why did Elisha tell his servant to "fear not..."? *II Kings 6:8–17*

? After Elisha prayed that the eyes of his servant might be opened, what did his servant see, and what happened to the Syrian army? *II Kings 6:17–18*

? How did Elisha tell the king of Israel to treat the captive Syrians? *II Kings 20–23*

6. I and II Chronicles

a) Historical books emphasizing events in the Southern Kingdom during the period covered in the books of Samuel and Kings

(For a chronology of the kings of Judah and Israel, see *The New Westminster Dictionary of the Bible*, p. 540. Also, please see this book's index for additional questions on the kings.)

? True or false? The period of Hebrew history covered in I and II Chronicles is approximately the same period covered in the books of Samuel and Kings.

? The book of I Chronicles begins with a genealogy, starting with Adam. Genealogies appear often in the Old Testament. What is a genealogy?

? II Chronicles begins with a story about David's son, who was known to be a very wise king. Who was he? *II Chronicles 1:1*

b) Queen of Sheba visits Solomon *II Chronicles 9:1–12*

? The queen of Sheba visited Solomon in Jerusalem. What did this queen give King Solomon? *I Chronicles 9:9*

c) Kingdom divided; Rehoboam first king of Judah; Jeroboam first king of Israel *II Chronicles, ch. 10; I Kings 15:1*

? Division of the United Kingdom occurred about 926 BCE. Which portion of the divided land was also called "Ephraim" — the Northern Kingdom or the Southern Kingdom? *The New Westminster Dictionary of the Bible*, p. 274. (An example of "Ephraim" used for the whole country may be found in Hosea 11:3.)

? Rehoboam, son of Solomon, was the first king of Judah. What unwise thing did Rehoboam do, causing the ten tribes of the north to leave the house of David forever? *I Kings 12:12–14; II Chronicles 10:6–16*

? Who was Jeroboam, son of Nebat? (See a Bible dictionary.)

? When the ten tribes separated from the two southern tribes called Judah, Jeroboam, son of Nebat, became king of Israel. Jeroboam's father was an official under Solomon, but he was not descended from Solomon. Was Jeroboam a good king? *II Chronicles, ch. 13*

d) Asa, third king of Judah, aided by prophet Azariah *II Chronicles, chs. 14, 15; I Kings, chs. 15, 16*

? A prophet named Azariah, the son of Oded, encouraged Asa, the third king of Judah, to be strong. "Be ye strong...for your work shall be rewarded." What did Asa and the Hebrew people do as a result of Azariah's speech? *II Chronicles 15:1–12*

e) Jehoshaphat, fourth king of Judah *II Chronicles, chs. 17 to 20; 21:1; I Kings, ch. 22*

? Jehoshaphat, son of Asa, turned to God for help during his reign in the Southern Kingdom. The country prospered during his twenty-five year reign. Was the Southern Kingdom known as Israel or Judah? *II Chronicles 17:1 to 21:1*

? During this king's reign in the Southern Kingdom, the Moabites and Ammonites invaded Judah. This Hebrew king and his people prayed and fasted. The king said to God, "our eyes are upon thee." As a result, the enemy destroyed itself. Please name this good king. *II Chronicles 17:1 to 21:1*

? Jehoshaphat, king of Judah, received this assurance at a crisis point during his reign: "Be not afraid ... by reason of this great multitude; for the battle is not yours, but God's." What became of Judah's enemies? *II Chronicles 20:20–24*

f) Ahaz, twelfth ruler of Judah *II Chronicles, ch. 28; II Kings, ch. 16; Micah 1:1; Isaiah 1:1*

? King Ahaz, ruler of Judah, said: "Because the gods of the kings of Syria help them, therefore will I sacrifice to them, that they may help me." What was the result of this decision? *II Chronicles 28:23*

g) Hezekiah, thirteenth ruler of Judah *II Chronicles, chs. 29 to 32; II Kings, chs. 18 to 20; Isaiah, chs. 36 to 39; Hosea 1:1*

? True or false? The Lord saved Hezekiah and the inhabitants of Jerusalem from the hand of the king of Assyria. *II Chronicles 32:22*

? Who was Hezekiah? (See a Bible dictionary.)

h) Manasseh, fourteenth ruler of Judah *II Chronicles 33:1–22; II Kings, ch. 21*

? Manasseh, one of the kings who reigned in Jerusalem, used witchcraft and other evil practices. Finally, "when he was in affliction, he besought the Lord his God, and humbled himself greatly." How did Manasseh show he was reformed? *II Chronicles 33:1–20*

i) Josiah, sixteenth ruler of Judah   *II Chronicles, chs. 34, 35; Jeremiah 1:1–3; II Kings, chs. 22, 23*

? During Josiah's reign, workmen began to repair the temple in Jerusalem. Hilkiah, the high priest, found the Book of the Law. Both the king and the people were deeply moved by the passages read from Deuteronomy, and they determined to rid their country of idolatry. Josiah died in a battle with the Egyptians at Megiddo. Please name the prophet who mourned for Josiah. *II Chronicles 35:25*

j) Zedekiah, last king of Judah   *II Chronicles 36:9–21; Jeremiah, chs. 37 to 39, 52; II Kings, chs. 24, 25*

? Did King Zedekiah, Josiah's son, hearken unto the words of the Lord spoken by the prophet Jeremiah? *Jeremiah 37:1, 2*

7. Ezra

? Ezra was a priest, scribe, and leader of the Hebrew people. He was born in Babylonian captivity, but received permission to lead an expedition of Hebrews to Judah. Please name the Persian king who gave Ezra permission to go to Jerusalem in 458 BCE. *Ezra 7:1–8*

? Please name the priest who "brought the law before the congregation both of men and women, and all that could hear with understanding…. And he read therein … from the morning until midday … and the ears of all the people were attentive unto the book of the law." *Nehemiah 8:2, 3*

? Ezra, a priest and scribe, lived during a time of Hebrew captivity. A Persian king named Artaxerxes allowed Ezra to lead a large group of Jewish exiles back to Jerusalem. According to the book of Ezra, how did Ezra feel about the marriage of Israelites with foreigners? *Ezra, chs. 7–10*

? The book of Ezra tells the story of the Jews' return from Babylonia under the leadership of Sheshbazzar. About eighty years later, a priest named Ezra led another group of exiles back to Jerusalem. Please name the two Persian kings who allowed these returns. *Ezra 1:1, 2; 7:1–8*

8. Nehemiah   (See Figure 12)

? Artaxerxes, a Persian king, lived in Sushan. Who was his cupbearer? *Nehemiah 2:1*

? What Hebrew leader helped his people rebuild the wall around Jerusalem in only fifty-two days? *Nehemiah 1:1; 2:4–6; 6:15*

? Please name the important city where Nehemiah's ancestors lived. *Nehemiah 2:3, 11*

Figure 12: Nehemiah helps to rebuild the walls of Jerusalem.

? Nehemiah was a great Hebrew leader who loved God and cared about his people. What did Nehemiah help his people do? *Nehemiah 1:1; 2:4–6; 6:15*

? Please name the Hebrew who said to King Artaxerxes: "Why should not my countenance be sad, when the city, the place of my fathers' sepulchres, lieth waste, and the gates thereof are consumed with fire?" *Nehemiah 1:1; 2:1–3*

? While the Hebrew people lived in captivity under the rule of foreign kings, their holy city, Jerusalem, was left in ruins by invading armies. Finally, Nehemiah rebuilt Jerusalem's walls. Nehemiah was cupbearer to which Persian king?
- Nebuchadnezzar
- Artaxerxes
- Darius

Nehemiah 2:1

? What did Nehemiah request when King Artaxerxes asked him why he was so sad? *Nehemiah 2:4, 5*

? Which king gave Nehemiah permission to go to Jerusalem? *Nehemiah 2:1, 6*

? Nehemiah was sad when he learned Jerusalem was in ruins. But he stopped crying and started praying. Please name the Persian king who helped Nehemiah. *Nehemiah 2:1, 6*

? Please name the three men who were unhappy to hear that someone was coming to help the children of Israel rebuild the wall around Jerusalem. *Nehemiah 2:10*

? Who taunted and mocked Nehemiah and the other Hebrews as they worked to rebuild the wall of Jerusalem? *Nehemiah 2:19*

? How did Nehemiah answer his enemies? *Nehemiah 2:20*

? When their adversaries would not stop bothering Nehemiah and the Israelites while they were building the wall, Nehemiah asked his people to work in an unusual way. Please explain. *Nehemiah 4:15–18*

? Nehemiah was a Hebrew living in captivity. He was cupbearer to the Persian King Artaxerxes. What "great work" was Nehemiah able to accomplish, despite enemy suggestions designed to stop the project? *Nehemiah 1:1; 2:4–6; 6:15*

? How many messages did Sanballat send Nehemiah? *Nehemiah 6:1–5*

? Sanballat, Tobiah, and Geshem laughed at and despised the Hebrews who were rebuilding the wall of Jerusalem. Who sent these enemies this message: "I am doing a great work, so that I cannot come down: why should the work cease?" *Nehemiah 1:1; 6:3*

Figure 13: Esther, the Hebrew queen of Persia, and King Xerxes

? Why did Sanballat, Tobiah, and Geshem want to stop Nehemiah's work of rebuilding the wall of Jerusalem? *Nehemiah 4:1, 2*

? Did enemy threats ever stop Nehemiah from doing his good work? *Nehemiah, chs. 4 to 6*

? Who helped Nehemiah rebuild the wall of Jerusalem?

? Enemies of the Hebrews tried to scare Nehemiah and his friends away from their work of rebuilding the wall. When that didn't stop the Hebrews, what did they try?

? Sanballat and his friends tried to stop Nehemiah from rebuilding the wall around Jerusalem. Nehemiah's work wasn't stopped, because he himself didn't stop it. The work was wrought of God. How long did it take to complete the wall? *Nehemiah 6:15*

? How was Nehemiah able to keep from being deceived by Sanballat, Tobiah, and Geshem?

9. Esther   (See Figure 13)

? Which book of the Bible is a narrative probably prepared for reading in Jewish homes during the celebration of Purim? *The New Westminster Dictionary of the Bible, p. 782*

? What two books in the Old Testament are named for women?

? Esther, a beautiful young woman from Judah, married a rich and powerful king of Persia named Ahasuerus (also known as Xerxes). Please name the man who raised Esther and who warned Esther of a plot to assassinate the king. *Esther 2: 5–7, 21–23; The New Westminster Dictionary of the Bible, p. 21*

? Mordecai, Queen Esther's cousin, was loyal and helpful to the king of Persia, Ahasuerus (also known as Xerxes). Haman was the villain in the book of Esther. What became of Haman? *Esther 7:10*

? The beautiful Esther married a king of Persia and was able to save her people from extermination. Please name Esther's powerful husband. *Esther 1:1–4; 2:17*

Figure 14: Even during hard times, Job still loves God.

C. Books of Poetry and Wisdom Literature

(In Hebrew Scripture, Job, Proverbs, and Ecclesiastes are categorized as Wisdom Literature. In English Bibles, these three books, along with Psalms and Song of Solomon, are known as poetical books. Many other Old Testament books, especially those of the prophets, also include poetry.)

1. Job (See Figure 14)

? Please name the man from the land of Uz who was "perfect and upright, and one that feared God...." *Job 1:1*

? Was Job an upright man? *Job 1:1*

? The book of Job attempts to answer the question, "Why does a righteous man suffer?" Although Job suffers terrible losses, God eventually restores his health and prosperity. What physical problem plagues Job? *Job 2:7*

? How many sons and daughters does Job have? *Job 1:2; 42:13*

? Seeing Job's tremendous grief, three friends, Eliphaz, Bildad, and Zophar, come to comfort him. How long do they sit with him in silence? *Job 2:11–13*

? In the Old Testament, who says in discouragement to his three friends: "Let the day perish wherein I was born"? *Job 3:1–3*

? Who made the following statement, which is well known because of its inclusion in Handel's *Messiah* oratorio? "I know that my redeemer liveth, and that he shall stand at the latter day upon the earth." *Job 19:1, 25*

? "Who hath put wisdom in the inward parts? or who hath given understanding to the heart? who can number the clouds in wisdom?" God asks these questions of whom? *Job 38:36, 37*

? Please fill in the blanks: "Acquaint now thyself with him, and be at _____: thereby good shall come unto _____." *Job 22:21*

? "The Lord blessed the latter end of Job more than his beginning," according to the book of Job. Please complete this sentence: "the Lord turned the captivity of Job, when _____ _____ _____ _____ _____." *Job 42:10*

? Do Bible scholars know the name of the author of Job? (See, for instance, *The New Westminster Dictionary of the Bible*, pp. 496–498.)

? Who are Eliphaz, Bildad, and Zophar? *Job 2:11*

? Although parts of the book of Job are written in prose, Job is a poetic book and is the first of five books grouped together in English Bibles. Please name the other four Books of Poetry and Wisdom Literature.

2. Psalms

? Which book of the Bible is a collection of religious poems?

? True or false? The book of Psalms includes:
- hymns of praise,
- hymns of penitence,
- hymns of thanksgiving, and
- hymns of prayer.

? How many psalms are in the book of Psalms?

? Many poems included in the book of Psalms are attributed to one of Israel's national heroes. Please name him.

? The psalms number 150. Although scholars question the authorship of the psalms, almost half of them are attributed to one poet. Please name him.

? Please fill in the blanks: "Blessed is the man that _____ not in the counsel of the ungodly, nor _____ in the way of sinners, nor _____ in the seat of the scornful." *Psalms 1:1*

? In the Bible, where is it written: "let all those that put their trust in thee rejoice: let them ever shout for joy, because thou defendest them ..."? *Psalms 5:11*

? Please fill in the blanks: "Let the words of my _____, and the meditation of my _____, be acceptable in thy sight, O Lord, my _____ , and my redeemer." *Psalm 19:14*

? Please fill in the blanks: "The Lord is my _____; I shall not want. He maketh me to lie down in _____ pastures: he leadeth me beside the still _____." *Psalm 23:1, 1*

? The famous Twenty-third Psalm is attributed to David. The psalm begins: "The Lord is my shepherd." What do you know about David's life and career?

? "The Lord is my shepherd; I shall not want." This is the beginning of which psalm?

? Please recite Psalm 23.

? Please fill in the blanks: David said, "____ _____ is my shepherd." *Psalm 23:1*

? The following verses are from which psalm? "Yea, though I walk through the valley of the shadow of death, I will fear no evil: for thou art with me; thy rod and thy staff they comfort me." *Psalm 23:4*

? One of the psalms states: "the meek shall inherit the earth." Who repeats this idea in his Sermon on the Mount? *Psalm 37:11; Matthew 4:23; 5:5*

? Please fill in the blanks: "God is our refuge and _____, a very present help in _____." *Psalm 46:1*

? Please read aloud part of the Ninety-first Psalm.

? Please recite the first verse of the Ninety-first Psalm.

? "He that dwelleth in the secret place of the most High shall abide under the shadow of the Almighty." This is the first verse of which psalm? *Psalm 91:1*

? A verse in Psalm 91 assures us that God will deliver us "from the snare of the fowler...." What is a fowler? *Psalm 91:3*

? In Matthew's account of Christ Jesus' temptation by the devil, Satan is described as able to talk to Jesus. During their conversations, which one quotes the Ninety-first Psalm: "he shall give his angels charge concerning thee..."? *Matthew 4:5, 6*

? The Old Testament was written in the Hebrew language. Each stanza of Psalm 119 begins with a different letter of the Hebrew alphabet. How many letters are in the Hebrew alphabet? *The One Volume Bible Commentary*, Dummelow, p. 372; *The New Westminster Dictionary of the Bible*, p. 373

? Which Psalm begins: "Make a joyful noise unto the Lord, all ye lands. Serve the Lord with gladness: come before his presence with singing"?
- Psalm 23
- Psalm 100
- Psalm 91
- Psalm 1
- Psalm 121
- Psalm 46

? Please read aloud Psalm 121.

? Please read the first four verses of Psalm 137. Is the author referring to:
- a time during the United Kingdom,
- a time during Moses' leadership, or
- a time of captivity in Babylonia?

? What musical instruments are mentioned in the last psalm, number 150?

? Please match:

    1. Psalm 23   a. "Make a joyful noise unto the Lord, all ye lands."

    2. Psalm 100   b. "The Lord is my shepherd; I shall not want."

    3. Psalm 91   c. "He is my refuge and fortress...."

? Which quote is from Psalm 121 and which is from Psalm 91?

- "He that dwelleth in the secret place of the most High shall abide under the shadow of the Almighty."
- "I will lift up mine eyes unto the hills, from whence cometh my help."

? Hebrew poetry occurs in many books of the Bible, including Genesis, Exodus, I and II Samuel, Proverbs, Lamentations, Isaiah, Matthew, and Luke. The poetry is "rhythmical and regular in form" and employs parallelism. In which book of the Bible is the largest collection of poetry? *The New Westminster Dictionary of the Bible, pp. 757–758*

3. Proverbs

? Which book of the Bible is made up of the short sayings "of Solomon the son of David, king of Israel; to know wisdom and instruction; to perceive the words of understanding..."? *Proverbs 1:1, 2*

? The book of Proverbs is a collection of wise sayings or maxims. The authors of the sayings are uncertain. Although the book was traditionally credited to Solomon, most scholars now regard it as having been in process for many years. Why do you suppose Solomon was credited with having written this book of the Bible? *I Kings 3:6, 9–12*

? True or false? Many of the proverbs make observations about proper conduct.

? Where does wisdom come from, according to the author of Proverbs? *Proverbs 2:6*

? Please fill in the blanks: "Trust in the Lord with all thine _____; and lean not unto thine own _____. In all thy ways _____ him, and he shall direct thy _____." *Proverbs 3:5, 6*

? What does Proverbs say about "they that tarry long at the wine"? *Proverbs 23:29–32*

? Fill in the blanks: "A word fitly spoken is like apples of _____ in pictures of _____." *Proverbs 25:11*

? In which book of the Bible can we read a description of a virtuous woman who "reacheth forth her hands to the needy" and "openeth her mouth with wisdom"? *Proverbs 31:10–31*

Figure 15: Old Jerusalem

That Ye May Teach the Children

? Which of the following is known as "a poetical book on practical piety"? *The New Westminster Dictionary of the Bible*, p. 771
- Genesis
- Proverbs
- Esther
- Luke

4. Ecclesiastes

? Which book of the Bible contains "the words of the Preacher, the son of David, king in Jerusalem"? *Ecclesiastes 1:1*

? In which book of the Old Testament does the Preacher admit: "whatsoever mine eyes desired I kept not from them..."? *Ecclesiastes 2:10*

? The author of Ecclesiastes built himself houses; planted vineyards and gardens; gathered silver and gold; got servants and singers to entertain himself, and "withheld not ... from any joy." Did all these things make him happy? *Ecclesiastes 2:4, 5, 7–11*

? Please fill in the blanks: "To every thing there is a season, and a time to every purpose under the heaven: A time to be born, and a time to _____; a time to plant, and a time to pluck up that which is _____...." *Ecclesiastes 3:1,2*

? "To every thing there is a season, and a time to every purpose under the heaven," writes the author of Ecclesiastes. Please fill in the blanks from these examples: "A time to rend, and a _____ to sew; a time to keep silence, and a time to _____." *Ecclesiastes 3:1, 7*

? Do you think the following statement is true? "Wisdom is better than weapons of war...." *Ecclesiastes 9:14–18 (to:)*

? Of the following Old Testament authors, who seeks to find some profit in life through indulgence in the pleasures of vast wealth?
- Moses,
- Daniel,
- the Preacher, or
- Job

? Which Old Testament book is characterized by the phrase "all is vanity"? *Ecclesiastes 1:2, 14; 2:17, 19, 23; 3:19; 4:4, 8, 16; 12:8*

? What do you think this verse from Ecclesiastes means? "If the tree fall toward the south, or toward the north, in the place where the tree falleth, there it shall be." *Ecclesiastes 11:3*

? Please fill in the blanks. At the end of the book of Ecclesiastes, the author concludes that "the whole duty of man" is to: "Fear God, and _____ _____
_____." *Ecclesiastes 12:13, 14*

? Who in the Bible says, "all is vanity"? *Ecclesiastes 1:2*

5. Song of Solomon

? Which book of the Old Testament is a collection of love poems?

? "The flowers appear on the earth; the time of the singing of birds is come, and the voice of the turtle is heard in our land; the fig tree putteth forth her green figs, and the vines with the tender grape give a good smell." Please use a Bible concordance to determine in which book of the Bible this sentence is found. *Song of Solomon 2:12, 13*

? Please name the Bible author who compares his love "to a company of horses in Pharaoh's chariots." *Song of Solomon 1:9*

D. The Books of the Major Prophets

1. Isaiah

? Isaiah is the first of five books of the major prophets. Please name the other four books of the major prophets.

? The prophet Isaiah was a married man with two sons. He lived in Jerusalem and prophesied during the reigns of four kings of Judah. Please name the four kings who were contemporaries of Isaiah. *Isaiah 1:1*

? According to Isaiah, "they shall mount up with wings as eagles; they shall run, and not be weary; and they shall walk, and not faint." Who are "they"?
- the "children of Israel"
- the Gentiles
- "they that wait upon the Lord"
Isaiah 40:31

? Different Bible writers have portrayed God in different ways. Please match:
    1. God as Shepherd   a. Isaiah 6:1–5
    2. God as King   b. Psalm 23
    3. God as Creator   c. Isaiah 40:28

a) Prophecy concerning war *Isaiah 2:4*

? Please fill in the blanks: "they shall beat their swords into _____ , and their spears into pruninghooks: nation shall not lift up _____ against nation, neither shall they learn _____ any more." *Isaiah 2:4; compare with Micah 4:1–5*

b) Messianic prophecies *Isaiah 7:14; 9:6, 7; 11:1, 2; 35:4, 5; 40:15; 42:1; 53:15; 61:1*

? In which book of the Bible can you read this prophecy? "Behold, a virgin shall conceive, and bear a son, and shall call his name Immanuel." *Isaiah 7:14* (Teachers should note that it was New Testament writers who assigned new meanings and messianic interpretation to the words written in the book of Isaiah and in other Old Testament books. The original authors assigned their own meanings to their words.)

? Matthew quotes the following prophecy from Isaiah. Please fill in the blanks: "Behold, a virgin shall conceive, and bear a _____, and shall call his name _____." *Isaiah 7:14; Matthew 1:23*

? Both Matthew and Luke mention Jesse in their genealogies of Jesus. Who was Jesse? *Ruth 4:21, 22; Isaiah 11:1, 2; Matthew 1:1–17; Luke 3:23–38*

? In which book of the Bible can you find this verse: "For unto us a child is born, unto us a son is given: and the government shall be upon his shoulder: and his name shall be called Wonderful, Counsellor, The mighty God, The everlasting Father, The Prince of Peace"? *Isaiah 9:6*

? "And there shall come forth a rod out of the stem of Jesse, and a Branch shall grow out of his roots: And the spirit of the Lord shall rest upon him...." Whose coming is prophesied? From which book of the Bible is this verse? *Isaiah 11:1, 2*

? Which of the two Gospel genealogies given for Jesus fulfills the prophecy of Isaiah: "there shall come a rod out of the stem of Jesse..."? *Isaiah 11:1, 2; Matthew 1:1–17; Luke 3:23–38*

? Please fill in the blanks: "Prepare ye the way of the _____, make straight in the desert a highway for our God." *Isaiah 40:3*

? "Be strong, fear not: behold, your God will come with vengeance, even God with a recompence; he will come and save you. Then the eyes of the blind shall be opened, and the ears of the deaf shall be unstopped." This prophecy appears in which book of the Bible? *Isaiah 35:4, 5*

? Whose words did John the Baptist quote when he said: "The voice of one crying in the wilderness, Prepare ye the way of the Lord, make his paths straight ...?" *Matthew 3:3; Isaiah 40:3–5; see also Mark 1:3; Luke 3:4, 5*

?   Fill in the blanks: "Every valley shall be _____, and every mountain and hill shall be made _____: and the crooked shall be made _____, and the rough places _____...." *Isaiah 40:4*

?   Please fill in the blanks: "He shall feed his flock like a _____; he shall gather the lambs with his arm, and carry them in his bosom, and shall _____ lead those that are with young." *Isaiah 40:11; John 10:11–14*

?   Jesus is sometimes called the "man of sorrows." Please tell another name by which he is identified. See, for example: *Isaiah 53:3; Matthew 1:16; Luke 2:11; John 13:13*

?   Please fill in the blanks: "The Spirit of the Lord God is upon me; because the Lord hath anointed me to _____ good tidings unto the _____...." *Isaiah 61:1*

?   Who was sent by God "to bind up the brokenhearted" and "to proclaim liberty to the captives"? *Isaiah 61:1; Luke 4:1421*

?   Who fulfilled this prophecy from Isaiah? "The spirit of the Lord God is upon me; because the Lord hath anointed me to preach good tidings unto the meek; he hath sent me to bind up the brokenhearted, to proclaim liberty to the captives, and the opening of the prison to them that are bound...." *Isaiah 61:1; Luke 4:14–21*

?   Jesus refers to a prophecy made by "Esaias" while in the synagogue at Nazareth. What Old Testament prophet is called Esaias in the New Testament? *Luke 4:14–21; Isaiah 61:1*

?   What book of the Bible contains many prophecies about the coming of the Messiah? *Isaiah 7:14; 9:6; 42:1; 40:1–5; 53:1–5; 61:1*

?   Which of the following books of the Bible is identified with messianic prophecies?
- Leviticus
- Isaiah
- Proverbs

?   What are some of the Old Testament prophecies about the Messiah? *Deuteronomy 18:15, 17, 18; Micah 5:2; Isaiah 7:14; 9:6; 40:1–5; 42:1; 53:1–5; 61:1*

?   Please name two Old Testament prophets who foretold the coming of Christ. *Micah 5:2; Isaiah 7:14; 9:6; 42:1; 53:1–5; 61:1*

c) Hezekiah shows treasures to Babylonians *Isaiah 39:1–8*

?   Hezekiah, one of the kings of Judah, was a devoted servant of God. Under his leadership, the Hebrews destroyed their idols and renewed the practice of giving tithes to the Levites. At one point Hezekiah made the mistake of showing treasures to the Babylonians. Who then foretold their loss? *Isaiah 39:1–8* (For additional questions concerning Hezekiah, see sections under *I and II Kings* and *I and II Chronicles* and the index of this book.)

? Hezekiah, king of Judah, once showed some Babylonian envoys "the house of his precious things." What did Isaiah, the prophet, foretell would become of all these precious things? *Isaiah 39:1–8*

2. Jeremiah

a) Active during the reigns of Josiah, Jehoiakim, and Zedekiah, kings of Judah *Jeremiah 1:1–3*

? Jeremiah was a major Hebrew prophet who had a lasting influence on his people. He was an active prophet for over forty years. Please name a king who was Jeremiah's contemporary. *Jeremiah 1:1–3*

? Jeremiah spoke out courageously regarding Judah's disobedience. For most of his life, he was persecuted for this courage and honesty. Jeremiah was beaten, mocked, threatened and imprisoned. At one point, the men of his village plotted to kill him. Who commanded Jeremiah to write his prophecies in a book? *Jeremiah 36:1–3*

? Please name the prophet who sorrowfully wrote: "Oh, that my head were waters, and mine eyes a fountain of tears, that I might weep day and night for the slain of the daughter of my people!" *Jeremiah 9:1*

? Which prophet foretold the victory of Nebuchadnezzar, king of Babylon? *Jeremiah 27:1, 6, 7*

? What did Baruch do for Jeremiah? *Jeremiah 36:4*

? Baruch was a scribe and a friend of Jeremiah. What did a scribe do? *The New Westminster Dictionary of the Bible*, pp.94, 841

? Who was Jeremiah's disciple and successor? *The Golden Bible Atlas*, Terrien, p. 53; *The New Westminster Dictionary of the Bible*, pp. 94, 287

? During the time of Jeremiah, the tiny kingdom of Judah was caught in the struggle between two strong empires, Egypt and Babylon. Nebuchadnezzar punished Judah for trying to revolt and destroyed much of Jerusalem, including the temple, in 586 BCE. Was Nebuchadnezzar from Egypt or Babylon? *II Kings 24:1; Jeremiah 27:6*

3. Lamentations

? Who is credited as the author of the book of Lamentations?

? What did Jeremiah lament in Lamentations? *Lamentations 1:1, 6–8*

4. Ezekiel

? Ezekiel was a prophet who taught and encouraged the people during an era of captivity and exile. Was Ezekiel also a priest? *Ezekiel 1:2, 3*

? Ezekiel is one of five books sometimes called the books of the major prophets in the English Bible. Please name the other four.

? True or false? Ezekiel is an Old Testament book of prophecy.

? When Ezekiel "saw visions of God," he described "the appearance of the likeness of the glory of the Lord." "As the appearance of the bow that is in the cloud in the day of rain, so was the appearance of the brightness round about." Is Ezekiel considered a major or minor prophet in the English Bible? *Ezekiel 1:1, 28*

? What Bible character relates that he was set down in the "midst of the valley which was full of bones" and was told to say, "O ye dry bones, hear the word of the Lord"? *Ezekiel 37:1, 4, 7*

? Who was the biblical author who describes a man "whose appearance was like the appearance of brass, with a line of flax in his hand, and a measuring reed..."? *Ezekiel 40:2, 3*

5. Daniel

a) Daniel and the king's meat *Daniel 1:3–20*

? Who was a child during the reign of Nebuchadnezzar, king of Babylon, but nevertheless "purposed in his heart that he would not defile himself with the portion of the king's meat, nor with the wine which he drank"? *Daniel 1:3–20*

? When Daniel was young, he was taken captive with other Hebrews to Babylon. Daniel "purposed in his heart" that he would not eat the king's meat nor drink the king's wine. Who was the Babylonian king in this story? *Daniel 1:3–20*

? Who ate pulse instead of the king's meat for ten days, proving their countenances fairer and fatter in flesh than all the children who ate the king's meat? *Daniel 1:3–20*

? Daniel, Hananiah, Mishael and Azariah were able to prove to the master of the eunuchs that their countenances were "fairer and fatter in flesh than all the children which did eat ... the king's meat." What did they eat and drink during the ten day testing period? *Daniel 1:3–20*

? Daniel said to Melzar: "Prove thy servants, I beseech thee, ten days; and let them give us pulse to eat and water to drink." At the end of ten days, how did the countenances of Daniel and his friends compare to the other children? *Daniel 1:15*

Figure 16: Daniel was safe in the lions' den.

? Daniel said, "give us pulse to eat, and water to drink." What is pulse? *Daniel 1:12*

? Daniel was a young Hebrew taken into exile, along with many others, during the reign of King Jehoiakim (about 609–598 BCE) of Judah when Nebuchadnezzar was king of Babylon. Who lived first: Daniel or David?

b) Three Hebrew boys and the fiery furnace   *Daniel 3:1–30*

? What are the names of the three Hebrew boys who were cast into the fiery furnace? *Daniel 3:20*

? Why were Shadrach, Meshach, and Abed-nego "cast into the midst of the burning, fiery furnace"? *Daniel 3:14, 15*

? Who was king in the province of Babylon when Shadrach, Meshach, and Abed-nego were cast into the burning, fiery furnace? *Daniel 3:1–30*

? Why did the Hebrews, Shadrach, Meshach, and Abed-nego, refuse to worship the golden image set up by the king? *Daniel 3:1–30*

? What did King Nebuchadnezzar see after the three men "fell down bound" in the fiery furnace? *Daniel 3:25*

? The much-loved story of three Hebrew boys saved from the burning, fiery furnace by God is in the book of Daniel. Please tell the new names given to Daniel, Hananiah, Mishael, and Azariah. *Daniel 1:6, 7*

c) Belshazzar and the handwriting on the wall   *Daniel 5:1–6*

? During a great feast, Belshazzar, Nebuchadnezzar's son, commanded that the golden and silver vessels taken out of the temple in Jerusalem be used for their wine. Shortly there-after, something very strange and scary happened. What did Belshazzar see? *Daniel 5:1–6*

d) Daniel in the lions' den   *Daniel 6:1–28* (See Figure 16)

? Is the story of Daniel in the lions' den in the New Testament or in the Old Testament?

? In the story of Daniel in the lions' den, what is the name of the king? *Daniel 6:1*

? Why was Daniel cast into the lions' den? *Daniel 6:1–28*

? How many times a day did Daniel pray to God? *Daniel 6:10*

? Who wanted to have Daniel killed? *Daniel 6:4*

? What did the princes and presidents get King Darius to do? *Daniel 6:7, 8*

? How did the king feel when he knew Daniel would be killed for disobeying the law?
Daniel 6:13, 14

? Why couldn't the new law made by King Darius be changed? *Daniel 6:15*

? Was Daniel angry with the king and the princes and presidents? *Daniel 6:1–28*

? How did the king pass the night while Daniel was in the lions' den? *Daniel 6:18*

? What did Daniel say when he saw King Darius the next morning? *Daniel 6:21, 22*

? What protected Daniel in the lions' den? *Daniel 6:22*

? What new law did King Darius decree after God saved Daniel from the lions?
Daniel 6:25–27

E. The Books of the Minor Prophets

1. Hosea

? Which book is the first of the minor prophets in the order of their arrangement in the
Bible? *Abingdon Bible Handbook,* Blair, pp. 148–149

? Hosea married a woman named Gomer, who was unfaithful. Gomer left Hosea for a man
"who could give her a life of luxury." Does Hosea forgive Gomer? *Hosea 1:2, 3; An Outline of
the Bible: Book by Book,* Landis, p. 76

? The prophet Hosea worked to rouse his people, those who lived in Israel, the northern
Hebrew kingdom. The people would not listen, and Israel and its capital, Samaria, were
destroyed and her people dispersed. Who conquered Israel in about 722 BCE? *II Kings
17:6; Teaching the Scriptures,* Robinson, p. 37; *The Golden Bible Atlas,* Terrien, p. 50

? The book of Hosea contains a parable for the people of Israel. The prophet writes that just
as he loves and forgives his unfaithful wife, God will love and forgive the unfaithful
Israel. Please name Hosea's wife. *Hosea 1:2, 3*

? Hosea's contemporaries included Amos, Micah, Isaiah, and Hezekiah, king of Judah. Was
Hosea a prophet of Israel or Judah? *An Outline of the Bible: Book by Book,* Landis, p. 75; *Teaching
the Scriptures,* Robinson, p. 37

2. Joel

? In the Old Testament there are twelve books known as the books of the minor prophets.
Hosea begins this section. Please name the following three books. *Abingdon Bible Handbook,*
Blair, p. 148

? The text of the short book of Joel is in poetic form. Little is known about the author. A much loved and quoted verse is found in the second chapter of Joel. Please read aloud Joel 2:25.

? "I will restore to you the years that the locust hath eaten" is a much loved biblical promise. In what book is it written? *Joel:2:25*

3. Amos

? Of the twelve minor prophets, who wrote that he was a "herdman"? *Amos 1;1; 7:14; Abingdon Bible Handbook, Blair, p. 148*

? Amos, a citizen of Tekoa, was sent of God to warn the people about Assyria. He courageously warned the Israelites to return to the worship of Yahweh and protested against ecclesiastical decadence. Did the Israelites of that period heed Amos's warnings? *Amos 1:1*

? Amos was contemporary with the prophet Hosea. He rebuked the rich for oppressing the poor. Amos prophesied, "Israel shall surely be led away captive out of their own land." How was this prophecy fulfilled? *Amos 7:11; The Golden Bible Atlas, Terrien, p. 50; Getting Better Acquainted with Your Bible, Shotwell, p. 18*

? Of the Old Testament prophets, who taught the timeless message that privilege implies responsibility? *The New Westminster Dictionary of the Bible, p. 40*

? A plumbline is "a heavy weight suspended from a line." It is an instrument used by carpenters in building to determine the accuracy and precision of their work. In which Old Testament book is it written: "Then said the Lord, Behold, I will set a plumbline in the midst of my people Israel..."? *Amos 7:8; Getting Better Acquainted with Your Bible, Shotwell, p. 94*

4. Obadiah

? Obadiah is the shortest book of the Old Testament. How many verses make up this short book of prophecy? *An Outline of the Bible: Book by Book, Landis, p. 80*

5. Jonah

? What had the Lord prepared to swallow up Jonah? *Jonah 1:17*

? Please name the city that God told Jonah to visit. *Jonah 1:1, 2*

? Why did God want Jonah to go to Nineveh? *Jonah 1:2; 3:1, 2*

? What did Jonah do when God first told him to go to Nineveh and warn the people against their wickedness? *Jonah 1:3*

? Who was the Old Testament prophet who heard the word of the Lord saying, "Arise, go to Nineveh," but he disobeyed and took a ship going to Tarshish? *Jonah 1:2*

? What did it mean in Bible times to "cast lots"? *Jonah 1:7; The New Westminster Dictionary of the Bible, p. 567*

? How long was Jonah in the belly of the great fish? *Jonah 1:17*

? Jonah prayed while he was in the belly of the great fish for three days and three nights. What was the result of this prayer? *Jonah 2:1, 10; 3:3*

? Scholars debate whether the story of Jonah actually happened. Some consider it an allegory. The central message is that God is the God of all peoples and that His love extends to all. Nineveh was the capital of what great nation? *An Outline of the Bible: Book by Book, Landis, pp. 81–82*

? Who was thrown off a ship headed toward Tarshish after he explained to the mariners, "for my sake this great tempest is upon you"? *Jonah 1:3, 12*

? What happened to the sea after the mariners cast Jonah into the water? *Jonah 1:15*

? Once Jonah finally got to Nineveh to convert the people, did they turn from their evil ways? *Jonah 3:10*

? After his successful mission to Nineveh, Jonah becomes angry with God. Why? *Jonah 3:5–10; 4:1–4*

? Outside the city of Nineveh, a gourd vine shelters Jonah. According to the story, God first causes the vine to spring up overnight and then lets the vine wither and droop. How does this make Jonah feel? *Jonah 4:8, 9*

? Nineveh, a city in Bible times, was the capital of the Assyrian Empire. Two prophets, Nahum and Zephaniah, proclaimed the fall of Nineveh. Enemies did indeed destroy it in 612 BCE. What prophet preached in Nineveh before the time of Nahum and Zephaniah and caused the people to repent? *Nahum 3:7; Matthew 12:41*

? What lessons do we learn from the story of Jonah?

? Who said this: "For as Jonas was three days and three nights in the whale's belly; so shall the son of man be three days and three nights in the heart of the earth"? *Matthew 12:40*

6. Micah

? "They shall beat their swords into plowshares, and their spears into pruninghooks: nation shall not lift up a sword against nation, neither shall they learn war any more." This prophecy by Micah echoes another Old Testament prophet. Which one? *Isaiah 2:1–5; Joel 3:10; Micah 4:1–5*

? The prophet Micah lived in Judah, the Southern Kingdom, during the reign of King Hezekiah. Please read aloud the messianic prophecy recorded in Micah 5:2.

? "But thou, Bethlehem Ephratah, though thou be little among the thousands of Judah, yet out of thee shall he come forth unto me that is to be ruler in Israel; whose goings forth have been from of old, from everlasting." In which book of the Bible does this messianic prophecy appear? *Micah 5:2*

? Finish this verse from Micah: "what doth the Lord require of thee, but to do justly, and to love mercy, and to walk humbly with thy _____." *Micah 6:8*

? Some Bible scholars note that Micah has given "the classic definition of a simple practical religion, which has not been surpassed." Please read aloud this "classic definition" in *Micah 6:8. The New Westminster Dictionary of the Bible*, p. 616

7. Nahum

? "The Lord is good, a strong hold in the day of trouble; and he knoweth them that trust in him." Please use a Bible concordance to determine in what book of the Old Testament this sentence appears. *Nahum 1:7*

8. Habakkuk

? Who was the prophet who wrote about God: "Thou art of purer eyes than to behold evil"? *Habakkuk 1:1, 13*

9. Zephaniah

? According to the first verse of Zephaniah, who was the king of Judah during this prophet's activity? *Zephaniah 1:1*

10. Haggai

? During the time of the Persian Empire, Haggai and Zechariah were two prophets who helped rouse Zerubbabel and the Hebrew people to build a new temple on the site of the old temple in Jerusalem. During what king's reign had the first temple been built? See temple in a Bible Dictionary.

11. Zechariah

? "Rejoice greatly, O daughter of Zion; shout, O daughter of Jerusalem: behold, thy King cometh unto thee: he is just, and having salvation; lowly, and riding upon an ass, and upon a colt the foal of an ass." Please use a Bible concordance to determine in which book of the Old Testament this verse is located. *Zechariah 9:9 (Matthew 21:4, 5 and John 12:15* are often noted in connection with this verse. However, as with all messianic prophecies, the meaning of this verse was not the same for the author of Zechariah and the New Testament writers.)

12. Malachi

? Please name the last book of the Old Testament.

? In the Hebrew language "Malachi" means messenger. Malachi is the last of a section in English Bibles known as the Books of Prophecy. Is Malachi in the Old Testament or the New Testament?

? Who prophesied: "unto you that fear my name shall the Sun of righteousness arise with healing in his wings?" *Malachi 4:2*

Notes

That Ye May Teach the Children

III. New Testament

A. Gospel record of Christ Jesus' life and ministry

1. Background: Matthew, Mark, Luke, John

? What four books of the Bible contain essentially all we know of the works and words of Jesus?

? Please name the first four books of the Bible in the New Testament.

? What four books of the Bible are known as the Gospels?

? What does *Gospel* mean? *The New Westminster Dictionary of the Bible, p. 339*

? Which three books of the Bible are called the *synoptic Gospels*? *The New Westminster Dictionary of the Bible, p. 340*

? The Gospel of Mark is generally thought to have been written before the other three Gospels. It is the shortest of the four books. Does Mark include any information about the birth of Jesus?

? The Gospel of Luke indicates that it was written for an individual named Theophilus. Please check a Bible concordance. Is Theophilus mentioned in any other book of the Bible? *Luke 1:3; Acts 1:2*

? The Gospel of John does not mention Jesus' birth, childhood, baptism, temptation, transfiguration or ascension. This Gospel does not give the text of any parables. The author DOES write about some of Jesus' healing works. Please cite an example. *John 4:46–54; 5:2–9; 9:1–7; 11:1–57*

? Which two books of the Bible tell the beloved Christmas story? *Matthew 1:18–25; 2:1–23; Luke 1:26–35, 37, 38; 2:1–20*

? Matthew and Luke tell the beloved Christmas story. Which books of the Bible tell the Easter story?

? In what book of the Bible do we learn the story of John the Baptist's birth? *Luke 1:5–80*

? What is the first story in the Gospel of Mark? *Mark, ch. 1*

? "In the beginning was the Word, and the Word was with God, and the Word was God." Which of the Gospels begins with this verse? *John 1:1*

? What is the opening verse of the Gospel of John? *John 1:1*

? Does the Gospel of John begin with the story of Jesus' birth?

? What place was known as the city of David in biblical times? *Luke 2:4, 11*

? Most scholars believe that several of the New Testament epistles were written before the Gospels. Why do you suppose the Gospels were put first in the arrangement of the twenty-seven New Testament books?

? Using the verse from John 1:17, please match the following:
   1. Moses   a. grace and truth
   2. Jesus   b. the law

? True or false? No man hath seen God at any time. *John 1:18*

2. John the Baptist, who prepared the way for Jesus   *Matthew 3:1, 2, 58; Mark 1:1–11; Luke 1:5–80; 3:1–22; John 1:6–8*

? Who were John the Baptist's parents? *Luke 1:5–25, 57–80*

? What angel appeared to Zacharias and said "thy wife Elisabeth shall bear thee a son, and thou shalt call his name John"? *Luke 1:13, 19*

? What was the angel Gabriel's message to the righteous priest, Zacharias? *Luke 1:5–25*

? Who told Zacharias that his son, John, would "make ready a people prepared for the Lord"? *Luke 1:5–19*

? Why was Zacharias not able to speak until after John was born? *Luke 1:18–20*

? Who was Zacharias? *Luke 1:5*

? Please name a woman in the New Testament who was barren and then "brought forth a son." *Luke 1:5–25, 36, 57–80*

? Who was the babe who "leaped" in his mother's womb, according to the Gospel of Luke? *Luke 1:41–44*

? How much older than Jesus was John the Baptist? *Luke 1:30, 31, 36*

? In which book of the Bible can you read the story of John the Baptist's birth? *Luke 1:5–25, 57–80*

? According to the book of Luke, who was the Roman emperor when "the word of God came unto John the son of Zacharias in the wilderness"? *Luke 3:1, 2*

? Tiberius Caesar, the second Roman emperor, is mentioned by name in which of the four Gospels? *Luke 3:1, 2*

? When they came to John the Baptist for baptism, John said: "O generation of vipers, who hath warned you to flee from the wrath to come?" To whom was John speaking? *Matthew 3:1, 2, 5–8*

3. Genealogies of Jesus   *Matthew 1:1–17; Luke 3:23–38; Isaiah 11:1, 2*

? True or false? The Bible records two genealogies for Christ Jesus. *Matthew 1:1–17; Luke 3:23–38; Getting Better Acquainted with Your Bible, Shotwell, p. 224; The Interpreter's Bible, Vol. 8, pp. 82–83*

? Jacob had twelve sons: Reuben, Joseph, Simeon, Benjamin, Levi, Dan, Judah, Naphtali, Issachar, Gad, Zebulun, and Asher. Which one of these sons is listed in Matthew's genealogy as an ancestor of Jesus? (Please note a slight variation in New Testament spelling.) *Matthew 1:2*

? Isaiah foretold that the Messiah would "come forth a rod out of the stem of Jesse." Both Mary and Joseph were descended from Jesse. According to *The Interpreter's Bible*, the genealogy in Luke is Mary's, although Joseph's name is substituted. Matthew gives Joseph's genealogy. What do you know about Jesse? *Isaiah 11:1, 2; Matthew 1:1–17; Luke 3:23–38; Getting Better Acquainted with Your Bible, Shotwell, p. 224; The Interpreter's Bible, Vol. 8, pp. 82–83*

4. Jesus' birth and early life   (See Figure 17)

a) Christmas story, which tells of Jesus' birth   *Matthew 1:18–25; 2:1–23; Luke 1:26–35, 37, 38; 2:1–20; Isaiah 7:14; Micah 5:2; Hosea 11:1*

? In which Old Testament book does this prophecy appear: "Behold, a virgin shall conceive, and bear a son, and shall call his name Immanuel"? *Isaiah 7:14*

? Matthew explains that Emmanuel means "God with us." Emmanuel is another name for whom? *Matthew 1:21–23*

? Isaiah and Matthew both speak of Emmanuel (spelled "Immanuel" in Isaiah.) What does Emmanuel mean, according to Matthew? *Matthew 1:23; Isaiah 7:14*

? Throughout its history, Palestine had times of independent rule by the Hebrew people themselves. The various empires that controlled Palestine, however, determined much of

Hebrew history. During which empire was Jesus born — the Greek or the Roman?
The New Westminster Dictionary of the Bible, p. 810

? Christ Jesus was born during which empire:
  • Persian,
  • Greek, or
  • Roman?

? Who was the king of Judaea at the time Jesus was born? *Matthew 2:1; Luke 1:5*

? Christ Jesus was the son of a virgin named Mary. His father was God. Please name the man who later married Mary and became Jesus' legal father. *Matthew 1:18–25*

? Who told Joseph: "Fear not to take unto thee Mary thy wife: for that which is conceived in her is of the Holy Ghost. And she shall bring forth a son, and thou shalt call his name JESUS"? *Matthew 1:20–21*

? Who was told by an angel that "with God nothing shall be impossible"? *Luke 1:34–37*

? In what town was Jesus born? *Matthew 2:1; Luke 2:1–7*

? Where was Jesus born? *Luke 2:1–7*

? Please give another name for "the city of David." *Luke 2:4, 11*

? Why did Mary and Joseph happen to be in Bethlehem, rather than Nazareth, their home-town, when Jesus was born? *Luke 2:1–7*

? Why was Jesus born in a manger, rather than the inn? *Luke 2:7*

? Christ Jesus was born during the time of the Roman Empire. The Gospel of Luke notes: "there went out a decree from Caesar Augustus, that all the world should be taxed." Who was Caesar Augustus? *Luke 2:1; Teaching the Scriptures*, Robinson, p. 46

? "Where is he that is born King of the Jews? for we have seen his star in the east, and are come to worship him." Who came to Jerusalem and asked this question? *Matthew 2:1, 2*

? According to Saint Matthew: "there came wise men from the east to Jerusalem, saying, Where is he that is born King of the Jews? for we have seen his star in the east, and are come to worship him." For whom were the wise men looking? *Matthew 2:1, 2*

? Who gave Jesus gifts — gold, frankincense, and myrrh? *Matthew 2:1, 11*

? What did the wise men bring Jesus? *Matthew 2:11*

Figure 17: Mary, Joseph, and baby Jesus

? Herod (also known as Herod the Great) gathered all the chief priests and scribes and demanded of them where Christ should be born. They said: "In Bethlehem of Judaea: for thus it is written by the prophet...." Who is the prophet they quote? *Matthew 2:4–6; Micah 5:2; A Commentary on The Holy Bible, Dummelow, p. 626*

? What king "slew all the children that were in Bethlehem, and in all the coasts thereof, from two years old and under," hoping to slay Jesus — the King of kings? *Matthew 2:16*

? How were the wise men from the east warned that they should not return to Herod (known as Herod the Great) after worshipping Christ Jesus in the manger? *Matthew 2:12*

? Why was the visit to Jesus by "wise men from the east" so important? *Matthew 2:1; The New Westminster Dictionary of the Bible, "Magi," p. 579*

? The visit of the wise men to see Jesus signified "that salvation was to be extended to all people." By what other name are the wise men known? *The New Westminster Dictionary of the Bible, "Magi," p. 579*

? Luke tells us that shepherds went to see the babe in the manger. Who told them he was there? *Luke 2:8–16*

? Who came to see the infant Jesus? *Luke 2:15 and Matthew 2:1*

? The angel of the Lord said: "Fear not: for, behold, I bring you good tidings of great joy, which shall be to all people. For unto you is born this day in the city of David a Saviour, which is Christ the Lord." To whom was the angel speaking? *Luke 2:8–14*

? Please fill in the blanks: "Glory to _____ in the highest, and on earth _____, good will toward men." *Luke 2:14*

? Why did Joseph take Mary and the young child Jesus into Egypt? *Matthew 2:1315*

? Matthew writes that Joseph took "the young child and his mother" into Egypt. Matthew notes that this event fulfilled that which was spoken by the prophet Hosea. Please read aloud Hosea's messianic prophecy in Hosea 11:1. *Matthew 2:14, 15*

? How long did Joseph, Mary, and Jesus stay in Egypt? *Matthew 2:13–15; 19–21*

? Please tell the story of Jesus' birth. *Matthew 1:18–25; 2:1–23; Luke 1:2635, 37, 38; 2:1–20*

(1) Simeon *Luke 2:21–35*

? About how old was Christ Jesus when Simeon, a just and devout man at the temple in Jerusalem, said to God: "mine eyes have seen thy salvation ... A light to lighten the Gentiles, and the glory of thy people Israel"? *Luke 2:21–35*

Figure 18: Jesus talks with wise men in the temple.

? Joseph and Mary marvelled at the things Simeon said about their new baby Jesus. Simeon, a just and devout man, said: "Lord ... mine eyes have seen thy salvation ... A light to lighten the Gentiles...." Where did this take place? *Luke 2:25, 27, 30–32*

? When Jesus was just a baby, Mary and Joseph took him to the temple in Jerusalem. Please name the devout man who, according to Luke, took Jesus "up in his arms and blessed God" and said: "Lord ... mine eyes have seen thy salvation ... A light to lighten the Gentiles, and the glory of thy people Israel." *Luke 2:25–35*

(2) Anna *Luke 2:36–38*

? Who was Anna, the prophetess? *Luke 2:36–38*

? Please name the widow who visited the temple in Jerusalem daily and recognized the baby Jesus as the Messiah. *Luke 2:36–38*

b) Temple visit at age twelve *Luke 2:40–52* (See Figure 18)

? With whom did Jesus live when he was a boy? *Luke 2:40–42*

? How old was Jesus when he tarried behind at the temple in Jerusalem, listening, questioning, and giving answers to the wise men there? *Luke 2:42, 43, 46*

? Passover, known also as the feast of unleavened bread, commemorates the deliverance of the children of Israel from Egypt and their hasty departure with Moses. When Jesus was twelve, where did he and his parents go to celebrate the passover? *Luke 2:40–52*

? When Jesus was twelve years old, he stayed behind at the temple in Jerusalem talking with wise teachers and doctors. What did Jesus mean when he said, "I must be about my Father's business"? *Luke 2:49*

? What happened to Jesus when he was in Jerusalem at age twelve? *Luke 2:41–52*

5. Christ Jesus' ministry and teachings

a) Jesus baptized by John *Matthew 3:1–17; Mark 1:1–11; Luke 3:1–23; John 1:1–18*

? Who was John the Baptist?

? Who baptized Jesus in the River Jordan? *Matthew 3:13–17*

? Please name the "man sent from God" who came "to bear witness of the Light, that all men through him might believe .... He was not that Light, but was sent to bear witness of that Light." *John 1:6–8*

? Who saw Jesus coming and said: "Behold the Lamb of God, which taketh away the sin of the world"? *John 1:29*

? Where were Jesus and John the Baptist when they heard "a voice from heaven saying, This is my beloved Son, in whom I am well pleased"? *Matthew 3:13, 16, 17*

b) Jesus tempted in the wilderness *Matthew 4:1–11; Mark 1:12, 13; Luke 4:1–13*

? True or false? Jesus fasted forty days and forty nights. *Matthew 4:2*

? How long had Jesus fasted when the tempter came to him in the wilderness and said: "If thou be the Son of God, command that these stones be made bread"? *Matthew 4:1–13*

? Who tempted Jesus to turn stones into bread, cast himself down from a pinnacle, and accept all the kingdoms of the world as his own? *Matthew 4:1–11*

? Matthew records that Satan tempted Jesus in the wilderness by suggesting three things. What were these three temptations? *Matthew 4:1–11*

? Who came and ministered unto Jesus in the wilderness after the temptation, when the devil left him? *Matthew 4:1–11*

? "Thou shalt worship the Lord thy God, and him only shalt thou serve." Jesus spoke these words to the devil during his temptation in the wilderness. Which commandment is Jesus quoting? *Matthew 4:10; Exodus 20:3–6*

? How did the first commandment help Jesus? *Matthew 4:8–11*

? Did Jesus eat anything during the forty days he was tempted of the devil in the wilderness? *Luke 4:2*

? "Get thee behind me, Satan: for it is written, Thou shalt worship the Lord thy God, and him only shalt thou serve." Who said this to the devil when tempted with worldly power? *Luke 4:8*

c) The first disciples: Andrew, Simon Peter, Philip, and Nathanael *John 1:35–51*

? According to John's Gospel, who was the disciple who "findeth his own brother Simon, and saith unto him, We have found the Messias, which is, being interpreted, the Christ"? *John 1:40, 41*

? The Aramaic name given by Jesus to the apostle Simon was Cephas, which means "rock or stone." Please give the name that is the Greek equivalent of Cephas and by which the disciple Simon is generally known. *John 1:42; The New Westminster Dictionary of the Bible, p. 154*

? Which disciple went to Nathanael and said: "We have found him, of whom Moses in the law, and the prophets, did write, Jesus of Nazareth, the son of Joseph"? *John 1:45*

? When Jesus saw this disciple coming toward him for the first time, Jesus said: "Behold an Israelite indeed, in whom is no guile." Who was this disciple? *John 1:47*

? Nathanael was one of the twelve disciples. The Bible notes that he was from Cana in Galilee. Please tell of at least one event in Jesus' life that took place in Cana. *John 2:1–11; 4:46–54; 21:1, 2*

? Please name the city of Andrew, Simon Peter, and Philip. *John 1:44*

? Where was Jesus when he made the water wine? *John 4:46–53*

? According to the book of Luke, who was the Roman emperor when Jesus began his public ministry in 28 CE? *Luke 3:1*

? Changing the water into wine at a marriage in Cana of Galilee was Jesus' first "miracle." Were the disciples with Jesus at this marriage? *John 2:1–11*

? Who encouraged Jesus to produce wine for the wedding? *John 2:1–5*

d) First passover: Jesus drives moneychangers from temple *John 2:13–25*

? Who overturned the tables of the moneychangers in the temple of God at Jerusalem? Compare John's version to the synoptic Gospels, which place the temple cleansing during Jesus' last week. *John 2:13–25; compare with Matthew 21:12–14; Mark 11:15–19; Luke 19:45, 46*

e) Jesus instructs Nicodemus; the new birth discourse; "God so loved the world" *John 3:1–21*

? Not all the Pharisees were bad! A certain Pharisee, a ruler of the Jews, came to Jesus by night and said to him: "Rabbi, we know that thou art a teacher come from God: for no man can do these miracles that thou doest, except God be with him." Please name this wise Pharisee. *John 3:1–21*

? Nicodemus was "a man of the Pharisees ...a ruler of the Jews." Who told Nicodemus: "Except a man be born again, he cannot see the kingdom of God"? *John 3:1–5*

? Please fill in the blanks: "For God so _____ the world that he gave his only begotten _____, that whosoever believeth in him should not _____, but have everlasting _____." *John 3:16*

f) Jesus' conversation with woman of Samaria; water of life discourse
John 4:1–42

? John records the story of Jesus meeting a woman at Jacob's well. Jesus asks her for a drink of water. During their conversation, "the woman saith unto him, Sir, I perceive that thou art a prophet." From what country is the woman? *John 4:4–42*

? Why did the woman of Samaria say to Jesus: "Sir, I perceive that thou art a prophet"? *John 4:4–19*

? Where was Jesus when he met the woman of Samaria and "saith unto her, Give me to drink"? *John 4:5–7*

? When Jesus was at Jacob's well in Samaria, he said: "whosoever drinketh of the water I shall give him shall never thirst; but the water that I shall give him shall be in him a well of water springing up into everlasting life." To whom was Jesus speaking? *John 4:3–30, 39–42*

? Which commandment do you think Jesus had in mind when he talked with the Samaritan woman at the well? *John 4:16–19*

? Why was the woman of Samaria surprised at Jesus' request for a drink of water? *John 4:5–30, 39–44*

? Jesus came from a little town called Nazareth in Galilee. Please name a neighboring country whose people had no dealings with the Jews. *Mark 1:9; John 4:3,4,9; Luke 2:40–52*

? The Jews and Samaritans disagreed on which was the correct holy center of worship — Jerusalem or Mt. Gerizim. Who cut through the controversy with this observation: "the true worshippers shall worship the Father in spirit and in truth"? *John 4:19–29*

g) Imprisonment of John the Baptist *Matthew 4:12; Mark 1:14; Luke 3:19, 20*

? Who ordered the imprisonment of John the Baptist? *Luke 3:19, 20*

h) Commencement of public work in Galilee *Matthew 4:12–17; Mark 1:14, 15; Luke 4:14, 15; John 4:43–54*

? What prompted Jesus to leave Nazareth, his home town, and go to Capernaum, a town bordering the Sea of Galilee? *Matthew 4:12–17*

? True or false? Capernaum was on the sea coast. *Matthew 4:12–17*

? When Jesus healed the son of a nobleman, the author of John called it Jesus' "second miracle." In what town in Galilee was the nobleman's son when he was healed? *John 4:46–54*

i) First rejection at Nazareth *Luke 4:16–31*

? Did Jesus ever teach in the synagogues? *Luke 4:16–24; Mark 1:21*

? Where was Jesus when he read Isaiah's prophecy: "The Spirit of the Lord is upon me, because he hath anointed me to preach the gospel to the poor; he hath sent me to heal the brokenhearted, to preach deliverance to the captives…"? *Luke 4:16–24; Isaiah 61:1*

? Was Jesus aware of the Old Testament prophecies about himself found in Isaiah? (Please note that the Greek form of the name, Esaias, is used in the New Testament of the King James Version.) *Isaiah 35:5, 6; 42:1; 61:1; Luke 4:16–21; Matthew 12:14–18*

? "Esaias" is the New Testament spelling for the prophet Isaiah. In how many books of the New Testament is Esaias mentioned by name? (Please use a Bible concordance.)

? Was Jesus aware of the Old Testament stories about Elijah and Elisha? (In the King James Version of the New Testament the Greek forms of their names are used: Elias and Eliseus.) *Luke 4:24–27*

? One Sabbath day in Nazareth the Jews in the synagogue were "filled with wrath." They tried to kill Jesus by throwing him down a hill, but Jesus "went his way." Why were these people so angry? *Luke 4:16–31; Isaiah 61:1*

j) Call of the Four: Simon, Andrew, James, and John; great draught of fishes
Matthew 4:18–22; Mark 1:16–20; Luke 5:1–11

? Simon had toiled all night with his fishing partners, James and John, the sons of Zebedee. They had taken nothing. These fishermen were washing their nets when Jesus entered Simon's ship and asked if he could teach the press of people from the ship. What happened next? *Luke 5:1–11*

? Please list the following events in their proper order, using Matthew's Gospel as a guide:
- Jesus comes to John the Baptist for baptism.
- Jesus gives the Sermon on the Mount.
- Jesus invites Peter and Andrew to be disciples.
- Jesus is tempted in the wilderness.

k) Second passover: discourse on the Son and the Father at the pool of Bethesda *John 5:1–47*

? Who instructed his listeners to "search the scriptures"? *John 5:39*

? How did Jesus respond to those who accused him of "making himself equal with God"? *John 5:17–19*

l) Plucking ears of corn; discussion of Sabbath   *Matthew 12:1–8; Mark 2:23–28; Luke 6:15*

? Who objected when the disciples began to pluck and eat ears of corn on the Sabbath day? *Matthew 12:1–8; Mark 2:23–28; Luke 6:15*

? When the Pharisees objected to the disciples' plucking corn on the Sabbath, Jesus mentioned an Old Testament character who ate shewbread from "the house of God" when he was hungry. Who did Jesus mention? *Matthew 12:1–8; Mark 2:23–28; Luke 6:1–5; I Samuel 21:1–6*

m) Sermon on the Mount   *Matthew, chs. 5 to 7; Luke 6:20–49* (See Figure 19)

? In his Sermon on the Mount, Christ Jesus teaches us how to pray. What does he teach about prayer and our "closet"? *Matthew 6:6*

? Who gave the Sermon on the Mount?

? True or false? The Sermon on the Mount begins with the Ten Commandments. *Matthew, ch. 5*

? Fill in the blanks: "Let your light so _____ before men, that they may see your good works, and glorify your Father which is in _____." For help, see the Sermon on the Mount. *Matthew 5:16*

? In his Sermon on the Mount, does Christ Jesus instruct us to put our light: under a bushel or on a candlestick? *Matthew 5:14–16*

? In his Sermon on the Mount, does Christ Jesus refer to his listeners as: "the salt of the earth" or "the light of the world"? *Matthew 5:13, 14*

? In what sermon does Jesus say: "Think not that I am come to destroy the law, or the prophets: I am not come to destroy, but to fulfil"? *Matthew 5:1, 17*

? "Lay not up for yourselves treasures upon earth, where moth and rust doth corrupt, and where thieves break through and steal," said Jesus in his Sermon on the Mount. What should we "lay up" for ourselves? *Matthew 6:19, 20*

? Who said this? "No servant can serve two masters: for either he will hate the one, and love the other; or else he will hold to the one, and despise the other. Ye cannot serve God and mammon." *Luke 16:13; Matthew 6:24*

? "Consider the lilies of the field, how they grow; they toil not, neither do they spin: And yet I say unto you, That even Solomon in all his glory was not arrayed like one of these." Who said this? Who was Solomon? *Matthew 6:28, 29*

Figure 19: The Sermon on the Mount

That Ye May Teach the Children

? Who said this? "Ask, and it shall be given you; seek, and ye shall find; knock, and it shall be opened unto you." *Matthew 7:7*

? What is the Golden Rule? *Matthew 7:12*

? Who said this? "Love your enemies, do good to them which hate you...." *Luke 6:27* (Similar to *Matthew 5:43, 44*)

? According to Christ Jesus, who "love to pray standing in the corners of the streets, that they may be seen of men"? *Matthew 6:5*

? According to Matthew, immediately after giving the Sermon on the Mount, Jesus "was come down from the mountain" and "great multitudes followed him." What disease did the man have who was quickly healed when "Jesus put forth his hand and touched him"? *Matthew 8:1–3; Luke 5:12–16*

(1) Beatitudes *Matthew 5:1–12*

? Where are the Beatitudes?

? Who gave us the Beatitudes?

? The Beatitudes are part of what famous sermon? *Matthew, chs. 5–7*

? Finish this Beatitude: Blessed are the poor in spirit:___ *Matthew 5:3*

? Finish this Beatitude: Blessed are they that mourn:___ *Matthew 5:4*

? Finish this Beatitude: Blessed are the meek:___ *Matthew 5:5*

? Finish this Beatitude: Blessed are they which do hunger and thirst after righteousness:___ *Matthew 5:6*

? Finish this Beatitude: Blessed are the merciful:___ *Matthew 5:7*

? Finish this Beatitude: Blessed are the pure in heart:___ *Matthew 5:8*

? Finish this Beatitude: Blessed are the peacemakers:___ *Matthew 5:9*

? Finish this Beatitude: Blessed are they which are persecuted for righteousness' sake:___ *Matthew 5:10*

? Finish this Beatitude: Blessed are ye,___ *Matthew 5:11*

? Finish this Beatitude: Rejoice,___ *Matthew 5:12*

? Is the following Bible verse part of the Commandments or the Beatitudes? "Blessed are the pure in heart: for they shall see God." *Matthew 5:8*

? Which is the correct ending for the Beatitude which begins, "Blessed are the meek..."?
- for they shall obtain mercy.
- for they shall see God.
- for they shall inherit the earth.

Matthew 5:5

? Which of the following correctly completes this Beatitude? "Blessed are the pure in heart..."
- for they shall be filled.
- for they shall inherit the earth.
- for they shall see God.

Matthew 5:8

? According to the Beatitudes, which of the following blessings comes to the peacemakers?
- they shall see God.
- they shall inherit the earth.
- they shall be called the children of God.

Matthew 5:9

? What does *blessed* mean?

? What does *meek* mean? *Matthew 5:5*

? What does *righteousness* mean? *Matthew 5:6*

? "Happy are those whose greatest desire is to do what God requires: God will satisfy them fully!" Please say this Beatitude as given in the King James Version. *Good News Bible; Matthew 5:6*

? In Psalm 37 it is written: "the meek shall inherit the earth." Where else in the Bible do we find this phrase? *Matthew 5:5*

? Using the Beatitudes as your guide, please match the following:
1. poor in spirit
2. mourn
3. the meek
4. hunger and thirst after righteousness

a. be comforted
b. inherit the earth
c. kingdom of heaven
d. shall be filled

? Using the Beatitudes as your guide, please match the following:

1. mourn
2. meek
3. merciful
4. pure in heart
5. peacemakers

a. inherit the earth
b. see God
c. obtain mercy
d. called the children of God
e. be comforted

? The Beatitudes proclaim the good qualities we all want to express. Please recite the Beatitude that Jesus taught to stress each of the following qualities:

- meekness
- purity
- righteousness
- peacemaking
- mercy
- rejoicing

? Which well-known Bible verses require us to be merciful, pure-minded, peace-loving, and able to stand firm in the face of opposition? *Matthew 5:3–12*

? Knowing the Ten Commandments and the Beatitudes enables us to resist wrong and do right. Please give an example of how they have helped you or how they could help you in a particular situation.

? Which Beatitude best corresponds to the sixth commandment, "Thou shall not kill"? *Matthew 5:7, 9*

? Which Beatitude best corresponds to the seventh commandment, "Thou shalt not commit adultery"? *Matthew 5:8*

(2) The Lord's Prayer *Matthew 6:9–13; Luke 11:1–4*

? Who first spoke the Lord's Prayer?

? Where can you find the Lord's Prayer? *Matthew 6:9–13; Luke 11:1–4*

? How does the Lord's Prayer begin? *Matthew 6:9*

? Please fill in the blanks: "Give us this day our daily _____. And forgive us our debts, as we forgive our _____. And lead us not into _____, but deliver us from evil:" *Matthew 6:11–13*

? Please say the Lord's Prayer. *Matthew 6:9–13*

? In response to one of his disciple's request that he teach them to pray, Christ Jesus gave us the Lord's Prayer. What line has been added to the prayer, as we say it today? *Luke 11:2–4; Matthew 6:9–13*

? True or false? The Lord's Prayer is part of Christ Jesus' Sermon on the Mount found in chapters 5–7 in Matthew.

? Sometimes we call Christ Jesus our Lord. This means our master or our Way-shower. In which New Testament book can you find the Lord's Prayer?

(3) Parable of house built on rock   *Matthew 7:24–27; Luke 6:47–49*

? Who told the story of a wise man who built his house upon a rock and a foolish man who built his house upon the sand?   *Matthew 7:24–29*

? Jesus tells the story of a wise man who built a house. "And the rain descended, and the floods came, and the winds blew, and beat upon that house; and it fell not." Why did the house remain standing?   *Matthew 7:25*

? Who built his house upon the sand? When the rain descended, and the floods came, and the winds blew, the house fell, and "great was the fall of it."   *Matthew 7:26, 27*

? If you were going to build a house, would you build it upon rock or upon the sand? Why?

n) Inquiry of John the Baptist about Jesus   *Matthew 11:2–30; Luke 7:18–35*

? Where was John the Baptist when he heard about "the works of Christ"?   *Matthew 11:2*

? Two followers of John the Baptist came to Jesus. Why did Jesus tell them to "Go your way, and tell John what things ye have seen and heard; how that the blind see, the lame walk, the lepers are cleansed, the deaf hear, the dead are raised..."?   *Matthew 11:5; Luke 7:22*

o) Discourse: Christ's invitation to the weary   *Matthew 11:25–30*

? Fill in the blanks: "Come unto me, all ye that labour and are heavy _____, and I will give you _____. Take my yoke upon you and learn of me; For I am _____ and lowly in heart: And ye shall find rest unto your souls. For my _____ is easy, and my burden is _____."   *Matthew 11:25–30*

p) Jesus declares true kindred   *Matthew 12:46–50; Mark 3:31–35; Luke 8:19–21*

? Whom did Jesus say were his mother and his brethren?   *Matthew 12:50; Mark 3:35; Luke 8:19–21*

q) Tempest stilled   *Matthew 8:23–27; Mark 4:35–41; Luke 8:22–25*

? "There arose a great tempest in the sea, insomuch that the ship was covered with the waves...." What was Jesus doing when the disciples came to him, saying, "Lord, save us: we perish"? *Matthew 8:23–27, Mark 4:35–41; Luke 8:22–25*

r) Second rejection at Nazareth   *Matthew 13:53–58; Mark 6:1–6*

? Where was Christ Jesus when, according to Matthew, "he did not many mighty works there because of their unbelief." *Matthew 13:53–58*

s) The twelve sent out   *Matthew, ch. 10; Mark 6:7–13; Luke 9:1–6*

? Who said this? "Heal the sick, cleanse the lepers, raise the dead, cast out devils: freely ye have received, freely give." *Matthew 10:8*

? To whom was Jesus speaking when he said, "Heal the sick, cleanse the lepers, raise the dead, cast out devils: freely ye have received, freely give." *Matthew 10:1, 8*

? When Jesus sent his disciples to "preach the kingdom of God," what did he instruct them to take? *Luke 9:1–6*

t) Martyrdom of John the Baptist   *Matthew 14:1–12; Mark 6:14–29*

? Please explain the circumstances that led Herod Antipas (son of Herod the Great by his wife, Malthake) to behead John the Baptist. *Matthew 14:1–12; A Commentary on The Holy Bible, Dummelow, p. lxxxvi*

? Why was Herod Antipas hesitant to kill John the Baptist? *Matthew 14:5*

? Who danced for Herod Antipas on his birthday? *Matthew 14:6*

? Herod Antipas made a foolish promise to the daughter of Herodias. What was the result? *Mark 6:17–30*

? Herod's wife, Herodias, hated John the Baptist because he condemned her marriage to Herod. Herodias and Herod both had divorced their first husband and wife to marry each other. How did Herodias plot to have John the Baptist killed? *Mark 6:14–29*

? Although the daughter of Herodias was not named in Scripture, a famous historian named Josephus wrote that her name was Salome. What was Salome's part in John the Baptist's death? *Matthew 14:1–12; Harper's Bible Dictionary, p. 35*

u) Multitude of five thousand fed   *Matthew 14:14–21; Mark 6:30–46; Luke 9:10–17; John 6:1–14*

? Who was able to feed a crowd of five thousand people with just five loaves and two fishes? *Matthew 14:14–21; Mark 6:34–44; Luke 9:2–17; John 6:1–14; 34–44*

? In John's account of Jesus' feeding the five thousand, two disciples talk to Jesus about feeding the multitude. Who are the two disciples mentioned by name? *John 6:3, 5–14*

v) Jesus walks on water   *Matthew 14:22–33; Mark 6:45–51; John 6:16–21*

? According to the Bible, who was able to walk on water? *Matthew 14:22–33; Mark 6:45–51; John 6:16–21*

? Where were the disciples when "Jesus went unto them, walking on the sea"? *Matthew 14:22–33*

w) Discourse on the bread of life at third passover   *John 6:22–71*

? Who said this? "I am the bread of life: he that cometh to me shall never hunger; and he that believeth on me shall never thirst." *John 6:35*

x) Four thousand fed   (Compare to account where five thousand are fed.) *Matthew 15:32–38; Mark 8:19*

? Once there were about four thousand people with Jesus. They had had nothing to eat for three days. What did Jesus do? *Matthew 15:32–39; Mark 8:1–9*

y) Peter's confession   *Matthew 16:13–20; Mark 8:27–30; Luke 9:18–21*

? The recognition that Jesus was "the Christ, the Son of the living God" was the rock upon which Jesus wanted the Christian church to be built. Who was the disciple who stated this truth? *Matthew 16:13–18*

? Jesus asked his disciples, "Whom do men say that I the Son of man am?" They said, "Some say that thou art John the Baptist: some, Elias; and others, Jeremias, or one of the prophets." Who were Elias and Jeremias? *Matthew 16:13–18; The New Westminster Dictionary of the Bible*

? To whom was Jesus speaking when he said: "upon this rock I will build my church..."? *Matthew 16:18*

? Who said this? "Thou art the Christ, the Son of the living God." *Matthew 16:16*

z) Jesus foretells crucifixion and resurrection   *Matthew 16:21–28; Mark 8:31–33; Luke 9:22–27; Luke 13:31,32*

? Jesus said to some Pharisees: "Go ye, and tell that fox, Behold, I cast out devils, and I do cures to-day and to-morrow, and the third day I shall be perfected." Who is Jesus calling a "fox"? *Luke 13:31, 32*

? What does it mean to be a prophet? *The New Westminster Dictionary of the Bible,* pp. 766–769

? Was Christ Jesus a prophet? *The New Westminster Dictionary of the Bible,* pp. 766–769

? How did Peter respond when Jesus foretold his own crucifixion? *Matthew 16:21–28; Mark 8:31–33*

aa) The transfiguration   *Matthew 17:1–13; Mark 9:2–13; Luke 9:28–36; II Peter 1:16–19*

? On the mount of transfiguration, Jesus' "face did shine as the sun." Who appeared with Jesus and talked with him? *Matthew 17:1–9; Mark 9:2–8; Luke 9:28–30; II Peter 1:16–19*

? Jesus knew ahead of time that he would be crucified, that he would rise from the dead, and that he would ascend. After his transfiguration, Jesus said: "Tell the vision to no man, until the Son of man be risen again from the dead." To whom was Jesus speaking? *Matthew 17:9*

? Please name three disciples who witnessed the transfiguration of Christ. *Matthew 17:1–9; Mark 9:2–8; Luke 9:28–36; II Peter 1:16–19*

? Three disciples witnessed Jesus' transfiguration. They were Peter, James, and John. It was Peter who said: "Master, it is good for us to be here: and let us make three tabernacles...." Who were the tabernacles to honor? *Mark 9:5*

? Who enthusiastically suggested at the transfiguration that the disciples build three tabernacles—one for Moses, one for Elias, and one for Christ Jesus? *Matthew 17:4; Mark 9:2–13; Luke 9:28–36*

bb) Coin in the fish's mouth   *Matthew 17:24–27*

? Jesus told Peter to go to the sea, cast an hook, "and take up the fish that first cometh up; and when thou hast opened his mouth, thou shalt find a piece of money...." What was Peter to do with this money? *Matthew 17:24–27*

? Jesus gave the following instructions regarding tribute money to a disciple: "Go thou to the sea, and cast an hook, and take up the fish that first cometh up; and when thou hast opened his mouth, thou shalt find ... money." Who received these instructions? *Matthew 7:24–27*

? In what unusual place did Peter find a piece of money enabling him to pay tribute for Jesus and himself? *Matthew 17:24–27*

cc) Sends forth the seventy *Luke 10:1–24*

? Who said this? "The harvest truly is great, but the labourers are few: pray ye therefore the Lord of the harvest, that he would send forth labourers into his harvest." *Luke 10:1, 2*

? Jesus "appointed other seventy also, and sent them two and two before his face into every city and place...." Did Jesus instruct these seventy to heal the sick? *Luke 10:1–9*

dd) Jesus attends the feast of tabernacles *John 7:1–31*

? "When Christ cometh, will he do more miracles than these which this man hath done?" On what occasion did the people in Judaea ask this question concerning Jesus? *John 7:1–31*

? Mosaic law required three annual celebrations called festivals or feasts. Scholars assume Jesus was customarily present at Jerusalem on these occasions. Please name at least one of these feasts. *The New Westminster Dictionary of the Bible*, p. 296; *Deuteronomy 16:16; John 7:1–31*

? Did Jesus observe Jewish holidays, such as passover and the feast of tabernacles? *John 2:13; 5:1; 7:2, 8–15; Matthew 26:17*

ee) Jesus forgives woman taken in adultery *John 8:1–11*

? In the Gospel of John there is a woman who breaks the commandment, "Thou shalt not commit adultery." Jesus told her accusers, "He that is without sin among you, let him cast first a stone at her." Who cast the first stone? *John 8:1–11*

? Who brought the woman taken in adultery to Jesus and said: "Moses in the law commanded us, that such should be stoned: but what sayest thou?" *John 8:1–11*

? When the scribes and Pharisees brought unto Jesus a woman taken in adultery, what did Jesus say to them? *John 8:1–11*

ff) Discourse: Christ the light of the world *John 8:12–30*

? Who said this? "I am the light of the world: he that followeth me shall not walk in darkness, but shall have the light of life." *John 8:12*

gg) Discourse: spiritual freedom *John 8:31–59*

? Who said this? "Ye shall know the truth, and the truth shall make you free." *John 8:31, 32*

hh) Discourse: the good shepherd *John 10:1–21*

? "He that entereth in by the door is the shepherd of the sheep. To him the porter openeth; and the sheep hear his voice…." Who is the shepherd, do you think, in this verse from John? *John 10:2, 3*

? Who said this? "I am come that they might have life, and that they might have it more abundantly." *John 10:7–10*

ii) Jesus at the house of Martha and Mary *Luke 10:38–42*

? A woman called Mary "sat at Jesus' feet and heard his word." Mary's sister "was cumbered about much serving … and said, Lord, dost thou not care that my sister hath left me to serve alone?" Please name Mary's sister. *Luke 10:38–42*

? Please name the two sisters of Lazarus. *John 11:1–3*

? Luke records the story where Jesus went to the house of Martha and Mary. How did Jesus respond when Martha complained that her sister wasn't helping her? *Luke 10:38–42*

jj) Discourse: trust in God's care *Luke 12:1–59*

? Who said this? "…a man's life consisteth not in the abundance of the things which he possesseth." *Luke 12:15*

? Please fill in the blanks: "Take no thought for your life, what ye shall _____; neither for the body, what ye shall _____ _____." *Luke 12:22*

? Christ Jesus said: "Consider the lilies how they grow: they toil not, they spin not; and yet I say unto you, that Solomon in all his glory was not arrayed like one of these." Who was Solomon? *I Kings 10:18–27; Luke 12:27*

kk) Dines at chief Pharisee's house *Luke 14:1–24*

? During an eventful meal in the house of the chief Pharisee, Jesus healed a man of dropsy and told two parables. On what day of the week did this take place? *Luke 14:1–24*

ll) Teachings on forgiveness, faith, service *Luke 17:1–10*

? What did Christ Jesus say the apostles might do if they had "faith as a grain of mustard seed"? *Matthew 17:20; Luke 17:5, 6*

? What did Jesus teach regarding forgiveness? *Luke 17:3, 4*

mm) Blessing little children   *Matthew 19:13–15; Mark 10:13–16; Luke 18:15–17*

? Who said this? "Suffer the little children to come unto me." *Mark 10:14*

? Occasionally, the disciples did something which "much displeased" Jesus. This was the case when the disciples rebuked those who brought young children to him. What was Jesus' response to the children? *Mark 10:16*

? Jesus once said, "Allow the children to come to Me...." [sic] Who had been discouraging the people from bringing little children to him? *Mark 10:13, 14; See The Amplified Bible and The New Testament in Modern English, Revised Edition, J. B. Phillips*

nn) Instructions to one desiring eternal life   *Matthew 19:16–22; Mark 10:17–31; Luke 18:18–30; compare with Luke 10:25–37*

? Jesus told the young man who desired eternal life to keep the commandments. The young man said, "All these things have I kept from my youth up." What did he lack? *Matthew 19:16–22*

? A young man desiring eternal life came to Jesus and asked what he should do. After Jesus told him, the young man "went away sorrowful...." Why? *Matthew 19:16–22*

? A young man came to Jesus and asked: "Good Master, what good thing shall I do, that I may have eternal life?" How did Jesus respond? *Matthew 19:16–22*

? Did Jesus know the Ten Commandments given by God and written down by Moses? *Matthew 4:1–11; 12:1–13; 19:16–22; Mark 10:17–24; John 8:1–11*

? True or false? In his encounter with one desiring eternal life, Jesus points out the importance of following the fifth, sixth, seventh, eighth and ninth commandments. *Mark 10:19*

? What do you think is important to do to inherit eternal life, according to Christ Jesus' teachings? *Luke 10:25–37; 18:18–30*

oo) Supper at Bethany; anointed by a woman   *Matthew 26:6–13; Mark 14:3–9; John 12:1–8*

? About a week before his crucifixion, Jesus was at supper in the town of Bethany in the home of Simon the leper. A woman, Mary, anointed Jesus with expensive ointment. According to the Gospel of John, Judas Iscariot objected to this. Why? *Matthew 26:6–13; Mark 14:3–9; John 12:1–8*

6. Jesus' Parables

a) New cloth on old garment *Matthew 9:16; Mark 2:21; Luke 5:36*

? "No man putteth a piece of new cloth unto an old garment, for that which is put in to fill it up taketh from the garment, and the rent is made worse." In this short parable, what does *rent* mean? *Matthew 9:16*

b) New wine in old bottles *Matthew 9:17; Mark 2:22; Luke 5:37–39*

? According to Jesus' parable, why don't men put new wine into old bottles? *Matthew 9:17; Mark 2:22; Luke 5:37–39*

c) Two debtors forgiven *Luke 7:41–50*

? Tell the short parable told by Jesus at Simon the Pharisee's house. *Luke 7:36–50*

d) Sower and the seed *Matthew 13:1–23; Mark 4:1–20; Luke 8:4–15*

? In Jesus' parable of the sower and the seed, what are the four places where the seed fell? *Matthew 13:3–8, 18–23; Mark 4:3–8,14–20; Luke 8:4–15*

? In the parable of the sower and the seed, what is Jesus' interpretation of the seed? *Luke 8:11–15*

? In his parable of the sower and the seed, Jesus speaks of one that heareth the word, but "the care of this world, and the deceitfulness of riches, choke the word, and he becometh unfruitful." Is this person like the seed in stony places or in thorns? *Matthew 13:3–8, 18–23*

? In his explanation of the sower and the seed parable, Jesus likens those who receive the word of God with joy but fall away in time of temptation to which of the following: the seed on the rock, or the seed which fell among thorns? *Luke 8:13*

e) Natural growth of the seed *Mark 4:26–29*

? Who said this? "For the earth bringeth forth fruit of herself; first the blade, then the ear, after that the full corn in the ear." *Mark 4:28*

f) Wheat and the tares *Matthew 13:24–30, 36–43*

? In Jesus' parable of the wheat and the tares, an enemy planted weeds in with the good seed. Why did the householder tell his servants to let them both grow together until the harvest? *Matthew 10:24–30*

g) Mustard seed *Matthew 13:31, 32: Mark 4:30–32: Luke 13:18, 19; 17:5, 6*

? True or false? Christ Jesus said the kingdom of God is like a grain of mustard seed, which a man took, and cast into his garden; and it grew into a tree. *Luke 13:19*

? In Jesus' parable of a grain of mustard seed, what happens to the mustard seed? *Luke 13:18, 19*

? What example did Jesus give the apostles of what they might do if they had "faith as a grain of mustard seed"? *Matthew 17:20; Luke 17:5, 6*

h) Leaven *Matthew 13:33; Luke 13:20, 21*

? According to Christ Jesus, what is "like leaven, which a woman took and hid in three measures of meal, till the whole was leavened"? *Matthew 13:33; Luke 13:20, 21*

i) Hid treasure *Matthew 13:44*

? Please tell the short parable about treasure hid in a field. *Matthew 13:44*

j) Pearl *Matthew 13:45, 46*

? "The kingdom of heaven is like unto a merchant man, seeking goodly pearls...." This is the beginning of a parable recorded in Matthew. What did the merchant man do when he "found one pearl of great price"? *Matthew 13:45, 46*

k) Net *Matthew 13:47–50*

? In one parable Christ Jesus compared the kingdom of heaven with a net. It "was cast into the sea, and gathered of every kind." Once the net was full, what did the fishers do? *Matthew 13:47, 48*

l) Unmerciful servant *Matthew 18:23–35*

? Two parables told by Jesus have to do with talents. One parable outlines what three servants did with the talents given to them. The other parable tells of a servant's debt of 10,000 talents forgiven, and yet he was unmerciful to his fellow servant. What is a *talent?* *Young People's Bible Dictionary*, Smith, p. 144

m) Good Samaritan *Luke 10:25–37*

? Who first told the famous parable of the Good Samaritan? *Luke 10:30–37*

? A certain lawyer tempted Jesus saying, "Master, what shall I do to inherit eternal life?" Jesus answered, "What is written in the law?" Did the lawyer know the law? *Luke 10:25–29*

? A certain lawyer knew the law from Deuteronomy. "But, he, willing to justify himself, said unto Jesus, And who is my neighbour?" How did Jesus answer? *Luke 10:28–37*

? What did the Samaritan do for the man who fell among thieves that the priest and Levite did not do? *Luke 10:29–37*

? Who helped the man who went down from Jericho and fell among thieves: a priest, a Levite, or a Samaritan?

? Who was neighbour unto him that fell among thieves — the priest, the Levite, or the Samaritan? *Luke 10:30–37*

? What qualities did the Good Samaritan express? *Luke 10:25–37*

? Please tell of a time when you did something loving like the Good Samaritan. *Luke 10:25–37*

n) Importunate friend *Luke 11:5–8*

? The parable of the importunate friend illustrates "how perseverance in prayer brings its answer." What does *importunate* mean? *Getting Better Acquainted with Your Bible,* Shotwell, p.285

? Jesus tells a parable in which someone goes to a friend and urgently demands that the friend lend him three loaves, even though it is midnight. Why does the individual in the parable need the loaves? *Luke 11:6*

o) Rich fool *Luke 12:16–21*

? In one of Jesus' parables a certain rich man said to himself: "…take thine ease, eat, drink, and be merry." Why, in the parable, did God respond "Thou fool"? *Luke 12:19, 20*

p) Watchful servants *Luke 12:35–38*

q) Goodman of the house *Luke 12:39, 40; compare with Matthew 24:43, 44*

r) Faithful and faithless stewards *Luke 12:42–48; compare with Matthew 24:45–51*

s) Barren fig tree   *Luke 13:6–9*

? In Jesus' parable of the barren fig tree, what happens to the tree if it does not bear fruit? *Luke 13:6–9*

? In one of Jesus' parables, a certain man had a fig tree planted in his vineyard. For how many years had this man found no fruit on his fig tree? *Luke 13:6–9*

t) Wedding guest   *Luke 14:7–11*

? Christ Jesus made the following comment in a parable he told at the house of one of the chief Pharisees. Please fill in the blanks: "For whosoever exalteth himself shall be _____; and he that humbleth himself shall be _____." *Luke 14:11*

u) Great supper   *Luke 14:15–24*

? "A certain man made a great supper, and bade many...." Those invited made excuses for not attending the supper. Whom did the master then invite, according to Jesus' parable? *Luke 14:21*

v) Counting the cost of discipleship   *Luke 14:28–35*

w) Lost sheep   *Matthew 18:11–14; Luke 15:3–7*   (See Figure 20)

? If a man has 100 sheep and one of them goes astray, what does the man do? *Matthew 18:12*

? In the parable of the lost sheep, how many sheep does the man leave to seek the one that has gone astray? *Luke 15:4*

x) Lost piece of money   *Luke 15:8–10*   (See Figure 21)

? Jesus tells of a woman who loses something. She lights a candle, sweeps the house, and seeks diligently till she finds it. What did she lose? *Luke 15:8–10*

y) Prodigal son   *Luke 15:11–32*

? Please name the parable in which Jesus tells of a father and his two sons. The younger son wasted his inheritance in riotous living. When he came home again, in humility, his father rejoiced. "For this my son was dead, and is alive again...." *Luke 15:11–32*

? In the parable of the prodigal son, Jesus said that the father had compassion on his son and ran and kissed him. Which of the following qualities best describes the father:
  - meek,
  - merciful, or
  - courageous?

Figure 20: A shepherd finds his lost sheep.

Figure 21: A woman sweeps her house looking for a lost coin.

That Ye May Teach the Children

? In one of Jesus' parables, a father's younger son left home and wasted all his goods. Then there arose a mighty famine, and the hungry son returned home. What did the father do? *Luke 15:11–32*

? Who first told the parable of the prodigal son? *Luke 15:11–32*

? Please tell the story of the prodigal son. *Luke 15:11–32*

? Of the following parable characters, who was known for showing mercy:
- the prodigal son,
- the Good Samaritan,
- the father of the prodigal son, or
- the brother of the prodigal son?

z) Unjust steward *Luke 16:1–13*

? Who said: "No servant can serve two masters: for either he will hate the one, and love the other; or else he will hold to the one and despise the other. Ye cannot serve God and mammon"? *Luke 16:13*

aa) Lazarus and the rich man *Luke 16:19–31*

? Who first told the parable of a rich man and a beggar named Lazarus? *Luke 16:20*

? In Jesus' parable of a rich man "in hell" and a beggar named Lazarus, who is the patriarch who talks to the rich man? *Luke 16:22–25*

? One of the parables Jesus told is about a certain rich man and a beggar named Lazarus. After Lazarus died, he was "carried by the angels into Abraham's bosom." After the rich man died, he wanted Lazarus to return to warn the rich man's five brothers. What was Abraham's reply? *Luke 16:29–31*

? In one of Jesus' parables, a rich man wants to warn his five brothers against doing evil. The rich man proposes that Lazarus, once risen from the dead, might persuade them. Did Abraham agree? *Luke 16:29*

bb) Unprofitable servants *Luke 17:7–10*

cc) Unrighteous judge *Luke 18:1–8*

dd) The Pharisee and the publican *Luke 18:9–14*

? Luke records a parable told by Jesus about two men who went up into the temple to pray. One prayed thus: "God, I thank thee, that I am not as other men are, extortioners, unjust, adulterers...." The other man, Jesus explained, was humble. Which was the prayer of the Pharisee? *Luke 18:9–14*

? Jesus told a parable about two men who went up into the temple to pray. Match the appropriate adjective to each man:
   1. Pharisee   a. humble
   2. publican   b. self-righteous

? What lesson was Jesus trying to teach when he told the parable of the Pharisee and the publican going to the temple to pray? *Luke 18:9–14*

? Where in the Bible do you learn the importance of meekness? *Luke 18:9–14; Matthew 5:5; Numbers 12:3; Psalms 22:26; 25:9; Isaiah 29:19*

ee) Labourers in the vineyard *Matthew 20:1–16*

? In one parable told by Jesus, a man who is a householder hires labourers into his vineyard. How much does he agree to pay them for their day's work? *Matthew 20:1, 2*

ff) Ten pounds *Luke 19:11–27*

Parables told during Jesus' last week

gg) Two sons Matthew *21:28–32*

? Christ Jesus rebuked "the chief priests and elders of the people" when he told a parable of two sons. He showed the hypocrisy of the son who behaved like the chief priests. Who was doing the will of his father? *Matthew 21:28–32*

hh) Vineyard, or wicked husbandmen *Matthew 21:33–46; Mark 12:1–12; Luke 20:9–19*

ii) Marriage of the king's son *Matthew 22:1–14*

jj) Fig tree and young leaves *Matthew 24:32, 33; Mark 13:28, 29; Luke 21:29–31*

kk) Household and porter watching *Mark 13:34–36*

ll) Ten virgins   *Matthew 25:1–13*

?   In the parable of the ten virgins, what did the five foolish virgins request from the five wise virgins?   *Matthew 25:8*

?   In Jesus' parable of the ten virgins, the foolish girls requested oil from the wise ones. How many of the virgins were wise? How many were foolish?   *Matthew 25:1–13*

?   In the parable of the ten virgins, the five wise and five foolish "all slumbered and slept" as they waited for the bridegroom. At what time was the cry made, "Behold, the bridegroom cometh; go ye out to meet him"?   *Matthew 25:6*

mm) Talents   *Matthew 25:14–30*

?   In Jesus' parable of the talents, a man gives his three servants talents "according to his several ability." To one servant he gave five talents; to another, two; and to another, one. What did each servant do with his talents?   *Matthew 25:14–30*

nn) Parable review

?   What is a parable?

?   The four Gospels record over thirty different parables told by Christ Jesus. Some are long stories (for example, the sower and the seed), while others are very short. Please name three short parables that begin "the kingdom of heaven is like unto _____."   *Matthew ch. 13; Luke ch. 13*

?   How many parables told by Christ Jesus can you name?

?   According to the Gospels, what is like a pearl of great price, a net, a grain of mustard seed, leaven, and a treasure hid in a field?   *Matthew 13; Luke 13:18–21*

?   Which of the following is not a parable told by Jesus?
- the Good Samaritan
- Noah's ark
- the ten virgins
- the sower and the seed
- the Sermon on the Mount

?   Please tell a parable Jesus told.

? Who compared the kingdom of heaven to these things?
- leaven,
- a grain of mustard seed,
- a net, and
- a treasure hid in a field.

? Two parables are included in Christ Jesus' Sermon on the Mount. One teaches us to light a candle and put it on a candlestick. The other advises building our house upon a rock. In what book is the Sermon on the Mount? *Matthew 5:14–16; 7:24–27*

? In which of Jesus parables would you find the following sayings?
- "Some fell among thorns." *Matthew 13:7*
- "Which now of these three, thinkest thou, was neighbour unto him that fell among the thieves?" *Luke 10:36*
- "Bring hither the fatted calf, and kill it; and let us eat, and be merry…." *Luke 15:23*

? Over thirty parables told by Christ Jesus are recorded in three Gospels. Which Gospel does not record any parables? *An Outline of the Bible: Book by Book,* Landis, p. 113

7. Specific healings by Christ Jesus

a) Nobleman's son *John 4:46–54*

? Who wanted Christ Jesus to come to Capernaum to heal his son and said, "Sir, come down ere my child die"? *John 4:49*

? The Gospels reveal that Christ Jesus could heal individuals without being personally present with them. For instance, where was Jesus when he healed the nobleman's son who was sick at Capernaum? *John 4:46*

? Jesus was in Cana of Galilee when he healed the son of a nobleman who was in Capernaum. What was wrong with the nobleman's son? *John 4:52*

? Where was Jesus when he made the water wine? *John 4:46; 2:1–11*

? After talking with Christ Jesus, the nobleman began his return trip to Capernaum. Who met him and said, "Thy son liveth"? *John 4:51*

b) Man with unclean spirit in synagogue *Mark 1:21–28; Luke 4:31–37*

? Who healed a man, "which had a spirit of an unclean devil," in the synagogue at Capernaum? *Luke 4:33–35*

? Who said to Jesus: "Let us alone; what have we to do with thee, thou Jesus of Nazareth? Art thou come to destroy us? I know thee who thou art; the Holy One of God"? *Luke 4:33, 34*

? Did Jesus ever heal in the synagogue? *Luke 4:33–35*

? Jesus healed a man with an unclean spirit in a synagogue on the Sabbath. Who else was healed in a synagogue on the Sabbath? *Matthew 12:9–13; Mark 1:21–28; 3:1–5; Luke 4:31–37; 6:6–11*

c) Simon's wife's mother   *Matthew 8:14, 15; Mark 1:29–31; Luke 4:38, 39*

? The Gospels record a healing "when Jesus was come into Peter's house." Someone in Peter's family was lying down, "sick of a fever." Jesus healed her. Was the woman Peter's:
- daughter,
- wife,
- mother-in-law, or
- mother?

? Simon and Andrew lived in Capernaum, a town located on the shore of the Sea of Galilee. Jesus healed a number of people in Capernaum. Please name one. *Matthew 8:5–15*

d) Cleansing of a leper   *Matthew 8:2–4, Mark 1:39–45; Luke 5:12–15*

? Matthew, Mark, and Luke all recount Jesus' immediate cleansing of a leper. Do any of the Gospel accounts indicate whether or not Jesus touched the leper? *Matthew 8:3; Mark 1:41; Luke 5:13*

? Please tell the story, recorded in Luke, of Christ Jesus and the "man full of leprosy." *Luke 5:12–15*

e) One "sick of the palsy" (paralytic)   *Matthew 9:1–8; Mark 2:1–12; Luke 5:18–25*

? Four friends carried a man sick of the palsy so Christ Jesus might heal him. Mark records that "they uncovered the roof where he was" and "let down the bed." Why did they go to the housetop to get the paralytic to Jesus? *Mark 2:4*

? Who was healed of an illness after Jesus said to him, "Son, be of good cheer; thy sins be forgiven thee"? *Matthew 9:2*

? The Gospels tell of a time when "they brought to him a man sick of the palsy, lying on a bed: and Jesus seeing their faith said unto the sick of the palsy; Son be of good cheer; thy sins be forgiven thee." Who thought it was wrong for Jesus to do this? *Matthew 9:2, 3*

Figure 22: Jesus heals the man with the withered hand in the temple.

That Ye May Teach the Children

? In the town of Capernaum, Jesus healed a man "sick of the palsy." How many friends of the sick man carried him and let down his bed from the roof? *Mark 2:1–12*

? What was wrong with the man brought in a bed to Christ Jesus for healing and let down through the housetop? *Luke 5:18*

f) Infirm man at the pool of Bethesda   *John 5:1–19*

? True or false? Jesus enabled a man who had been sick thirty-eight years to get into the pool of Bethesda for his healing. *John 5:1–9*

? Before Jesus healed him, an infirm man at the pool of Bethesda in Jerusalem believed a certain superstition. What was that superstition? *John 5:1–9*

? Why did certain Jews say to say to the man who was cured at the pool of Bethesda, "it is not lawful for thee to carry thy bed"? *John 5:1–19*

? What happened at the pool called Bethesda in Jerusalem? *John 5:1–19*

? Where did the man, healed at the pool of Bethesda, see Jesus again? *John 5:1–16*

g) Man with a withered hand on the Sabbath   *Matthew 12:9–13; Mark 3:1–5; Luke 6:6–11* (See Figure 22)

? The Pharisees did not like it when Jesus healed the man with a withered hand on the Sabbath. Why? *Matthew 12:10, 14*

? Where was Jesus when he healed "a man whose right hand was withered"? *Luke 6:6*

? Jesus healed a man with an unclean spirit in a synagogue on the Sabbath. Who else was healed in a synagogue on the Sabbath? *Matthew 12:9–13; Mark 1:21–28; 3:1–5, Luke 4:31–37; 6:6–11*

h) Centurion's servant   *Matthew 8:5–13; Luke 7:1–10*

? Who healed a centurion's servant who was "sick, and ready to die"? *Luke 7:2, 3*

? Two of the Gospels tell of a centurion whose servant was "sick, and ready to die." The centurion sent friends to Christ Jesus saying, "Lord, trouble not thyself: for I am not worthy that thou shouldest enter under my roof...." What quality was the centurion expressing? *Luke 7:6*

? What is a *centurion*?

? A certain centurion of Capernaum said to Jesus, "I am not worthy that thou shouldest enter under my roof ... but say in a word, and my servant shall be healed." What did Jesus say and do then? *Luke 7:1–10*

? The elders of the Jews once came to Jesus begging him to help a certain centurion whose servant was sick. What good thing had the centurion done for the Jewish people? *Luke 7:4, 5*

? In what town did Jesus heal the centurion's servant who was "sick, and ready to die"? *Luke 7:1–10*

i) Widow's son raised from the dead *Luke 7:11–16*

? Christ Jesus "came nigh to the gate of the city" when a dead man was being carried out on a bier. The man, the only son of a widow, rose at Jesus' command. Where were they? *Luke 7:11, 12*

? Which one of the following people did Christ Jesus raise from the dead in the city called Nain?
   • Lazarus
   • the only son of a widow
   • Jairus's daughter
   Matthew 9:18, 19, 23–26; Mark 5:22–24, 35–43; Luke 7:1116; 8:41, 42, 49–56; John 11:1–54

j) Penitent woman anoints Jesus at Pharisee's house *Luke 7:36–50*

? Christ Jesus sat at meat in Simon the Pharisee's house. A woman brought an alabaster box of ointment, "And stood at his feet behind him weeping, and began to wash his feet with tears ... and anointed them with the ointment." Jesus healed this woman. What was her problem? *Luke 7:38*

? Did Jesus forgive the sins of the woman who came to anoint his feet at Simon the Pharisee' s house? *Luke 7:48*

? According to Luke, Jesus was at the home of a Pharisee, when a woman "which was a sinner" washed Jesus' feet with her tears, wiped them with her hair, and then anointed them with ointment. Please name the Pharisee in whose house this took place. *Luke 7:36–40*

? Please name the man who had these thoughts about Jesus: "This man, if he were a prophet, would have known who and what manner of woman this is that toucheth him: for she is a sinner." *Luke 7:39*

? Why did Christ Jesus forgive the sins of the woman who washed his feet at Simon the Pharisee's house? *Luke 7:36–50*

k) Man possessed with a devil, blind and dumb *Matthew 12:22–37; Mark 3:20–30; Luke 11:14, 15, 17–23*

? Jesus instantly healed "one possessed with a devil, blind and dumb." Who said, immediately afterward: "This fellow doth not cast out devils, but by Beelzebub the prince of the devils"? *Matthew 12:24*

l) Gadarene demoniac (Legion) *Matthew 8:28–34; Mark 5:1–20; Luke 8:26–39*

? When Jesus came out of the ship in the country of the Gadarenes, there met him "a man with an unclean spirit." When Jesus asked him, "What is thy name?" he answered, "My name is Legion: for we are many." Where did this man live? *Mark 5:1–20*

? What happened to the herd of swine in the country of the Gadarenes when the unclean spirits entered into them? *Mark 5:13*

? The Gospels are filled with true accounts of healing. Did Jesus ever heal someone of insanity? *Matthew 8:28–34; Mark 5:1–20; Luke 8:26–39*

m) Jairus's daughter raised from the dead *Matthew 9:18, 19, 23–26; Mark 5:22–24, 35–43; Luke 8:41, 42, 49–56*

? Who healed Jairus's daughter when she was about twelve years old? *Mark 5:20–23*

? What did Jesus say to Jairus, the ruler of the synagogue, when people came from his house and reported his daughter was dead? *Matthew 9:18, 19, 23–26; Mark 5:22–24, 35–43; Luke 8:41, 42, 49–56*

? Christ Jesus raised Jairus's twelve-year-old daughter from the dead. Jairus was a ruler of the synagogue. How many of the Gospels report this healing? *Matthew 9:18, 19, 23–26; Mark 5:22–24, 35–43; Luke 8:41, 42, 49–56*

? A certain ruler came to Jesus "and worshipped him, saying, My daughter is even now dead: but come and lay thy hand upon her, and she shall live." Two Gospels, Mark and Luke, give the ruler's name. What is it? *Mark 5:22; Luke 8:41; compare with Matthew 9:18*

? According to Jewish law, touching a dead body would have rendered Jesus unclean. Whose hand did Jesus take when raising her from the dead? *Mark 5:39, 41; Luke 8:49, 54*

n) Woman with an issue of blood *Matthew 9:20–22; Mark 5:25–34; Luke 8:43–48*

? What did the woman with the issue of blood do in order to be healed by Jesus? *Matthew 9:20*

? What was wrong with the woman, healed by Jesus, who "had suffered many things of many physicians, and had spent all that she had, and was nothing bettered but rather grew worse"? *Mark 5:25, 26*

? Christ Jesus was on his way to heal Jairus's daughter when someone else needing help "touched his garment." Who was immediately made "whole"? *Mark 5:27, 34*

o) Two blind men *Matthew 9:27–31*

? True or false? Jesus once healed two blind men who followed him, crying, "Thou Son of David, have mercy on us." *Matthew 9:27–30*

? Why was Jesus sometimes called the Son of David? *Matthew 9:27; Isaiah 9: 6, 7; Luke 1:30–33; John 7:42*

p) Dumb demoniac *Matthew 9:32–34; Luke 11:14*

? Matthew records the following healing by Jesus: "they brought to him a dumb man possessed with a devil. And when the devil was cast out, the dumb spake...." Who claimed that Jesus "casteth out devils through the prince of the devils"? *Matthew 9:34; Luke 11:14*

? Luke records Jesus' healing of a dumb man. What was the dumb man able to do after "the devil was gone out"? *Luke 11:14*

q) Daughter of woman of Canaan/Syrophenicia *Matthew 15:21–28; Mark 7:24–30*

? According to the Gospel of Matthew, a woman of Canaan asked Jesus to heal her daughter who was "grievously vexed with a devil." The girl was "made whole from that very hour." Where did this healing take place? *Matthew 15:21–28*

? True or false? The Syrophenician woman was greatly offended by Jesus' statement: "it is not meet to take the children's bread, and to cast it unto the dogs." *Mark 7:24–30*

? A Syrophenician woman besought Jesus "that he would cast forth the devil out of her daughter." Why was Jesus hesitant, at first, to grant this Greek woman's request? *Matthew 15:21–28; Mark 7:24–30*

r) Man deaf and with "an impediment in his speech" *Mark 7:31–37*

? True or false? Christ Jesus healed a man who was deaf and had an impediment in his speech. *Mark 7:31–37*

s) Blind man at Bethsaida *Mark 8:22–26*

? A blind man saw "men as trees, walking;" then he "saw every man clearly." Who healed this blind man at Bethsaida? *Mark 8:24*

? Jesus healed a man named Bartimaeus near Jericho. He also healed a man in Bethsaida. What problem was healed for both men? *Luke 18:35–43; Mark 8:22–26*

t) Epileptic boy *Matthew 17:14–21; Mark 9:14–29; Luke 9:37–42*

? "Lord, have mercy on my son: for he is lunatic, and sore vexed: for ofttimes he falleth into the fire, and oft into the water." Who said this to Jesus?
  - the boy's father
  - the boy's mother
  Matthew 17:14–21

? Christ Jesus rebuked the foul spirit in an epileptic boy, saying: "Thou dumb and deaf spirit, I charge thee, come out of him, and enter no more into him." Who were unable to cast out this "dumb spirit" earlier? *Mark 9:25*

? Jesus said, "If thou canst believe, all things are possible to him that believeth." Who responded, with tears, "Lord, I believe; help thou mine unbelief"? *Mark 9:17–19, 21–29*

? A father, desperate to have his only child healed, came to Christ Jesus. Although the disciples had been unable to heal the boy, Jesus did. What was wrong with the boy? *Luke 9:38–43*

? "If ye have faith as a grain of mustard seed, ye shall say unto this mountain, Remove hence to yonder place; and it shall remove; and nothing shall be impossible unto you." What event preceded this statement by Jesus Christ? *Matthew 17:14–20*

u) Man born blind *John 9:1–41*

? In Jerusalem Jesus told a man to wash at the pool of Siloam. The man was obedient and was healed. What was the man's problem? *John 9:7*

? How did Jesus answer the disciples' question: "Master, who did sin, this man, or his parents, that he was born blind?" *John 9:2*

? Jesus healed a man. Afterwards, the Pharisees questioned the man. They inquired: "What sayest thou of him…?" He answered, "He is a prophet." Of what problem had this man been healed? *John 9:13, 17*

? What is a *prophet*? *John 9:17*

? Who said, "I am the light of the world" and then spat on the ground, made clay of the spittle, anointed the eyes of the blind man with the clay, and told him to wash in a pool? *John 9:1, 5, 6*

? The pool of Siloam in Jerusalem is at the end of a tunnel built for the purpose of conducting water from the Gihon spring into the city walls. The tunnel is 1749 feet long, and visitors to Jerusalem can walk through it. The tunnel is known as Hezekiah's tunnel. Who was Hezekiah? *II Chronicles 32:30; The New Westminster Dictionary of the Bible, pp. 880–882*

v) Woman bowed together eighteen years *Luke 13:10–17*

? The Gospel of Luke records a beautiful healing of "a woman which had a spirit of infirmity ... and was bowed together and could in no wise lift up herself." Jesus healed her, and "immediately she was made straight." How many years had she been bowed together? *Luke 13:11*

? According to Saint Luke, the ruler of the synagogue answered with indignation when Jesus healed the woman who had been bowed together eighteen years. Why? How did Jesus respond? *Luke 13:14–16*

? Who was indignant when Jesus healed a woman who had been bowed together eighteen years? *Luke 13:11–17*

w) Man with dropsy on the Sabbath *Luke 14:1–6*

? In New Testament times, the Pharisees, a major religious party of the Jews, emphasized strict conformity with law and tradition. This caused conflict with Christ Jesus. Did Jesus ever associate with Pharisees? *Luke 14:16; 7:36; 11:37*

? Where was Christ Jesus when he healed a certain man "which had the dropsy" on the Sabbath day? *Luke 14:1, 2*

? What lesson was Jesus trying to teach the Pharisees when he healed a certain man of dropsy? *Luke 14:1–6*

? Please give an example of an individual healed by Jesus on the Sabbath day. *Matthew 12:9–13; Mark 1:21–28; Luke 13:11–17; 14:1–6; John 5:2–19*

x) Lazarus raised from the dead *John 11:1–54*

? Please fill in the blank: Jesus raised _____, who had been in the grave four days. *John 11:17*

? Is the account of Lazarus being raised from the dead in the Old or New Testament?

? What was the first thing Jesus did when they took away the stone from Lazarus's grave? *John 11:41*

? Christ Jesus raised Lazarus from the dead at Bethany. Please name the two sisters of Lazarus. *John 11:19*

? Who cried with a loud voice, "Lazarus, come forth"? *John 11:41, 43*

? How many days had Lazarus "lain in the grave" when Jesus came to Bethany? *John 11:17*

? Jericho, Capernaum, Bethany, Nazareth, Jerusalem, and Nain are the names of some of the cities Jesus visited during his ministry. In which two of these cities did Jesus raise a man from the dead? *John 11:1–54; Luke 7:11–16*

? Who said this? "I am the resurrection, and the life: he that believeth in me, though he were dead, yet shall he live: And whosoever liveth and believeth in me shall never die." *John 11:25, 26*

? Who was healed after Jesus said: "Father, I thank thee that thou hast heard me. And I knew that thou hearest me always: but because of the people which stand by I said it..."? *John 11:42*

? When Jesus came to Bethany to raise Lazarus from the dead, Lazarus's sister, Martha, first met him. Then Mary came weeping. Why, do you suppose, did Jesus then weep? *John 11:35, 36*

? Lazarus and his two sisters, Mary and Martha, were close friends of Jesus. In what town did they live? *John 11:1*

y) Ten lepers *Luke 17:11–19*

? Luke records that Jesus cleansed ten lepers as he went to Jerusalem. Only one returned to give thanks. Was the grateful one an Israelite or a Samaritan? *Luke 17:16*

? True or false? In Saint Luke's account of ten lepers healed by Jesus, only one, a Samaritan, turned back to give thanks. *Luke 17:16*

? A certain Samaritan was one of ten individuals healed at one time by Christ Jesus. Yet, he was the only one to turn back and give thanks. Of what problem was he healed? *Luke 17:12*

z) Blind Bartimaeus and two blind men near Jericho *Matthew 20:29–34; Mark 10:46–52; Luke 18:35–43*

? Bartimaeus sat by the highway side begging. He cried out to Jesus saying, "Thou Son of David, have mercy on me." What did Bartimaeus want Jesus to do? *Mark 10:48, 51*

? When Bartimaeus called to Jesus for help, how did some of the bystanders respond?
Mark 10:48

? What did Bartimaeus do when the people told him to be quiet as Jesus passed by?
Mark 10:46–52; Luke 18:35–43

? What was blind Bartimaeus doing when Jesus passed by on his way out of Jericho?
Mark 10:46–52

? Who was rebuked by some people when he cried, saying, "Jesus, thou Son of David, have mercy on me"? *Luke 18:35–43*

? The Gospel of Mark gives us the name of a blind beggar in Jericho who was healed by Christ Jesus. Please name him. *Mark 10:46–52*

? As Jesus and the disciples were leaving Jericho, two men sitting by the way side cried out, "Have mercy on us, O Lord, thou son of David." Jesus had compassion on them. From what problem did he free them? *Matthew 20:29–34*

? True or false? Jesus was descended from King David. *Matthew 1:1–16*

? Jericho "is regarded as the oldest city in the world." Did Jesus ever go there? *Matthew 20:29–34; Mark 10:46–52; Luke 18:35–43; The New Westminster Dictionary of the Bible, p. 460*

aa) Zacchaeus *Luke 19:1–10*

? Luke tells the story of Zacchaeus, chief among the publicans. When Jesus passed through Jericho, Zacchaeus sought to see him, but could not because he was too short. What did Zacchaeus do that enabled him to see Jesus? *Luke 19:4*

? Did Christ Jesus heal Zacchaeus of sickness or sin? *Luke 19:8, 9*

? Why did Zacchaeus have to climb a sycamore tree in order to see Christ Jesus? *Luke 19:3*

? Zacchaeus, a publican, was "little of stature." Climbing a sycamore tree enabled him to see and speak to Jesus in Jericho. Was Zacchaeus rich or poor? *Luke 19:2*

? Was Zacchaeus joyful or fearful when Jesus announced: "to-day I must abide at thy house"? *Luke 19:5, 6*

? "Publicans were hated for their service to Rome and classed as sinners; they were also hated for their extortionary practices...." Please name the wealthy publican in Jericho who was converted to a disciple of Christ Jesus. *Luke 19:1–10; Getting Better Acquainted with Your Bible, Shotwell, p. 298*

? In what town did Zacchaeus live? *Luke 19:1, 2*

bb) Malchus's ear *Matthew 26:50–53; Mark 14:44,47; Luke 22:49–51; John 18:3, 10, 11*

? Peter cut off the right ear of Malchus, servant of the high priest, with a sword when Judas Iscariot and the band of men came to get Jesus. According to Luke, what happened next? *Luke 22:49–51*

cc) Overview of healings

? Please name someone who Jesus raised from the dead. *Matthew 9:18, 19, 23–26; Mark 5:22–24, 35–43; Luke 7:11–16; 8:41, 42, 49–56; John 11:1–54*

? Besides his own resurrection, Jesus raised three people from the dead. Please name them. *Matthew 9:18, 19, 23–26; Mark 5:22–24, 35–43; Luke 7:11–16; 8:41, 42, 49–56; John 11:1–54*

? Despite the Pharisees' rules, Jesus often healed on the Sabbath day. How many healings that occurred on the Sabbath can you think of? *Matthew 12:10–14; Luke 13:10–17; 14:1–6; John 5:2–19*

? True or false? Jesus healed people of blindness, fever, leprosy, deafness, and dropsy.

? In what town did these events occur?
- Jesus healed a centurion's servant who was sick of the palsy.
- Jesus healed a man with an unclean spirit in the synagogue.
- Jesus healed a man let down through the roof.
Matthew 8:5–10; Mark 1:21–27; 2:1–12

? Which of the following healings by Jesus were not performed on the Sabbath?
- man with a withered hand
- thirty-eight year invalid at pool of Bethesda
- man born blind
- woman bowed together eighteen years
- man with dropsy
Matthew 12:9–14; Mark 3:1–5; Luke 6:6–11; 13:10–17; 14:1–6; John 5:2–19; 9:1–25

? At least three of those healed by Jesus on the Sabbath had long-standing physical problems. Please tell how long:
- the woman was bowed together
- the man was blind
- the man at the pool of Bethesda was an invalid
Luke 13:10–17, John 5:2–19; 9:1–25

? The Gospels record that Christ Jesus healed the following four people. What do they have in common besides being healed by Jesus?
- the nobleman's son
- Jairus's daughter
- Syrophenician girl
- epileptic boy

(Use a Bible concordance to find the citations for these stories.)

? How many healings of children are recorded in the four Gospels? *Matthew 9:18, 19, 23–26; 15:21–28; 17:14–21; Mark 5:22–24, 35–43; 7:24–30; 9:14–29; Luke 8:41, 42, 49–56; 9:37–42; John 4:46–54*

? In the Gospels are numerous examples of Jesus healing people of sin, disease, and death. Of which malady were these people healed?
- Jairus's daughter
- Zacchaeus
- Bartimaeus
- Lazarus

? Please tell who was healed of the following maladies:

1. blindness		a. Simon's wife's mother	
2. a fever		b. centurion's servant	
3. palsy		c. Syrophenician woman's daughter	
4. unclean spirit		d. Bartimaeus	

8. The last week of Christ Jesus' ministry

(The "Harmony of the Gospels" used in this portion of the outline is based on one from *The New Westminster Dictionary of the Bible*, pp. 342–349. The assignment of days of the week for the following events, which is commonly done in reference books such as *The New Westminster Dictionary of the Bible*, is disputed by some scholars because of difficulties reconciling the Gospel of John with the synoptic Gospels. Teachers may wish to emphasize the events of Jesus' last week with little or no reference to the exact chronology, since it is debatable.)

a) Triumphal entry into Jerusalem *Matthew 21:1–11; Mark 11:1–11; Luke 19:29–44; John 12:12–19; Zechariah 9:9*

? Jesus rode a colt, the foal of an ass, as prophesied by Zechariah. A "very great multitude spread their garments in the way; others cut down branches from the trees, and strawed them in the way." Where was Jesus going? *Matthew 21:1–11; Luke 19:29–32; John 12:15; Zechariah 9:9*

? Who sent two of his disciples saying, "Go ye into the village over against you; in the which at your entering ye shall find a colt tied, whereon yet never man sat: loose him, and bring him hither." *Mark 11:1–10; compare with Matthew 21:1–11; Luke 19:29–32; John 12:12–16; Zechariah 9:9*

b) Barren fig tree cursed; second cleansing of the temple *Matthew 21:12–17; Mark 11:15–19; Luke 19:45–48*

? Where was Jesus when he "overthrew the tables of the moneychangers, and the seats of them that sold doves"? *Mark 11:15*

? What was Jesus' explanation for why he "cast out them that sold and bought in the temple" at Jerusalem? *Mark 11:17*

c) Teachings, including "Render ... unto Caesar," two great commandments, widow's mites, prophecy regarding destruction of the temple *Matthew 22:15 to 24:31; Mark 12:13 to 13:27; Luke 10:25–28; 20:20 to 21:28; Deuteronomy 6:5*

? Who praised the poor widow who threw two mites (which make a farthing) into the treasury? *Mark 12:41–44; Luke 21:1–4*

? Who said this? "Render therefore unto Caesar the things which are Caesar's; and unto God the things that are God's." *Matthew 22:21; Mark 12:17; Luke 20:25*

? Solomon built the first temple in Jerusalem. It was destroyed by the Babylonians. Zerubbabel led the building of the second temple on the same site. The second temple was superseded by a larger one begun during the reign of Herod the Great. This third temple was destroyed by the Romans. Who foretold the destruction of Herod's temple? *Mark 13:1, 2; compare with Matthew 22:15 to 24:31; Luke 20:20 to 21:28*

d) Last Supper *Matthew 26:17–35; Mark 14:12–31; Luke 22:7–38; John, chs. 13 to 17; I Corinthians 11:20*

? What is the "Lord's Supper"? *I Corinthians 11:20; Matthew 26:17–19; Luke 22:17–20*

? What important religious ceremony, which is still observed by members of the Jewish faith today, did Jesus celebrate the night before he was crucified? *Mark 14:13–17*

? Where was Jesus when he prayed to God, saying: "Father, if thou be willing, remove this cup from me: nevertheless not my will, but thine, be done." *Luke 22:39–46*

? After Jesus and his disciples ate the feast of the passover, later known as the Last Supper, Jesus prepared to wash his disciple's feet. Who said, "Thou shalt never wash my feet"? *John 13:1–14*

? When the disciple Thomas asked Jesus: "we know not whither thou goest; and how can we know the way," how did Jesus respond? *John 14:5–7*

e) Gethsemane: betrayal and arrest *Matthew 26:30–56; Mark 14:26–52; Luke 22:39–53; John 18:1–12*

? Where was Jesus when he prayed to God, saying: "Father, if thou be willing, remove this cup from me: nevertheless not my will, but thine, be done"?

? To whom did Jesus ask this question: "betrayest thou the son of man with a kiss?" *Luke 22:45–48*

? What happened to the money Judas Iscariot received for betraying Jesus? *Matthew 27:57*

? According to the Gospel of Matthew, how did Judas Iscariot die? *Matthew 27:36; compare with Acts 1:16–20*

? Jesus asked his disciples to pray. When he rose up from prayer, however, he found them sleeping. Where did this happen? *Luke 22:39–46*

? After the Last Supper, some of Jesus' disciples followed him to the Mount of Olives where he prayed in the garden of Gethsemane. Jesus said unto them, "Pray that ye enter not into temptation." Did the disciples follow Jesus' instruction? *Luke 22:39–46*

? Who fell asleep "for sorrow" while Jesus prayed at Gethsemane at the Mount of Olives? *Luke 22:39–46*

? In the garden of Gethsemane, Simon Peter cut off the right ear of the high priest's servant. Luke records that Jesus "touched his ear, and healed him." Please name the servant. *Luke 22:39, 50, 51; compare with Matthew 26:51; Mark 14:47; John 18:10*

? According to Luke, where was Jesus when he healed the right ear of the servant of the high priest? (The ear had just been cut off with a sword.) *Luke 22:39, 50, 51; compare with Matthew 26:51; Mark 14:47; John 18:10*

f) Trials

(1) Before Annas *John 18:12–14, 19–24*

? When Jesus was arrested, he was first taken before Annas. Was Annas a Jewish official or a Roman official? *John 18:12–14, 19–24*

(2) Before Sanhedrin (Caiaphas is high priest) *Matthew 26:57, 59–68; Mark 14:53, 55–65; Luke 22:54, 55, 63–65, 66–71*

? The Sanhedrin functioned as a supreme court for the Jews in religious matters. It consisted of seventy-one Sadducees and Pharisees with the high priest presiding. At what point in his life did Jesus appear before the council, later called the Sanhedrin? *Matthew 26:57, 59–68; Mark 14: 53, 55–65; Luke 22:54, 55, 63–65, 66–71*

(3) **Before Pilate and Herod the tetrarch** *Matthew 27:2, 11–30; Mark 15:1–19; Luke 23:1–25; John 18:28 to 19:16*

?   Who was Pilate? *John 18:33–40*

?   Who asked the question, "What is truth?" *John 18:38*

?   Pontius Pilate asked Jesus the question, "What is truth?" How did Jesus respond? *John 18:38*

?   Why, do you suppose, did Jesus not respond to Pilate's question, "What is truth?" *John 18:38*

?   Did Pilate find fault with Jesus? *Matthew 27:21–26; Mark 15:1–19; Luke 23:13–24; John 18:33–40*

?   Only the Gospel of Luke mentions Jesus' trial before Herod the tetrarch. (Also known as Herod Antipas, he was a son of Herod the Great by his wife, Malthace.) What did Jesus say in his defense before Herod the tetrarch? *Luke 23:8–12; The New Westminster Dictionary of the Bible, pp. 382–383*

g) Peter's denials *Matthew 26:58, 69–75; Mark 14:54, 66–72; Luke 22:56–62*

?   When the cock crowed, Peter went out and "wept bitterly." Why? *Matthew 26:75; Luke 22:62*

?   How many times did Peter deny knowing Jesus after the arrest in the garden of Gethsemane? *Matthew 26:69–75; Mark 14:54, 66–72*

h) Crucifixion and burial *Matthew 27:31–61; Mark 15:24–47; Luke 23:33–56; John 19:18–42*

?   In which city or town was Jesus crucified? *John 12:12, 13*

?   Where was the place in Jerusalem where they crucified Jesus? *Matthew 27:33; Mark 15:22; Luke 23:33; John 19:17*

?   Matthew writes that Jesus prophesied: "the Son of man shall be betrayed unto the chief priests and unto the scribes, and they shall condemn him to death, and shall deliver him to the Gentiles to mock, and to scourge, and to crucify him: and the third day he shall rise again." Where did Jesus prophesy that all this would take place? *Matthew 20:17–19; compare with Mark 10:32–34 and Luke 18:31–33*

?   Each year at the passover the Roman governor released unto the people any one prisoner they most wanted released. Pilate asked if he should release Jesus. Whom did the crowd select instead? *Matthew 27:15–26; Mark 15:6–15; Luke 23:13–25*

? True or false? Soldiers of the governor mocked Christ Jesus before they led him away to crucify him. *Matthew 27:27–31*

? In what ways did the soldiers mock Jesus before taking him to be crucified? *Matthew 27:27–31*

? Where was Jesus when he said: "Father, forgive them; for they know not what they do"? *Luke 23:33, 34*

? How did Jesus feel about those who mocked him and nailed him to the cross? *Luke 23:34*

? Who was crucified with Jesus? *Matthew 27:38; Luke 23:32, 33*

? According to Mark's Gospel, Jesus cried with a loud voice, saying: "My God, my God, why hast thou forsaken me?" These same words begin Psalm 22, which Jesus evidently knew. Where was Jesus when he said this? *Mark 15:32, 34*

? Please name the "good" and "just" man who, according to Luke, "went unto Pilate, and begged the body of Jesus ... and wrapped it in linen, and laid it in a sepulchre that was hewn in stone...." *Matthew 27:57–60; Mark 15:43–46; Luke 23:50–53; John 19:38–41*

l) Sealing of tomb; guard set   *Matthew 27:62–66*

? Why did the chief priests and Pharisees ask Pilate to seal and guard the tomb where Jesus lay? *Matthew 27:62–64*

9. From resurrection to ascension

a) Visit of the women   *Matthew 28:1–10; Mark 16:1–8; Luke 24:1–11*

? According to Jesus' own prophecy, how many days after his crucifixion would he rise again? *Mark 8:31*

? According to Matthew, who told Mary Magdalene and the other Mary who came to see the sepulchre: "Fear not ye: for I know that ye seek Jesus, which was crucified. He is not here: for he is risen, as he said"? *Matthew 28:1–8*

? True or false? Jesus told Mary Magdalene and the other Mary not to tell anyone yet that they had seen him risen from the dead. *Matthew 28:10*

? Who was Salome and what did she do? *Mark 15:40; 16:1–8*

? To whom did Jesus first appear after the resurrection? *Matthew 28:1, 9; John 20:11–17; (Mark 16:9)**

(* Scholars believe verses 9–20 of chapter 16 in Mark were not part of the original book. These twelve verses were added very early, perhaps at the beginning of the second century. Thus, the Mark references are in parentheses.)

b) Visit of John and Peter to the empty sepulchre; return of Mary Magdalene
Luke 24:12; John 20:1–18

c) Walk to Emmaus *Luke 24:13–35; (Mark 16:12, 13)*

? Toward which village were Cleopas and another of Christ's disciples walking when Jesus joined them after his resurrection? *Luke 24:13–35*

? Christ Jesus appeared to two disciples as they walked "into the country" to a "village called Emmaus." Luke gives the name of one of them who spoke to Jesus the evening of his resurrection. Please name him. *Luke 24:13–35; compare with Mark 16:12,13*

? Who said this? "Did not our heart burn within us, while he talked with us by the way, and while he opened to us the scriptures?" *Luke 24:32*

? What happened as Cleopas and another follower of Jesus travelled to Emmaus from Jerusalem? *Luke 24:13–35*

? After his resurrection, Christ Jesus appeared to two disciples walking to a village called Emmaus. When did Cleopas and the other disciple finally recognize Jesus: When he expounded the Scriptures? Or when he broke bread with them? *Luke 24:13–35*

d) Jesus appears to disciples, except Thomas *Luke 24:36–49; John 20:19–24; (Mark 16:14)*

? The book of Luke notes that one time Jesus ate "a piece of a broiled fish, and of an honeycomb." Why was this significant to the disciples? *Luke 24:42*

e) Jesus appears to disciples, including Thomas *John 20:25–29*

? Which disciple is known for saying the following: "Except I shall see in his hands the print of the nails, and put my finger into the print of the nails, and thrust my hand into his side, I will not believe." *John 20:25*

f) Appearance to seven disciples at Sea of Galilee *John 21:1–23*

? How many of the disciples shared the morning meal with Jesus on the seashore after his resurrection? *John 21:1–14*

? At the Sea of Tiberias (also called the Sea of Galilee) Jesus shared a morning meal with seven of his disciples. Three times he asked Peter, "Simon, son of Jonas, lovest thou me?" What was the significance of this exchange occurring three times? *Matthew 26:75; John 21:1–23*

? Please name the disciples who were with Jesus at the Sea of Tiberias after his resurrection. *John 21:1, 2*

? What did Simon Peter do when he realized it was the risen Jesus Christ who stood on the shore? *John 21:7*

? Please recount what happened at the Sea of Tiberias when Jesus appeared to seven of his disciples. *John 21:1–23*

g) Jesus' final instructions   *Matthew 28:16–20; (Mark 16:15–18)*

? According to the book of Matthew, what were Jesus' final instructions to his disciples? *Matthew 28:16–20*

h) The ascension at Mount of Olives   *Luke 24:50–53; Acts 1:1–12; (Mark 16:19, 20)*

? According to Luke, how did the apostles feel as they returned to Jerusalem after Jesus' ascension? *Luke 24:52*

? True or false? Forty days after Jesus' resurrection, he led a small group of Pharisees from Jerusalem out to the Mount of Olives and ascended. *Luke 24:50, 51; Acts 1:1–3, 9–12; The New Westminster Dictionary of the Bible, p. 490*

? During the forty days from resurrection to ascension, about how many times did his followers see Jesus? *Matthew 28:9, 10; (Mark 16:9–14); Luke 24:9–53; John 20:11–29; 21:1–23; I Corinthians 15:7, 15; Getting Better Acquainted with Your Bible, Shotwell, p. 329*

I) Closing words of John's Gospel   *John 20:30, 31; 21:24, 25*

? The following words are written at the end of which Gospel? "And there are also many other things which Jesus did, the which, if they should be written every one, I suppose that even the world itself could not contain the books that should be written." *John 21:25*

10. The apostles' roles in Jesus' ministry

a) Jesus' preparation for choosing the twelve   *Luke 6:12, 13*

? What did Jesus do all night before he chose his twelve apostles? *Luke 6:12, 13*

b) Listing of the twelve *Matthew 10:2–4; Mark 3:16–19; Luke 6:13–16; John 1:44–51; 21:16; Acts 1:13;*

? An *apostle* is "one sent forth, a messenger." How many apostles did Jesus have? *Matthew 10:2–4; Mark 3:16–19; Luke 6:13–16; The New Westminster Dictionary of the Bible,* p. 53 (Note to teachers: The number of disciples or apostles Jesus had can become a more complicated question if you discuss the seventy. This question, with the simple answer of twelve, is intended for young children.)

? Here are the names of six disciples: Simon, Simon, James, James, Judas, Judas. One Simon was renamed Peter. One James was the son of Zebedee. One Judas betrayed Jesus. Please tell something about the other Simon, the other James and the other Judas. *Matthew 10:2–4; Mark 3:16–19; Luke 6:13–16; The New Westminster Dictionary of the Bible,* p. 53

? Scholars are not sure who wrote the four Gospels. They were written anonymously. However, many years ago two of the four Gospels were attributed to two disciples. Please name the two disciples who have Gospels named after them.

? Of the following persons, who was NOT among Jesus' original twelve disciples? (Please name two who were not among the original twelve.)
  - Matthew
  - Mark
  - Luke
  - John

? Please name ten of the twelve apostles. *Matthew 10:2–4; Mark 3:16–19; Luke 6:13–16, John 1:44–51; 21:1–6; Acts 1:13; The New Westminster Dictionary of the Bible,* p. 53

? Please give a general description of the twelve disciples. What kind of men were they? Where were they from? What did they do that was important? *The New Westminster Dictionary of the Bible,* pp. 53–54

? Was Judas Iscariot one of the twelve disciples? *Matthew 10:2–4*

? Of the following persons, who was NOT one of Jesus' twelve disciples?
  - James, the son of Zebedee
  - Judas, also called Thaddaeus
  - Elijah, the Tishbite
  - John, brother of James and son of Zebedee
  - Thomas, called Didymus

? Was Mark one of the original twelve disciples? *Acts 12:12*

? Who were the two disciples Jesus called "sons of thunder"? *Mark 3:17*

? Of the following persons, who was NOT one of Jesus' twelve disciples?
- Bartholomew (usually considered the same person as Nathanael)
- Matthew
- Philip
- Andrew
- David
- Simon Peter

? The twelve disciples included three sets of brothers. They were: James and John (the sons of Zebedee), James and Judas, and who? *Luke 6:13–16*

? Bethsaida was the home city of at least three of the disciples. Please name them. *John 1:44*

c) Call of Simon, Andrew, James, and John *Matthew 4:18–22; Mark 1:16–20; Luke 5:1–11; John 1:40, 41*

? Of the disciples, who found his brother and said unto him: "We have found the Messias, which is, being interpreted, the Christ"? *John 1:40, 41*

? Who was Simon Peter's brother? *Matthew 4:18; Mark 1:16; John 1:40,41; Luke 6:14*

? Whom did Jesus say he would make "fishers of men"? *Matthew 4:19; Mark 1:16–18*

? Who was Simon Peter?

? Jesus once asked his disciples: "whom say ye that I am?" Which disciple answered, "Thou art the Christ"? *Mark 8:27–29*

? Simon (called Peter) and Andrew were brothers who left their nets to become "fishers of men." The original twelve disciples included two other sets of brothers. Please name the two sons of Zebedee. *Matthew 4:18–22*

? Simon, Andrew's brother, is usually known by the Greek equivalent of his name: Peter. Who called this disciple "Cephas," which means "rock or stone" in Aramaic? *Matthew 16:13–19; John 1:42; The New Westminster Dictionary of the Bible, p. 154*

? Please name the region where John, the son of Zebedee, who was sometimes called "the beloved disciple," grew up. *Matthew 27:55, 56*

? In the fourth Gospel the author writes enigmatically about the disciple "whom Jesus loved." It is not actually known who this disciple was. A tradition regarding the disciple's identity has developed since the New Testament was written. Who is sometimes called "the beloved disciple" (a term not actually used at all in the King James Version)? *John 13:23; 19:26; 20:2; 21:7, 20; The Cambridge Companion to the Bible, p. 540*

? When Jesus was on the cross, to whom did he commit the care of his mother? *John 19:26*

d) Philip and Nathanael: their calling and association with Jesus   *John 1:43–51*

? Who was the disciple who went to Nathanael and said: "We have found him, of whom Moses in the law, and the prophets, did write, Jesus of Nazareth, the son of Joseph"? *John 1:45*

? When Jesus saw this disciple coming toward him for the first time, Jesus said: "Behold an Israelite indeed, in whom is no guile." Who was this disciple? *John 1:47*

? Nathanael was one of the twelve disciples. The Bible notes that he was from Cana in Galilee. Please tell of at least one event in Jesus' life that took place in Cana. *John 21:1, 2; John 2:1–11; 4:46–54*

? What was probably the other name for Nathanael — the one used in lists naming the twelve disciples? *Matthew 10:2–4; Mark 3:16–19; Luke 6:14–16; John 1:44–51; 21:1–6; Acts 1:13*

? Please explain how Nathanael became a disciple of Jesus. *John 1:44–50*

? Jesus showed himself to his disciples on several occasions after he was risen from the dead. Was Nathanael present the time Jesus told seven of the disciples to cast their net on the right side of the ship? *John 21:2–6, 9, 12, 14*

e) Peter's mother-in-law healed   *Matthew 8:14, 15; Mark 1:29–31; Luke 4:38–40*

? The synoptic Gospels each relate a time in Capernaum when Jesus healed a disciple's wife's mother of a fever. Please name the disciple.

f) Call of Matthew (Levi)   *Matthew 9:9–13; 10:3; Mark 2:13–17; Luke 5:27–32*

? Please name the disciple who was sitting at the receipt of custom when Jesus called him to follow him. *Matthew 9:9; compare with Mark 2:14 and Luke 5:27*

g) Three present at healing of Jairus's daughter   *Matthew 9:18–26; Mark 5:22–43; Luke 8:41–56*

? Who were the three disciples present when Jesus raised Jairus's daughter? *Mark 5:22–43; compare with Matthew 9:18–26*

? Peter, James and John were with Jesus when he raised Jairus's daughter. How old was Jairus's daughter when this incident occurred? *Mark 5:42; Luke 8:4*

h) Peter's confession   *Matthew 16:13–20; Mark 8:27–30; Luke 9:18–21*

? When Jesus asked his disciples, "whom say ye that I am?" who quickly responded, "Thou art the Christ"? *Mark 8:27–30*

i) Three with Jesus at the transfiguration *Matthew 17:19; Mark 9:2–10; Luke 9:28–36*

? Please name the three disciples who were with Jesus at the transfiguration.

j) Jesus' instructions to disciples, including Peter's question re: forgiving one's brother *Matthew 18:21, 22; Mark 9:33–50; Luke 9:46–50*

? Where was Jesus when "he took a child" and set him in the midst of the disciples and said, "Whosoever shall receive one of such children in my name, receiveth me"? *Mark 9:33–37*

k) Request of James and John *Matthew 20:20–29; Mark 10:35–45*

? Who said to Jesus: "Grant that these my two sons may sit, the one on thy right hand, and the other on the left, in thy kingdom"? *Matthew 20:20, 21*

l) Jesus' betrayer, Judas Iscariot, at the garden *Matthew 26:36–46; Mark 14:32–42; Luke 22:39–51; John 18:1*

? Jesus went to the garden of Gethsemane to pray. Peter, James, and John were with him. Then, Judas arrived with "a great multitude with swords and staves" to arrest Jesus. What was the prearranged signal Judas used to let the officials know who was Jesus? *Matthew 26:36–46*

? At the garden of Gethsemane, one of the disciples "smote the servant of the high priest, and cut off his right ear." Why did he do this? According to Luke, what was Jesus' response? *Luke 22:50, 51*

m) Peter's fall after Jesus' prophecy at Last Supper *Mark 14:30; Luke 22:31–38, 54–62*

? At the Last Supper, Jesus has a conversation with his disciple Simon Peter and makes an interesting prophecy about Peter. What does Jesus prophesy? *Luke 22:34*

n) Doubting Thomas sees Jesus after resurrection *John 20:9–21, 24–29*

? One of the twelve disciples was named Thomas, also called Didymus. How did he earn the nickname "doubting Thomas" (a term not used in the Bible)? *John 20:9–29*

o) Jesus instructs Peter to "Feed my sheep" *John 21:14–17*

? Please tell what happened at the Sea of Tiberias (more commonly called the Sea of Galilee) after Jesus' resurrection. *John 6:1; 21:14–17; The New Westminster Dictionary of the Bible, "Tiberias," p. 946*

? To whom was Jesus speaking when he said, "Feed my sheep"? *John 21:14–17*

B. The Acts of the Apostles

? The book, The Acts of the Apostles, was very likely written by the same individual who wrote the Gospel of Luke. Please tell a story related in Acts.

1. The early church in Jerusalem (ca. 30–35 CE)

a) Matthias chosen an apostle *Acts 1:12–26*

? In the first chapter of Acts, Luke records that the apostles prayed about a replacement for Judas Iscariot. Please name the new apostle who was "numbered with the eleven...."
Acts 1:26

b) Day of Pentecost *Acts 2:1–47*

? Pentecost was originally a Jewish festival celebrating the end of the grain harvest. It became significant to the Christian church because of what occurred on that notable first Pentecost after Jesus' resurrection and ascension. Please tell what happened on that day, according to the book of Acts. *Acts 2:1–47*

? On what special day were the disciples "all with one accord in one place"? *Acts 2:1*

? Why did some of those present in Jerusalem on the day of Pentecost mock the disciples, saying they were "full of new wine"? *Acts 2:4–13*

? On the day of Pentecost, Peter endeavors to explain the events by quoting an Old Testament prophet. Who does Peter quote? *Acts 2:17–21; Joel 2:28–32*

? About how many people were baptized and "added unto them" on the day of Pentecost? *Acts 2:41*

c) Peter and John heal lame man at Beautiful gate of temple *Acts 3:1–11*

? Who said, "Silver and gold have I none; but such as I have give I thee"? *Acts 3:6*

? Tell the story of the lame man healed by Peter and John. *Acts 3:2–16*

d) Gamaliel *Acts 5:21–42*

? A Pharisee named Gamaliel advised the authorities in Israel to leave the apostles alone, saying: "for if this counsel or this work be of men, it will come to nought: But if it be of God, ye cannot overthrow it...." Is this story from Isaiah, Acts, or Revelation?
Acts 5:34, 38, 39

? Who was Gamaliel? *Acts 5:34–39; 22:3* (Please see a Bible dictionary.)

e) Stephen *Acts 6:1–15; 7:1–60*

? Stephen is described in the Bible as "a man full of faith and of the Holy Ghost." Nonetheless, Stephen was executed. How? *Acts 6:5, 6; 7:59, 60*

? What early Christian is described as having "the face of an angel"? *Acts 6:1*

2. Church spreads throughout Judea, Samaria (ca. 35–47 CE)

a) Philip the evangelist *Acts 8:5–40; 21:8*

(1) With Simon, the sorcerer *Acts 8:5–24*

? Philip the evangelist baptized Simon, a sorcerer in Samaria. Simon erred when he offered money for the power to confer the Holy Ghost. Who rebuked Simon? *Acts 8:5–24*

? A sorcerer named Simon had long "bewitched the people of Samaria," according to the book of Acts. Philip the evangelist converted and baptized many people in Samaria, including Simon. What did Simon later do which caused Peter to rebuke him? *Acts 8:5–24*

? Please name the sorcerer in Samaria who long "bewitched the people" with sorceries, but was converted to Christianity by Philip the evangelist. *Acts 8:5–24*

(2) With the Ethiopian *Acts 8:27–40*

? The evangelist Philip explains the life and teachings of Jesus to a powerful Ethiopian man. The Ethiopian asks: "what doth hinder me to be baptized?" In which book of the Bible can you read this story? *Acts 8:36*

? Directed by an angel, this New Testament evangelist went along the road from Jerusalem to Gaza. After a time, he met, preached to, and baptized the Ethiopian eunuch. Please name this man of good report, full of "the Spirit" and of wisdom. *Acts 6:5; 8:4–39; The New Westminster Dictionary of the Bible, p. 745*

b) Peter heals Aeneas *Acts 9:32–35*

? Of the twelve disciples, who came down to Lydda and healed a man named Aeneas, who "had kept his bed eight years, and was sick of the palsy"? *Acts 9:32–35*

? When Peter healed Aeneas, "all that dwelt at Lydda and Saron saw him, and turned to the Lord," according to the book of Acts. Why was this healing so impressive to the people living in Lydda and Saron? *Acts 9:32–35*

c) Peter raises Dorcas (Tabitha)   *Acts 9:36–43*

? What was the name of the woman in Joppa who was "full of good works" and who made "coats and garments"? *Acts 9:36–41*

? Who raised a woman named Dorcas (also called Tabitha) from the dead in Joppa? *Acts 9:36–41*

? Peter raised Tabitha (also called Dorcas) from death. The book of Acts notes that Peter sent out the weeping widows and "kneeled down, and prayed." Please name the place where this healing occurred. *Acts 9:36–43*

d) Cornelius's conversion   *Acts 10:1–48*

? When Simon Peter was in Joppa, three men came to him and asked him to go with them to a centurion's home. The centurion was not Jewish, but he was "a devout man." Peter went with the three servants to the centurion's home and spoke these profound words: "I perceive that God is no respecter of persons." Please name the centurion. *Acts 10:1–48*

? A centurion named Cornelius was baptized a Christian in Caesarea. Why was this event significant in the history of the early church? *Acts 10:1–48*

e) Church at Antioch of Syria   *Acts 11:22–30*

? Please name the "good man" who went to Antioch from Jerusalem to teach the people about Christ Jesus. He was "full of the Holy Ghost and of faith: and much people was added unto the Lord." *Acts 11:22, 24*

? The disciples were first called Christians in what location? *Acts 11:26*

f) Peter thrown into prison and freed by prayer   *Acts 12:3–18*

? Please name the king who "killed James the brother of John with the sword" and had Peter put in prison. *Acts 12:1, 2, 4* (To distinguish among the different individuals named *Herod* in the Bible, see *The New Westminster Dictionary of the Bible*, pp. 379–384.)

? Who was responsible for the early death of James the apostle, brother of John? *Acts 12:1, 2*

? What did members of the church do while Herod (Herod Agrippa I, son of Aristobulus and Bernice) kept Simon Peter in prison? *Acts 12:5; A Commentary on The Holy Bible*, Dummelow, p. 834

? Whom did Peter follow out of prison the night Herod Agrippa I "would have brought him forth"? *Acts 12:5–11*

? When Peter escaped from prison, he said: "Now I know of a surety, that the Lord hath sent his angel, and hath delivered me out of the hand of Herod...." Who answered the door when Peter knocked at the house of Mary, mother of John Mark? *Acts 12:11–13*

? Many members of the church were gathered together praying for Peter's release from prison. A young damsel named Rhoda excitedly informed them that their prayer was answered — Peter was at the gate! What did they first say to Rhoda? *Acts 12:15*

? Why didn't Rhoda open the gate for Peter when he arrived at the house of Mary (thought to be the mother of John Mark) after escaping from prison? *Acts 12:12–16; The New Westminster Dictionary of the Bible, pp. 587, 595*

C. Paul's life and ministry

1. Birth and early life *Acts 22:3, 4*

? According to the book of Acts, where was Paul born? *Acts 21:40 to 22:3*

? Please identify the individual who said: "I am a man which am a Jew of Tarsus, a city in Cilicia...." *Acts 21:39*

? What famous individual was born in Tarsus, a city in Cilicia, but was brought up in Jerusalem "at the feet of Gamaliel," the "leading rabbi of the day"? *Acts 22:3; Paul, Goodspeed, p. 10*

2. Saul's conversion *Acts 9:1–22*

? Who is described in Acts as "consenting" unto Stephen's death? *Acts 8:1*

? Please name the New Testament character who had this experience when journeying to Damascus: "there shined round about him a light from heaven: And he fell to the earth, and heard a voice...." *Acts 9:1–4*

? Who was healed of blindness in the city of Damascus and became one of the early Christians? *Acts 9:17–20*

? What happened to Saul as he was journeying to Damascus in search of disciples of Jesus? *Acts 9:1–22*

? Who said this: "Saul, Saul, why persecutest thou me?" *Acts 9:4–5*

? What disciple in Damascus was obedient to God's command in a vision and went and healed Saul of his blindness? *Acts 9:10–18*

? The Lord commanded Ananias to go to the house of Judas in Damascus and to restore a man's sight. Why was Ananias at first hesitant to this? *Acts 9:13*

3. Preaches in Damascus; escapes in basket over wall *Acts 9:20–25; II Corinthians 11:32, 33*

? Early in his career as a missionary, Paul's life was in jeopardy. How did the disciples help Paul escape from the Jews in Damascus who wanted to kill him? *Acts 9:25*

? Shortly after his conversion in Damascus, Paul "preached Christ in the synagogues." Soon "the Jews took counsel to kill him." How did Paul (still known as Saul) escape? *Acts 9:20–25*

? Some Jews plotted to kill Saul (later known as Paul.) The disciples helped Saul escape at night by lowering him down the city wall in a basket. Please name the city. *Acts 9:19–25 Then*

4. Converts Sergius Paulus in Cyprus *Acts 13:4–12*

? During their first missionary journey, Paul and Barnabas sailed to the island of Cyprus. Sergius Paulus, "a prudent man" was converted to Christianity during their stay. Who tried to keep Sergius Paulus "from the faith"? *Acts 13:8*

5. Heals crippled man in Lystra *Acts 14:6–18*

? As Paul preached the gospel at Lystra, there sat a certain man, "a cripple from his mother's womb, who never had walked." What did the man do when Paul said, "Stand upright on thy feet"? *Acts 14:10*

? Paul healed a man at Lystra who was "a cripple from his mother's womb." Onlookers concluded, "The gods are come down to us in the likeness of men." By which Greek god's name did they call Paul? *Acts 14:12*

6. Recovers from stoning *Acts 14:19–25*

? During his first missionary journey, Paul was stoned and supposed dead. "Howbeit, as the disciples stood round about him, he rose up...." Who accompanied Paul to Derbe the day after the stoning, as they continued their journey? *Acts 14:19, 20*

? Paul was stoned until he appeared to die. "Howbeit, as the disciples stood round about him, he rose up, and came into the city...." Please name another individual who was raised from the dead and whose story is told in the book of Acts. (Peter raises Tabitha, *Acts 9:36–43*; Paul raises Eutychus, *Acts 20:7–12*)

? In Bible times, stoning was usually fatal. Who lived to write of his perils as follows: "Thrice was I beaten with rods, once was I stoned, thrice I suffered shipwreck..."? *II Corinthians 11:25; Paul, Goodspeed, p. 49*

? Who joined Barnabas on a missionary journey to Cyprus, Antioch (called Pisidian), Iconium, Lystra, Derbe, and Perga? *Acts 13:1–5, 13, 14, 51; 14:5–7*

7. Council at Jerusalem* *Acts 15:1–35; Galatians 2:1–10*

(*Teachers: please note that Acts and Galatians give very different views of this council meeting. For further information, see, for example, *The Cambridge Companion to the Bible*, pp. 532–533)

? Dissension occurred in the early Christian church. Please explain the issue concerning the Gentiles that caused "much disputing." *Acts 15:1–35*

? After their first missionary journey, Paul and Barnabas went to Jerusalem to settle an important dispute that had come up within the early Christian community. What was the dispute? *Acts 15:1–35; Galatians 2:1–10*

8. Lydia helps Paul found church at Philippi *Acts 16:12–15*

? For his second missionary journey, "Paul chose Silas" to accompany him. In Philippi they met a woman who made her living by selling purple dyes or dyed goods. She listened to Paul and was baptized. Please name her. *Acts 15:40; 16:12–15*

? In which city did Paul and Silas meet "a certain woman named Lydia, a seller of purple" who was originally from Thyatira? *Acts 16:12–15*

? In Philippi Paul and Silas stayed with Lydia, their first convert to Christianity. She undoubtedly helped them found a church in that city. How did Lydia earn her living? *Acts 16:12–15*

9. Heals girl of soothsaying; Paul and Silas imprisoned, then freed *Acts 16:16–40*

? What was the reaction of her masters when Paul and Silas healed a "damsel possessed with a spirit of divination"? *Acts 16:16–22*

? Who travelled with Paul during his missionary journeys?
- Judas Iscariot
- Thomas
- Silas
- Elijah

? Why were Paul and Silas whipped and put into prison while they were in Philippi?
Acts 16:11–24

? Paul and Silas were in prison. "And suddenly there was a great earthquake... and every one's bands were loosed." What two things were Paul and Silas doing just before the earthquake? *Acts 16:25–26*

? Paul and Silas were once whipped and cast into prison by Roman magistrates for healing a "damsel possessed with a spirit of divination." What happened then? *Acts 16:16–26*

? Were Paul and Silas ever whipped? *Acts 16:23*

? "Sirs, what must I do to be saved?" Who asked Paul and Silas this question after witnessing an earthquake that freed them from prison? *Acts 16:27, 30*

? Paul kept the keeper of the prison in Philippi from killing himself by assuring him that none of the prisoners had escaped. Who later ordered that Paul and Silas be set free?
Acts 16:36

? Please name two Christian converts who lived in Philippi. *Acts 16:14, 15, 30–34*

10. Address in Athens *Acts 17:16–34*

? Please name the city in Greece where Paul saw an altar with the inscription, "TO THE UNKNOWN GOD"? *Acts 17:22–23*

? Who spoke to the men of Athens about God and said: "For in him we live, and move, and have our being"? *Acts 17:28*

? Who preached about God to the people in Athens, saying: "For in him we live, and move, and have our being ... For we are also his offspring"? *Acts 17:28*

? In his speech to the people of Athens, Paul explained God. Did the people of Athens subsequently found a Christian church? *Acts 17:15–34*

11. Joins Aquila and Priscilla in Corinth *Acts 18:1–18*

? What did Priscilla and Aquila, her husband, help Paul do? *Acts 18:1–3, 18, 26; Romans 16:3; II Timothy 4:19*

? After Paul departed from Athens, he came to Corinth. There, he abode with Aquila and his wife, Priscilla. According to the book of Acts, Paul, Aquila, and Priscilla had the same occupation. What was it? *Acts 18:1–3*

? Who was the early Christian largely responsible for founding the church at Corinth? *Acts 18:1–4*

? The Roman Emperor Claudius "commanded all Jews to depart from Rome," according to the book of Acts. Please name the husband and wife team, known for helping Paul advance the Christian cause, who left Italy because of Claudius's command. *Acts 18:1–3*

12. Paul in Ephesus

? What happened to the exorcists — "seven sons of one Sceva, a Jew, and chief of the priests" — after the evil spirit answered, "Jesus I know, and Paul I know; but who are ye?" *Acts 19:11–20*

? What caused many of the Jews and Greeks dwelling at Ephesus, who used "curious arts," to bring their books together and burn them before all men? *Acts 19:11–20*

a) Opposition from silversmiths *Acts 19:23–41*

? Why did Demetrius and the other silversmiths of Ephesus oppose the preaching of Paul? *Acts 19:23–41; The Cambridge Companion to the Bible, p. 472*

13. Raises Eutychus at Troas *Acts 20:7–12*

? Although Eutychus fell from a third story loft, he was raised from the dead through the prayers of Paul and his listeners. In which book of the Bible can you read this story? *Acts 20:7–12*

? Please name the man who was long preaching when Eutychus, "being fallen into a deep sleep ... fell down from the third loft, and was taken up dead." Was Eutychus healed? *Acts 20:9–12*

14. Paul in Jerusalem and Caesarea

a) Opposition to Paul by Christian and non-Christian Jews; Paul's arrest by Roman soldiers *Acts 21:17–36*

? Roman soldiers arrested Paul near the temple in Jerusalem. Why? *Acts 21:17–36*

b) Paul taken in custody to Caesarea *Acts 23:12–33*

(1) Trials before Felix, Festus, and King Agrippa
Acts 23:34 to 24:27; 25:1–12; 25:13 to 26:32

? Felix was the Roman governor in Caesarea during a time when Paul was held prisoner. The Bible notes that "Felix trembled" when Paul spoke about "righteousness, temperance, and judgment to come." Why did Felix tremble? *Acts 24:24, 25; The New Westminster Dictionary of the Bible, "Drusilla," p. 234*

? Drusilla, "a Jewess," is mentioned only once in the Bible. She was married to Felix, a Roman governor in Caesarea. Paul was arrested on the false charge of profaning the temple in Jerusalem. His trial took place before Felix. Did Felix free Paul? *Acts 24:1–23*

? Who was Felix's wife? *Acts 24:24, 25*

? Festus, the Roman governor who succeeded Felix, reinvestigated Paul's case and was satisfied that Paul was falsely accused of the "many and grievous complaints" laid against him by the Jews. The trials of Paul before Felix, then Festus and finally King Agrippa all took place in the Roman capital of Palestine. Please name this city located on the coast. *Acts, ch. 25*

? What king said unto Paul, "Almost thou persuadest me to be a Christian"? *Acts 25:23 to 26:32*

? Bernice was with her brother, King Agrippa, in Caesarea when Paul defended himself against the false accusations of certain Jews. What events of his life does Paul recount to Agrippa and Bernice during this trial? *Acts, ch. 26*

15. Journey to Rome

a) Shipwreck on Melita (Malta) *Acts, ch. 27*

? Why did Paul exhort his fellow ship passengers to be of good cheer, even though "neither sun nor stars in many days appeared"? *Acts 27:1, 2, 20–24, 41–44*

? What happened to the hinder part of Paul's ship after it ran aground? *Acts 27:41*

? Did Paul's prophecy about the shipwreck occur just as he said it would? *Acts 27:21, 22, 44*

? Please name the centurion, in charge of Paul and the other prisoners, who was shipwrecked with them on the way to Italy. *Acts 27:1, 2, 20–24, 41–44*

? What was the name of the island to which Paul and the other shipwrecked passengers escaped? *Acts 28:1*

? Why did the soldiers think they should kill Paul and the other prisoners after the ship-wreck? *Acts 27:42*

? In which book of the Bible can you read the story of Paul's protection when his ship ran aground on the island of Melita? *Acts 28:1*

? Why did the centurion named Julius keep his soldiers from killing the prisoners after their ship ran aground? *Acts 27:42, 43*

b) Paul healed of serpent bite; heals others of many diseases *Acts 28:2–10*

? Where was Paul when he healed the father of Publius who "lay sick of a fever"? *Acts 28:1, 8*

? Who healed the father of Publius, who "lay sick of a fever and of a bloody flux," on the island of Melita? *Acts 28:8*

? Did Paul ever heal the sick? *Acts 28:2–10*

16. Paul in Rome *Acts 28:17–31*

? Despite being bound with a chain, Paul was able to preach and to teach in Rome, according to the book of Acts. Were all Paul's listeners converted to Christianity? *Acts 28:20–24*

17. Miscellaneous questions on Paul

? Paul's tremendous ministry lasted twenty-five to thirty years. Did Paul live during the time of:
- Greek rule,
- Roman rule, or
- Persian rule?

? Was Paul one of Jesus' original twelve apostles? *Matthew 10:2–4; Mark 3:16–19; Luke 6:13–16; I Corinthians 1:1, 2; 15:9, 10*

? Who said this: "I am the least of the apostles, that am not meet to be called an apostle, because I persecuted the church of God. But by the grace of God I am what I am…"? *I Corinthians 1:1, 2; 15:9, 10*

? Who was Paul? (Please see a Bible dictionary.)

D. The New Testament Epistles

1. Romans

?   Please name the apostle who wrote a long letter "to all that be in Rome." *Romans 1:1–7*

?   Who wrote: "the good that I would I do not: but the evil which I would not, that I do"?
Romans 7:19

?   Please fill in the blanks: "For to be carnally minded is death; but to be spiritually minded
is _____ and _____." *Romans 8:6*

?   According to Paul, "to be carnally minded is death." What brings "life and peace," in the
words of Romans 8:6?

?   Please fill in the blanks: "And we know that all things work together for
_____ to them that love _____, to them who are the called according to his purpose." *Romans 8:28*

?   According to the book of Romans, "Who shall separate us from the love of Christ?"
Romans 8:35, 38, 39

?   Who wrote: "I am persuaded, that neither death, nor life, nor angels, ... nor height, nor
depth, nor any other creature, shall be able to separate us from the love of God..."?
Romans 8:38, 39

?   Do you think death, or life, or things present, or things to come, or height, or depth, or
any other creature, can separate you from the love of God? Why? *Romans 8:38, 39*

?   In his epistle to the Romans, Paul wrote: "Abhor that which is evil; cleave to that which is
good." What other instructions does Paul give in chapter 12 of Romans? *Romans 12:9–21*

?   Paul encouraged his fellow Christians to "bless" those who persecuted them. Did Paul do
this in his own life? How? *Romans 12:14; Acts 16:16–40*

?   Did Paul know the Ten Commandments given to the Hebrew people by Moses?
Romans 13:9

?   Who wrote to the Romans: "love is the fulfilling of the law"? *Romans 13:10*

?   In Romans, Paul explains that "he that loveth another hath fulfilled the law." He then
goes on to cite five commandments from Exodus. Please name these five commandments.
Romans 13:8–10

2. I and II Corinthians

? I and II Corinthians are books in the New Testament. Originally they were letters. Who wrote them?

? Paul wrote two epistles to the early Christians living in Corinth. Please name them.
I Corinthians 1:2

? Timotheus (also known as Timothy) was the son of Eunice and the grandson of Lois. They lived in Lystra and all became Christians. How did Paul feel toward Timotheus?
I Corinthians 4:17

? Why is Paul called an apostle? *I Corinthians 9:1, 2*

? In I Corinthians, Paul advises us to be "temperate in all things." What does temperate mean? *I Corinthians 9:25*

? One of the most beautiful and best known chapters of the Bible is chapter 13 of I Corinthians. Please read this chapter aloud.

? Please finish this verse: "And now abideth faith, hope, charity, these three: but the greatest of these is _____." *I Corinthians 13:13*

? According to Paul, are the following statements true or false? *I Corinthians, ch. 13*
  • Charity beareth all things.
  • Charity rejoiceth in the truth.
  • Charity suffereth long, and is kind.
  • Faith and hope are even greater than charity.
  • It is better to have knowledge than charity.

? Who is it that "comforteth us in all our tribulation"? *II Corinthians 1:3, 4*

? Paul wrote, "Thanks be unto God for his unspeakable gift." What is the gift?
II Corinthians 9:15

? Who wrote in an epistle that he had received stripes, been beaten with rods, stoned, suffered three shipwrecks and had often been in perils of waters, of robbers, etc.? Why did he "take pleasure in infirmities"? *II Corinthians 11:24–26; 12:10*

3. Galatians

? Who wrote a letter to the churches of Galatia? *Galatians 1:1, 2*

? Who was the early Christian who preached in "Arabia and returned again unto Damascus"? *Galatians 1:1, s15–17*

? Paul refers to Titus as his "partner and fellowhelper." Please name another early Christian who accompanied Paul and Titus to Jerusalem. *Galatians 2:1; II Corinthians 8:23*

? In Galatians we read: "whatsoever a man soweth, that shall he also reap." *Sow* means "to scatter, as seed, upon the earth for growth." What does *reap* mean? *Galatians 6:7, 8; Webster's Ninth New Collegiate Dictionary*

? Please fill in the blank: "For all the law is fulfilled in one word, even in this; Thou shalt _____ thy neighbour as thyself." *Galatians 5:14*

4. Ephesians

? What is the name of the epistle written to the people who lived in Ephesus? *Ephesians 1:1*

? Why should we follow the biblical command to "be kind one to another, tenderhearted, forgiving one another"? *Ephesians 4:32*

? What does the author of Ephesians suggest we "put on," that we "may be able to stand against the wiles of the devil"? *Ephesians 6:11–17*

? In Bible times, Ephesus was a city situated "at the junction of natural trade routes, and was on the main route from Rome to the East." Many Jews with Roman citizenship lived in Ephesus, and they maintained a synagogue where Paul preached during his stay there. Which epistle was sent to those who lived in Ephesus? *Ephesians 1:1; The New Westminster Dictionary of the Bible, p. 271*

? The author of Ephesians writes that we should "put on the whole armour of God." Please match the following:
    1. breastplate   a. of faith
    2. shield   b. of righteousness
    3. sword   c. of the Spirit
    Ephesians 6:11–17

? In which New Testament epistle do we read of the Christian's armour: the breastplate of righteousness, the shield of faith, the helmet of salvation, the sword of the Spirit? Please use a Bible concordance. *Ephesians 6:11–17*

? "Put on the whole armour of God, that ye may be able to stand against the wiles of the devil...." This message is in which book of the Bible? *Ephesians 6:11*

5. Philippians

? Who wrote a letter to the Philippians, which later became the eleventh book of the New Testament?

? Please name a book of the Bible that was originally a letter written by Paul to a church congregation.

? Philippians was likely written by Paul while he was in prison (probably in Rome.) Please look at the first chapter of Philippians and count how many times Paul uses the word "bonds."

? Who issued this invitation to all Christians: "Let this mind be in you, which was also in Christ Jesus"? *Philippians 2:5*

? Who said this? "Brethren, I count not myself to have apprehended: but this one thing I do, forgetting those things which are behind, and reaching forth unto those things which are before, I press toward the mark for the prize of the high calling of God in Christ Jesus." *Philippians 3:13, 14*

? Who encouraged the Philippians to: "Rejoice in the Lord alway" and "Let your moderation be known unto all men"? *Philippians 4:4, 5*

? The first European church founded by Paul was in Philippi. Paul's epistle to the Philippians was written from prison, perhaps in Ephesus or in Rome. Please read aloud the well-known advice given to this early church by Paul in Philippians 4:8.

? In the book of Philippians, we are told: "if there be any virtue, and if there be any praise, think on these things." What things? *Philippians 4:8*

? Please name the imprisoned author of a letter who exhorted his friends in Philippi to think on whatsoever things are true, honest, just, pure, lovely, and of good report? *Philippians 4:8, 9*

? Do you believe Paul when he writes in Philippians, "my God shall supply all your need..."? *Philippians 4:19*

6. Colossians

? Which book in the New Testament was originally a letter written "to the saints and faithful brethren in Christ which are at Colosse"? *Colossians 1:2*

? Scholars do not agree whether Paul was the author of Colossians. Paul never visited Colossae (spelled Colosse in the King James Version), though he may have written this epistle. Who is Epaphras? *Colossians 1:7, 8; 4:12; Philemon 1:23; Teaching the Scriptures,* Robinson, p. 83

? "Set your affection on things above, not on things on the earth." What does this verse from Colossians mean? *Colossians 3:2*

7. I and II Thessalonians

? I and II Thessalonians were both attributed to Paul. Scholars today agree that Paul wrote the first epistle, but debate the authorship of the second. In which letter (epistle) to the Thessalonians are these words: "Pray without ceasing"? *I Thessalonians 5:17*

? What man wrote at least one letter and perhaps two to the Thessalonians?

? Both Paul and his younger friend, Timothy, visited Thessalonica, the capital of Macedonia. Please read I Thessalonians 1:9 and tell whether most of the Christians there converted from Judaism or paganism. *I Thessalonians 1:9*

? The first letter to the Thessalonians is thought to be the oldest book in the New Testament. It was written by Paul to the Christians in Thessalonica, the capital of Macedonia. Aristarchus, a Macedonian of Thessalonica, travelled with Paul. In which three books of the Bible is Aristarchus mentioned? Please use a Bible concordance. *Acts19:29; 20:4; 27:2; Colossians 4:10; Philemon 1:24*

8. I and II Timothy

? In which of the epistles written to an individual do these words appear? "For God hath not given us the spirit of fear; but of power, and of love, and of a sound mind." *II Timothy 1:7*

? Although the letters to Timothy and Titus are attributed to Paul, most scholars today believe that Paul did not write them. Who was Timothy (also called Timotheus)? You may want to look in a Bible dictionary under "Timothy."

? Please fill in the blanks: "God hath not given us the spirit of fear; but of _____, and of _____, and of a sound _____ ." *II Timothy 1:7*

? The author of the second letter to Timothy observes: "from a child thou hast known the Holy Scriptures." What are the Holy Scriptures? *II Timothy 3:15*

9. Titus

? Titus was a trusted companion of Paul who is mentioned in several New Testament epistles. What do we learn about Titus in Galatians 2:3?

? The book of Titus is known as one of the "pastoral epistles," together with I and II Timothy. It was written by an experienced church leader to an associate named Titus. Titus was a Greek Gentile living in Crete. Where is Crete? *Titus 1:5; The New Westminster Dictionary of the Bible*, p. 706

10. Philemon

? Which one of Paul's epistles is addressed to a friend and concerns a runaway slave named Onesimus? *Colossians 4:7–9; Philemon, ch. 1*

? Most of Paul's letters were written to church congregations. Please name a letter written by Paul which was addressed to an individual.

11. Hebrews

? The book of Hebrews was written more in the form of an essay or a sermon than a letter. Unlike most of the epistles, there is no greeting at its opening. Scholars do not know who the author of Hebrews might have been, although they generally agree that it was not written by Paul. The book contains numerous references to people in the Old Testament. Please cite two examples. *Hebrews 11:1–40; An Outline of the Bible, Book by Book, Landis, pp. 154–155*

? In Hebrews we read that Christ Jesus was made a high priest after the order of Melchisdec (spelled Melchizedek in the Old Testament.) In what other books of the Bible is Melchizedek mentioned? *Genesis 14:18; Psalms 110:4; Hebrew 5:6, 10*

? "For ye have need of patience, that, after ye have done the will of God, ye might receive the promise." In which New Testament book can you find these words? Please use a Bible concordance. *Hebrews 10:36*

? Chapter 11 of Hebrews includes a list of elders who "obtained a good report" through faith. "By faith Enoch was translated.... Noah prepared an ark.... Abraham obeyed, and Moses forsook Egypt...." Please name at least three more "elders" mentioned in this chapter. *Hebrews, ch. 11*

? Please fill in the blank: "By faith _____ was translated that he should not see death; and was not found, because God had translated him: for before his translation ... he pleased God." *Hebrews 11:5*

? Using Hebrews, chapter 11, as a guide, please match the following:
   1. Noah   a. was translated.
   2. Moses   b. prepared an ark.
   3. Enoch   c. looked for a city which hath foundations.
   4. Abraham   d. forsook Egypt.

12. James

? Please fill in the blanks: "Every good gift and every perfect _____ is from above, and cometh down from the _____ of lights, with whom is no variableness, neither shadow of turning." *James 1:17*

13. I and II Peter

? The book of II Peter advises Christians to diligently work to attain these eight virtues: faith, virtue, knowledge, temperance, patience, godliness, brotherly kindness, and charity. What does *temperance* mean? *II Peter 1:5–7*

14. I, II, and III John

? True or false? The Bible tells us that God is love. *I John 4:8*

? Please fill in the blanks: "Behold, what manner of _____ the Father hath bestowed upon us, that we should be called the _____ of _____ : therefore the world knoweth us not, because it knew him not." *I John 3:1*

? "Beloved, let us love one another: for love is of God; and every one that loveth is born of God, and knoweth God." In what book of the Bible can you find this verse? *I John 4:7*

? Which book of the Bible includes this verse: "He that loveth not knoweth not God; for God is love"? *I John 4:8*

? Please fill in the blank. According to I John, if a man says, "I love God," and hateth his brother, he is a _____ . *I John 4:20*

15. Jude

? Please name the book of the Bible which is the last of the epistles.

? Please read aloud the benediction at the end of the book of Jude. *Jude 1:24, 25*

E. Revelation

? What is the last book in the Bible?

? Who wrote the book of Revelation? *Revelation 1:1, 2* (Teachers should note that scholars debate who was the author of this book. It may have been a John who lived after the apostle John.)

? In the first chapter of Revelation, John writes that "a great voice" told him to write the words of prophecy in a book. To whom was John supposed to send this book of Revelation? *Revelation 1:4, 10*

? Which book of the Bible contains messages sent by "John to the seven churches which are in Asia"? *Revelation 1:4*

? Where was John when he wrote Revelation? *Revelation 1:9*

Figure 23: Listening to God

That Ye May Teach the Children

? To which of the seven churches in Asia did John write this? "Hold that fast which thou hast, that no man take thy crown." *Revelation 3:7, 11*
- Ephesus
- Smyrna
- Pergamos
- Thyatira
- Sardis
- Philadelphia
- Laodicea

? In Revelation (chapters 2 and 3), six of the seven churches are rebuked. Which church received commendation from John? *Revelation 3:7–13*

? During his revelation, Saint John heard the words "I am Alpha and Omega" several times. What does Alpha mean?

? What does Omega mean? *Revelation 1:8, 11*

? Who writes in the Bible of his vision of a "great multitude ... of all nations, and kindreds" standing before the Lamb's throne "clothed with white robes"? *Revelation 7:9*

? In which book of the Bible can you read this description of an angel? "And I saw another mighty angel come down from heaven, clothed with a cloud: and a rainbow was upon his head, and his face was as it were the sun...." *Revelation 10:1*

? In the book of Revelation, who is clothed with a cloud with a rainbow upon his head? *Revelation 10:1*

? The Revelator writes in chapter 10: "I took the little book out of the angel's hand, and ate it up...." Was the book sweet or bitter? *Revelation 10:10*

? In the twelfth chapter of Revelation we read of a woman who "brought forth a man child, who was to rule all nations with a rod of iron." Please fill in the blanks that describe the woman: "clothed with the _____, and the _____ under her feet, and upon her head a _____ of twelve stars...." *Revelation 12:1*

? Which New Testament book describes "a great red dragon, having seven heads and ten horns, and seven crowns upon his heads"? *Revelation 12:3*

? Please describe the dragon as pictured in the twelfth chapter of Revelation. *Revelation 12:3*

? In Revelation, which angel fought against the great red dragon and cast him out of heaven? *Revelation 12:7–9*

? In what book of the Bible can you find these words: "Alleluia: for the Lord God omnipotent reigneth"? *Revelation 19:6*

? In what book of the Bible do these words appear? "And I saw a new heaven and a new earth: for the first heaven and the first earth were passed away; and there was no more sea. And I John saw the holy city, new Jerusalem...." *Revelation 21:1, 2*

? The book of Revelation is divided into seven main parts. These parts constitute seven visions and are themselves subdivided into seven parts. The seventh vision includes a detailed description of "new Jerusalem." In which chapter is the description of "that great city"? *Revelation, ch. 21*

? In which book of the Bible can you find this prophetic promise: "God shall wipe away all tears from their eyes; and there shall be no more death..."? *Revelation 21:4*

? What city, described in Revelation, "lieth foursquare" with the length and breadth and height of it equal? *Revelation 21:16*

? Chapter 21 of Revelation describes "new Jerusalem."
  - How many gates are there?
  - How many foundations are there?

? How many temples are there? *Revelation 21: 12, 14, 22*

? In the Revelator's vision of a new heaven and a new earth, he writes that "the city had no need of the sun ... to shine in it." Why was that? *Revelation 21:23*

? Please fill in the blanks. In Revelation, John writes of the holy city, "new Jerusalem." Then, "there came unto me one of the _____ angels which had the _____ vials full of the _____ last plagues...." *Revelation 21:9*

? Please give a brief description of the "new Jerusalem." *Revelation, ch. 21*

? Who said this? "I am the root and the offspring of David, and the bright and morning star." *Revelation 22:16*

? Which book of the Bible "is solely devoted to apocalyptic writing, weaving its message around a dramatic theme of seven sets of seven visions and seven letters to the seven churches of Asia Minor"? *Researched Bible Guide, July 1983, Vol. VI, No. 7, pg. 225*

? In which book of the Bible do we read about:
  - an angel clothed with a cloud with a little book open in his hand,
  - a great red dragon,
  - a city which lieth foursquare, and
  - a pure river of water of life?

? What is the Greek word for the revelation of Saint John? *The New Westminster Dictionary of the Bible, p. 801*

IV. Vocabulary Questions

ote to teachers: For most of the vocabulary questions, please have the children use a Bible dictionary to find the definition. There are many good Bible dictionaries, but children should generally use a one volume dictionary, such as Westminster's. For very young children, a volume such as Barbara Smith's *Young People's Bible Dictionary* is a good choice. Of course, many simple definitions may also be found in a regular Webster's dictionary. Use a concordance to find the word in the Bible.

? What does *abundance* mean? *Luke 12:15*

? The Greek word, *agape*, indicates a spiritual, universal sense of love. Several Bible passages use the word agape in the original Greek text. Which Testament was originally written in Greek? *Teaching the Scriptures*, Robinson, p. 1

? The *ark of the covenant* was made of shittim, or acacia, wood. It was overlaid with gold and had four rings into which carrying staves were inserted. The gold lid was known as the mercy seat. The contents of the ark were believed to be the two tablets of stone on which the Commandments were written. What happened to the ark of the covenant? *Exodus 25:10–22; Harpers Bible Dictionary*, Miller, p. 43

? The *Apocalypse* is a name frequently given to the last book of the Bible. Please name the last, or sixty-sixth, book of the Bible.

? What does *apostle* mean? *Matthew 10:2 ; The New Westminster Dictionary of the Bible*, p. 53

? Was Paul an *apostle*? *Romans 1:1; 11:13; I Corinthians 9:1, 2*

? What does *atonement* mean? *Leviticus 9:7*

? What is a *benediction*? Can you find an example of a benediction? *Numbers 6:24–26; II Corinthians 13:14*

? When the Jews were deported to Babylon, a famous psalm notes that they wept and hung their harps upon the willows. The *captives* asked, "how shall we sing the Lord's song in a strange land?" Please use a Bible concordance and find which psalm recorded the people's feelings "by the rivers of Babylon." *Psalm 137:1–4*

? The *captivity* of Judah began when Nebuchadnezzar, king of Babylonia, deported many Hebrews from their homes in Jerusalem. Please name someone who lived during this era of *captivity*. *Ezra, ch. 2; Daniel 1:1, 2, 21; The New Westminster Dictionary of the Bible*, pp. 148–149

? Daniel, Ezra, and Nehemiah were three Hebrews who lived away from their homeland during a period of *captivity*. Please name the Persian king who authorized the Jews to return to the land of their fathers. *Ezra 2:1; The New Westminster Dictionary of the Bible,* pp. 148–149

? A *centurion* was an officer in the Roman army who commanded one hundred soldiers. The Gospels recount a time when Jesus healed a centurion's servant. Please name another centurion mentioned in the New Testament. *Acts, ch. 10; Acts 27:1, 3, 43; Matt. 27:54; The New Westminster Dictionary of the Bible,* p. 154

? The Bible was written over a period of ten to twenty centuries. How long is a *century*? *Teaching the Scriptures,* Robinson, p. 1

? What is *chaff*? *Matthew 3:12*

? Please read chapter 13 of I Corinthians. What is *charity*?

? A *covenant* is an agreement. Please name someone from the Old Testament who had a *covenant* with God. *Genesis 6:18; 13:7; 15:18; 17:2, 4, 7, 11, 13, 14, 19* (For a more complete list of citations, see *The New Westminster Dictionary of the Bible,* pp. 188–190.)

? A *cupbearer* in Bible times held an important and prestigious position. To become a *cupbearer*, an individual would need to be very trustworthy and ethical. Please name someone who was *cupbearer* to a Persian king. *Nehemiah 1:1–11*

? What are the *Dead Sea Scrolls*? *The New Westminster Dictionary of the Bible,* pp. 217–218

? *Dogmatism* is "positiveness in assertion of opinion, especially when unwarranted or arrogant...." Can you think of a person in the Bible who was dogmatic? *Webster's Ninth New Collegiate Dictionary; Jonah 4:1–4*

? What does *Emmanuel* mean? (Spelled Immanuel in the Old Testament.) *Isaiah 7:14; Matthew 1:23*

? Paul probably wrote seven New Testament epistles: Romans, I and II Corinthians, Galatians, Philippians, I Thessalonians, and Philemon. He may have written II Thessalonians, Colossians, and Ephesians, though scholars debate the authorship of these books. The epistles to Timothy and Titus were probably not written by Paul. What is an *epistle*? *I Thessalonians 5:27*

? What does *eternal* mean? *Deuteronomy 33:27*

? The Bible mentions a number of times when there was "a famine in the land." What is a *famine*? See, for example, *Ruth 1:1.*

? What does it mean to *fast*? *II Chronicles 20:3*

? The prophet Ezekiel speaks of a "good fold" in the "high mountains of Israel." Please define a *fold*. *Ezekiel 34:14*

? What does *Gentile* mean? *Romans 2:9, 10*

? The lame man shall "leap as an hart" writes Isaiah. What is an *hart*? *Isaiah 35:6*

? *Herod* was the name of several rulers of Palestine and neighbouring areas. Herod the Great directed the building of the temple in Jerusalem and was living at the time Jesus was born. Herod Antipas is called Herod the tetrach in the New Testament. He married Herodias and had John the Baptist beheaded. Of these men named Herod, who consented to Jesus' crucifixion? *Luke 23:7–12* (See *Herod* in a Bible dictionary.)

? What were the *high places* in Old Testament times? *Numbers 33:50–52*

? *Importunate* means very "persistent in request or demand." Please tell the parable told by Jesus of the importunate friend. *Luke 11:5–13*

? When speaking of our Lord's greatness, the Psalmist comments that "his understanding is infinite." What does *infinite* mean? *Psalms 147:5*

? Who did King Saul try to kill with his *javelin*? *I Samuel 19:9*

? Matthew writes that Jesus went into the temple of God, and "the blind and the lame came to him in the temple; and he healed them." What does *lame* mean? *Matthew 21:14*

? True or False? The Old Testament was originally written in *Latin*, the language spoken by the Romans. *Teaching the Scriptures*, Robinson, pp. 1–2

? What does *leaven* mean? See, for example, *Exodus 12:15*

? What is a *leper*? *Leviticus 14:2*

? Please name the food on which the Israelites mainly subsisted during their forty year sojourn in the wilderness. *Exodus 16:15*

? What does *merciful* mean? See, for example, *Genesis 19:16.*

? Who is the *Messiah*? *John 1:40, 41*

? What are *messianic prophecies*? (See index of this book for further information.)

? What is *palsy*? *Matthew 9:2*

? What is a *parable*? *Matthew 13:10*

? A *parable* is "a method of speech in which moral or religious truth is illustrated from an analogy derived from common experience in life." Jesus taught using parables, but the Old Testament includes parables as well. Please tell the parable Nathan told King David. *II Samuel 12:1–14; The New Westminster Dictionary of the Bible, p. 700*

? True or false? All the *parables* of the Bible are contained in the New Testament. *The New Westminster Dictionary of the Bible, p. 700*

? What does the Jewish feast called *passover* celebrate? *Mark 14:1; Luke 2:41; John 13:1*

? *Passover* was the first of three annual festivals "at which all the men were required to appear at the sanctuary." Passover was also known as "the feast of unleavened bread." What is unleavened bread? *The New Westminster Dictionary of the Bible, pp. 705*

? Who were the *patriarchs*? *Acts 7:8*

? What is the title used for the king of Egypt? *Genesis 39:1; The New Westminster Dictionary of the Bible, pp. 740–741*

? In New Testament times, who were the *Pharisees*? *Matthew 3:7*

? Jesus spoke of the scribes and Pharisees, saying: "all their works they do for to be seen of men: they make broad their phylacteries...." What are *phylacteries*? *Matthew 23:6; Exodus 13:1–16; Deuteronomy 6:4–9; 11:13–21*

? According to one Bible dictionary, the *phylactery* was in the form of "a small case." The case for the forehead contained four compartments and was fastened with straps on the forehead. The other case was tied onto the left arm. "Phylacteries are worn by every male Jew during the time of morning prayer, except on the Sabbath and festivals...." Who mentioned *phylacteries* in the Gospels? *Matthew 23:6; The New Westminster Dictionary of the Bible, p. 751*

? Ten *plagues* were inflicted on Egypt during the time of Moses. Please give an example of a plague. *Exodus, chs. 7 to 12*

? When the children of Israel were in the wilderness, they were very unhappy about the lack of drinking water. They also longed for foods such as figs and pomegranates. What is a *pomegranate*? *Numbers 20:5*

? What does *preserve* mean? *Psalm 16:1*

? Who has been called
  - the *Prince of Peace,*
  - Saviour, and
  - the prince of the kings of the earth?

  Isaiah 9:6; Acts 5:31; Revelation 1:5

? What does *prodigal* mean? *Luke 15:11–32* (See a regular dictionary.)

? What is a *prophet?* *Deuteronomy 18:15*

? According to one Bible dictionary, a *prophet* is "an authoritative teacher of God's will," and "words are given to the prophet by God." Samuel, Amos, Elijah, Elisha and Jeremiah were all prophets. Please name another *prophet.* *John 4:19; The New Westminster Dictionary of the Bible,* pp. 766–769

? What is a *psaltery?* *Psalms 71:22*

? In his Sermon on the Mount, Jesus asks: "For if ye love them which love you, what reward have ye? Do not even the publicans the same?" Who were the *publicans*? *Matthew 6:46*

? Several Bible stories concern publicans, those who collected the Roman taxes. Please name a *publican.* *Luke 19:1–10*

? Why were tax collectors unpopular with most Hebrews in Bible times? *Luke 19:1–10; Getting Better Acquainted With Your Bible,* Shotwell, p. 298

? What does *reap* mean? *Galatians 6:7*

? Please explain what these words mean:
  • *resurrection*
  • *ascension*

? Who were the *Samaritans*? *Luke 10:25–37* (See a Bible dictionary.)

? Please name two Bible stories concerning individuals from Samaria.

? The highest Jewish governing body was composed of seventy-one members. Christ Jesus was tried before this group of elders. What was this governing assembly called? *Mark 15:1; The New Westminster Dictionary of the Bible,* pp. 187–188

? Jesus was tried before the council, also known as the *Sanhedrin.* Were any other early Christians taken before this council of seventy-one members? *Acts 4:5, 6, 15; 5:21, 27, 34, 41; 6:12; 22:30; 23:15; 24:20*

? What are the *Holy Scriptures,* which are "able to make thee wise unto salvation..."? *II Timothy 3:15* (Teachers, please note that for the New Testament Christians, the Holy Scriptures or Bible meant the Old Testament.)

? *Sedition* is the incitement of resistance to lawful authority, according to *Webster's Dictionary.* Please name someone in Moses' time who was guilty of *sedition.* *Numbers 12:1–15*

? The Vulgate is an early translation of the Old Testament into Latin. The *Septuagint* is another early translation of the Old Testament, done by Jewish scholars living in Alexandria, Egypt. The *Septuagint* became the Bible of the early Christian church. In what language was the *Septuagint* written? *Teaching the Scriptures*, Robinson, p. 2

? "Surely he shall deliver thee from the *snare* of the fowler, and from the noisome pestilence." What is a *snare*? *Psalm 91:3*

? One well-known parable told by Jesus begins: "A sower went out to sow his seed...." What does it mean to *sow* seed? *Luke 8:5*

? The first three Gospels of the New Testament are known as the *synoptic Gospels*. Please name them. *The New Westminster Dictionary of the Bible*, pp. 339–349

? What is a *talent*? *Matthew 25:14–29*

? Christ Jesus told a parable comparing the kingdom of heaven "unto a man which sowed good seed in his field: But while men slept, his enemy came and sowed tares among the wheat...." What are *tares*? *Matthew 13:25*

? In the book of Jonah, we read that "there was a mighty tempest in the sea." What is a *tempest*? *Jonah 1:12; Matthew 8:18, 23–27; Acts 27:20*

? A *tempest* is defined as a "violent wind, especially when accompanied by rain, hail or snow." Please name someone who experienced a *tempest*, according to the Bible. *Webster's Ninth New Collegiate Dictionary; Jonah 1:12; Matthew 8:18, 23–27; Acts 27:20*

? The Hebrew people built a *temple* in Jerusalem as a permanent house for Yahweh, their God. There are a number of Bible stories having to do with this temple. Please tell one.

? The Bible tells of two important men who were once shepherds: Moses and David. What is a *shepherd*? *Exodus 3:1; I Samuel 17:34*

? Which of the following is closest in meaning to *synagogue*?
  - patriarch
  - temple
  - publican
  - epistle

? What does *temporal* mean? *II Corinthians 4:18*

? *Urim* and *Thummin* were placed in the breastplate of the high priest when the people needed God's guidance making decisions. Please name Moses' brother, who was the first high priest and who served in that office for forty years. *Exodus, ch. 28*

? The Gospels recount a time when the disciples urged Jesus to send the multitude away so they could buy themselves *victuals* in the nearby villages. What are *victuals*? *Matthew 14:13–21*

? Is a *virgin*
- a married woman, or
- an unmarried woman?

? The term *Yahweh* is sometimes rendered Jehovah in English. Both words mean _____. *Exodus 6:3*

? An apostle named Simon was called Zelotes. This means that he was a *zealot*. What was a *zealot*? *Luke 6:15; Acts 1:13*

? What does *Zion* mean? *II Samuel 5:7*

Notes

That Ye May Teach the Children

V. Review Questions for Old and New Testaments

A. Old Testament Review Questions

? Please match the following mothers to their sons:
1. Sarah   a. Jacob
2. Hagar   b. Isaac
3. Rebekah   c. Joseph
4. Rachel   d. Ishmael

    (All these people are from the book of Genesis. The quickest way to match them is to look in a Bible dictionary.)

? In response to Balak, the king of Moab, this individual "suggested that if the Israelites could be seduced into...idolatry..., they would come under Yahweh's curse." Please name the Old Testament man who gained a terrible reputation for this suggestion.
Numbers, chs. 22 to 24; 31; The New Westminster Dictionary of the Bible, p. 90

? What was the relationship of each of the following pairs?
- Cain and Abel
- David and Jonathan
- Esau and Jacob
- Manasseh and Ephraim

Genesis 4:1, 2; 25:24–26; 41:50–52; I Samuel 18:1; 13:16

? Please identify this king: the son of David and Bathsheba who succeeded David as king of the United Kingdom. During his reign, the temple was built in Jerusalem. He eventually succumbed to idolatry and self-gratification. *I Kings 11:4*

? Please identify this prophet: he multiplied the meal and oil of a widow in Zarephath and later raised her son from death. He commanded that all the prophets of Baal be slain.
I Kings, ch. 17

? Early leaders of the Hebrew people were either prophets or kings. Samuel was a prophet; David was a king. Were the following leaders kings or prophets?
- Solomon
- Elijah
- Saul

? Were the following Hebrews prophets or kings?
- Samuel
- Elisha
- David

? Please identify this king: he succeeded his father, Asa, as king of Judah. During his twenty-five year reign, the kingdom prospered. He did "that which was right in the sight of the Lord." *II Chronicles 20:31, 32*

? Please tell something the following men had in common.
- Joseph, the son of Israel
- Samson, the Old Testament judge
- Jeremiah, a prophet of Judah
- John the Baptist
- Simon Peter, one of the twelve disciples
- Paul, the great apostle to the Gentiles

? Who was NOT an Old Testament queen?
- Bathsheba
- Jezebel
- Cleopatra
- Sheba

? Please match each husband listed below with his wife:

1. Jacob	a. Ruth
2. Boaz	b. Eve
3. Abraham	c. Rachel
4. David	d. Sarah
5. Adam	e. Bathsheba

? Please match the following Old Testament characters to their jobs:

1. Hagar	a. servant to Elisha
2. Gehazi	b. handmaid to Sarai
3. Nehemiah	c. hunter
4. Esau	d. king's cupbearer

? Please tell what these women had in common:
- Abimelech's wife
- Sarah, Abraham's wife
- Manoah's wife
- the Shunammite woman

Genesis 20:17, 18; 21:1–5; Judges 13:2–24; II Kings 4:12–17

? Job, Psalms, Proverbs, Ecclesiastes, and Song of Solomon make up a category of Old Testament books in English Bibles. Are they:
- the Law (or Books of Moses),
- Books of History,
- Books of Poetry and Wisdom Literature, or
- Books of Prophecy?

? Michal, the daughter of King Saul, was David's first wife. She never had any children, though David had numerous children by his other wives. Please name Michal's brother, who was a close friend of David's. *I Samuel 14:49*

? King David inspired loyalty in most of the people who knew him. His loyal followers included Saul's son, Jonathan, a priest named Zadok and his general, Joab. Unfortunately, one of David's sons had a traitorous nature and led a rebellion against his father. Please name this disloyal son. *II Samuel, chs. 13–19*

? In some Bible stories, the names of certain people were never recorded. An example is a short story told in chapter 13 of I Kings. A man of God from Judah heals King Jeroboam's paralyzed hand in Bethel. Soon thereafter, this man of God is killed by a lion. Who lied to this man of God and caused him to disobey God's command? *I Kings 13:18*

? One of the books of the Old Testament tells the story of a man terribly afflicted by Satan. Three friends come to comfort him, and he says to them: "Let the day perish wherein I was born." Who said this? *Job 3:3*

? Who was king when Shadrach, Meshach and Abed-nego were cast into the burning fiery furnace? *Daniel 3:1–30*

? In which book of the Bible may we read the story of Belshazzar, the Babylonian king who made a great feast and sacrilegiously drank wine out of vessels of gold and silver taken from the temple in Jerusalem? *Daniel, ch. 5*

? Please name two prophets who foretell the end of wars between nations? They both include this promise: "they shall beat their swords into plowshares, and their spears into pruninghooks...." *Isaiah 2:1–5; Micah 4:1–5; compare with Joel 3:10*

?   Who was NOT a prophet of God?
- Elijah
- Nebuchadnezzar
- Jeremiah
- Jonah

?   Three prophets who labored in the Northern Kingdom were Hosea, Amos and Jonah. Three prophets of the Southern Kingdom were Isaiah, Micah and Nahum. Did any of these prophets leave a written record of their work?

?   Amos and Hosea were both prophets who warned that Israel, the Northern Kingdom, would come to an end. Were the prophets correct? *Golden Bible Atlas,* Terrien, p. 50

?   Prophets were called of God to be teachers, preachers and writers. Please name three prophets. *The New Westminster Dictionary of the Bible,* pp. 766–760

B. New Testament Review Questions

?   Caesar Augustus was the first emperor of the Roman Empire. Please name someone important in the Bible who was born during the reign of Caesar Augustus. *Luke 2:1–7*

?   Please match the following events with the correct New Testament person:
1. healed of blindness	a. Lazarus
2. blessed the baby Jesus	b. Bartimaeus
3. raised from the dead	c. John
4. betrayed Jesus	d. Simeon
5. baptized Jesus	e. Judas Iscariot

?   Where in the Bible are the Beatitudes? *Matthew 5:1–12*

?   Who were the Pharisees and the Sadducees? *Matthew 16:12; John 10:23–33*

?   "He that entereth in by the door is the shepherd of the sheep. To him the porter openeth; and the sheep hear his voice." Who is the shepherd, do you think, in this verse from John? *John 10:2, 3*

?   Who cast lots for Jesus' garment and thereby fulfilled Scripture? *John 19:24; Psalms 22:18*

?   Jesus' followers saw him ten times after the resurrection. One incident occurred while two disciples walked along the road to Emmaus, a town about seven miles from Jerusalem. Please give the name of one of these disciples. *Luke 24:13–35; Getting Better Acquainted with Your Bible,* Shotwell, pp. 329–333

?   In which books of the Bible can you read the Easter story?

? Please tell the Easter story.

? According to Matthew, the last words Jesus said to his disciples before he ascended were: "lo, I am with you alway, even unto the end of the world. Amen." What does this mean to you? *Matthew 28:20*

? In Acts, who quotes Moses' prophecy about the coming Messiah? "The Lord thy God will raise up unto thee a Prophet from the midst of thee, of thy brethren, like unto me." *Deuteronomy 18:15; Acts 3:12–26*

? If you met someone who had never heard of Jesus Christ, how would you explain who he is?

? Please list the following events in chronological order, using Westminster's "Harmony of the Four Gospels" as a guide:
- Jesus heals a man with a withered hand on the Sabbath
- Jesus changes water to wine in Cana of Galilee
- Jesus tells the parable of the Good Samaritan
- Jesus washes the feet of his disciples in Jerusalem

The New Westminster Dictionary of the Bible, pp. 343–349

? Please match the following places to the events which occurred there:
1. Bethlehem   a. Jesus raised Lazarus from the dead.
2. Bethany   b. Followers of Jesus were first called Christians.
3. Antioch   c. On this isle John saw a vision of a new heaven and earth.
4. Patmos   d. Christ Jesus was born.

? Who do you associate with each of the following healings—Peter or Paul?
- lame man at temple gate
- damsel with spirit of divination
- crippled man at Lystra
- Aeneas, who was sick of the palsy

Acts 3:1–10; 9:32–35; 14:8–10; 16:16–18

? Did any of the disciples ever raise someone from the dead? *Acts 9:3642; 14:19, 20; 20:712;*

? In the book of Acts, there are three accounts of raising the dead by the apostles. Please name the three people raised from the dead. *Acts 9:3642; 14:19, 20; 20:7–12*

? Please match the following well-known Bible passages to the correct book, Revelation or Hebrews:
"Now faith is the substance of things hoped for, the evidence of things not seen."
"And I saw a new heaven and a new earth...."

C. Old and New Testaments · Combined Review Questions

? Please name the Old Testament prophet who wrote: "Behold, a virgin shall conceive, and bear a son, and shall call his name Immanuel." *Isaiah 7:14*

? Please match these women of the Bible to their description.
  1. Bathsheba   a. mother of Jesus
  2. Jezebel   b. worshipped Baal
  3. Ruth   c. mother of Solomon
  4. Mary   d. left Moab and went to Bethlehem

? Please match the following to the correct book:
  1. the Ten Commandments   a. Psalms
  2. Sermon on the Mount   b. Revelation
  3. "The Lord is my shepherd" c. Exodus
  4. story of Adam and Eve   d. Matthew
  5. "a great red dragon"   e. Genesis

? Are the following Bible verses from the Commandments or the Beatitudes?
     "Remember the Sabbath day, to keep it holy."
     "Blessed are the poor in spirit: for theirs is the kingdom of heaven."
     "Thou shalt not bear false witness against thy neighbour."

? Match each husband listed below with his wife:
  1. Moses   a. Mary
  2. Isaac   b. Ruth
  3. Joseph (New Testament)   c. Rebekah
  4. Boaz   d. Zipporah
  5. Abraham   e. Sarah

? The Bible includes a number of stories in which God preserves children. One example is God's care for the baby Moses found by Pharaoh's daughter in the ark of bulrushes. Please give another example of God's care for children. *Genesis 21:9, 10, 12–20; Exodus 1:8–10, 22; 2:1–10; Matthew 9:18, 19, 23–26; 15:21–28; Mark 7:24–30; Luke 9:38–43; John 4:46–54*

? Please match:
  1. coat of many colours   a. David
  2. burning bush   b. Noah
  3. sling and five stones   c. Joseph
  4. thirty pieces of silver d. Moses
  5. an ark of gopher wood   e. Judas Iscariot

? Please match the following people to the correct description:

1. Eli	a. high priest at the time of Jesus' crucifixion
2. Malchus	b. priest of the most high God who blessed Abram
4. Caiaphas	c. the high priest who trained Samuel
5. Melchizedek	d. servant of the high priest healed by Jesus

? Of the following people, who had no connection with the *temple* in Jerusalem?

- Jesus Christ
- Herod the Great
- Solomon
- Zerubbabel
- Abraham
- Nebuchadnezzar

? "God is love; and he that dwelleth in love dwelleth in God, and God in him." This verse is from which book of the Bible?

- Revelation
- Matthew
- Exodus
- I John

? Please match the following Bible characters to their first occupation:

1. Simon Peter, the disciple	a. fisherman
2. David, king of Israel	b. carpenter
3. Joseph, husband of Mary	c. shepherd

? Please match each Bible character to the peril from which he was saved by God:

1. Paul	a. fiery furnace
2. Daniel	b. poisonous viper
3. Shadrach	c. jaws of the lion

? Please give the earlier name used by each of the following Bible people:

- Abraham
- Israel
- Paul
- Peter
- Sarah

? Please match each Bible character's new name with the old name:

1. Simon	a. Abraham
2. Jacob	b. Sarah
3. Saul	c. Peter
4. Abram	d. Paul
5. Sarai	e. Israel

? Of the following Bible characters, who did NOT receive a new name?
- Jacob
- Sarai
- Abram
- David
- Saul (New Testament)
- Simon (an apostle—brother of Andrew)

? Please match each Bible character to the correct description:
1. Daniel   a. is anointed Israel's first king.
2. Samuel   b. escapes from a lions' den.
3. John the Baptist c. hears God speak when still a child.
4. Saul   d. prepares the way for Jesus.

? Please match the following Bible verses to the correct book: Genesis or I John
"There is no fear in Love, but perfect Love casteth out fear."
"And God said, let us make man in our image, after our likeness."

? Suicidal feelings are not unique to modern times. Please name some Bible people who were at one time suicidal. *I Kings 19:2–8, Matthew 4:5–7; 8:28–32; 27:3–5; Mark 5:1–20, Luke 4:9–13; 8:26–40; Acts 16:27, 28*

? The book of Peter states: "prophecy came not in old time by the will of man: but holy men of God spake as they were moved by the Holy Ghost." Please give an example of prophecy from the Bible. *II Peter 1:21*

? Many Old Testament prophets foretold the coming of Christ. These promises are called messianic prophecies. Please name two Old Testament prophets whose words were fulfilled in the New Testament. *Deuteronomy 18:15, 17, 18;
Isaiah 7:14; 9:7; 11:2; 35:4–6; 42:1–7; 49:6; 56:7; 60:1–3; Psalms 2:6, 7; 16:8–11; 22:16–18; 45:7; 69:9;
Jeremiah 23:5, 6; Daniel 2:44; 7:13, 14; Ezekiel 34:23; Hosea 11:1; Micah 5:2; Joel 2:28, 29;
Malachi 4:2; Getting Better Acquainted With Your Bible, Shotwell, p. 337*

? Jesus was familiar with the Old Testament and quoted from Scripture a number of times. Please name an Old Testament book which is quoted in the New Testament? (Those quoted more often, and listed in order of frequency quoted, include Deuteronomy, Isaiah, Psalms, Genesis, Exodus, Ezekiel, Daniel, Jeremiah, Leviticus, and Numbers.)

? Did Christ Jesus ever quote from the Old Testament?

> *Matthew 4:4* quotes *Deuteronomy 8:3*
> *Matthew 4:7* quotes *Deuteronomy 6:16*
> *Matthew 4:10* quotes *Deuteronomy 6:13*
> *Matthew 5:21* quotes *Exodus 20:13*
> *Matthew 5:27* quotes *Exodus 20:14*
> *Matthew 21:16* quotes *Psalms 8:2*
> *Matthew 27:46* quotes *Psalms 22:1*
> *Mark 10:7, 8* quotes *Genesis 2:24*
> *Mark 10:19* quotes *Exodus 20:12–17*
> *Luke 4:18, 19* quotes *Isaiah 61:1, 2*
> *Luke 7:27* quotes *Malachi 3:1*
> *Luke 19:46* quotes *Isaiah 56:7*
> *Luke 23:46* quotes *Psalms 31:5*
> See *Willmington's Guide to the Bible, p. 346*

? Using a Bible concordance, please locate the Old Testament verse quoted by Jesus in the following passages from the New Testament:

> *Matthew 4:4*
> *Matthew 4:7*
> *Matthew 4:10*
> *Matthew 5:21*
> *Matthew 5:27*
> *Matthew 21:16*
> *Matthew 27:46*
> *Mark 10:7, 8*
> *Mark 10:19*
> *Luke 4:18, 19*
> *Luke 7:27*
> *Luke 19:46*
> *Luke 23:46*

Notes

That Ye May Teach the Children

VI. **Bible Study Worksheets**

Bible Design

1. How many books are in the Old Testament?

2. How many books are in the New Testament?

3. What is the total number of books in the English Bible?

4. Where can you find the Ten Commandments?

5. Where are the Beatitudes?

6. In which book of the Bible can you find the Lord's Prayer?

7. Which translation of the Bible do we usually use in this Sunday School?

8. Please name the first four books of the New Testament, known as the Gospels.

9. Please name the first five books of the Bible, variously known as the Law, the Pentateuch, the Torah, or the Books of Moses.

10. What is the last book of the Bible?

11. Paul probably wrote seven New Testament epistles: Romans, I and II Corinthians, Galatians, Philippians, I Thessalonians, and Philemon. He may have written II Thessalonians, Colossians, and Ephesians, though scholars debate the authorship of these books. The epistles to Timothy and Titus were probably not written by Paul. What is an *epistle*? *Abingdon Bible Handbook, pp. 252–255*

Bible Themes

People approach reading the Bible in various ways. One approach is to read it chronologically, which is possible with a chronological Bible. Another approach is to read a book at a time. One common approach to reading the Bible is thematically. Please match each Bible passage with the word from the bottom of the page which best describes its theme or topic.

1. Samson, a Hebrew judge and Nazarite, is betrayed by Delilah.
   Judges 13:125; 16:4–30

2. Daniel and his Hebrew friends refuse the king's meat and eat pulse. *Daniel 1:1–21*

3. At God's direction, Noah builds an ark of gopher wood. *Genesis 6:5–22*

4. At the age of twelve years, Jesus tarries behind his parents at the temple in Jerusalem.
   Luke 2:41–52

5. Joshua sees the sun and moon stand still. *Joshua 10:6–15*

6. King David sets in motion plans concerning Uriah's wife, Bathsheba.
   II Samuel 11:1–27

7. Simon Peter escapes from prison. *Acts 5:17–42; 12:1–17*

8. Esau meets with his brother Jacob. *Genesis 33:1–5*

---

safety	angels	wisdom	food/sustenance
forgiveness	strength	light	covetousness

Literary Styles in the Bible

The Bible is a compilation of sacred writings. It is written in many different literary styles, including: history, prayers, songs, poetry, short stories, letters, proverbs, law, autobiography, parables, genealogy, sermons, orations, essays, drama, epic narratives, prophecy, biography and revelation. Many biblical books combine elements of these styles with teachings about God and theology.

Please read each of the following citations and match it with the literary style listed below.

1.   Deuteronomy 5:1–22

2.   Deuteronomy 31:30 to 32:44

3.   Romans, ch. 1

4.   Luke 3:23–38

5.   Luke 15:11–32

6.   Ruth (whole book)

---

short story   genealogy   song   law   letter   parable

Famous Quotations

Where in the Bible can you find these well-known words? Please write in the correct citation under each quote. Citations are at the bottom of the page.

1. "In the beginning God created the heaven and the earth."

2. "God is love; and he that dwelleth in love dwelleth in God, and God in him."

3. "Thou shalt have no other gods before me."

4. "Ye are the light of the world."

5. "Yea, though I walk through the valley of the shadow of death, I will fear no evil: for thou art with me; thy rod and thy staff they comfort me."

6. "Our Father which art in heaven, Hallowed be thy name."

7. "Glory to God in the highest, and on earth peace, good will toward men."

8. "In the beginning was the Word, and the Word was with God, and the Word was God."

9. "He that dwelleth in the secret place of the most High shall abide under the shadow of the Almighty."

Exodus 20:3	Genesis 1:1	Luke 2:14
Psalm 23:4	Matthew 5:14	John 1:1
I John 4:16	Matthew 6:9	Psalm 91:1

Chronology

Please number the following Bible characters and events in chronological order. Use a Bible time-line and a Bible dictionary for help. For example, look up "chronology" in *The New Westminster Dictionary of the Bible.*

_____ Isaac (son of Abraham and Sarah)

_____ Joshua (led the Israelites into Canaan)

_____ Nehemiah (probably returned to Jerusalem in 445 BCE)

_____ Jacob (son of Isaac who led his family to Egypt)

_____ Christ Jesus (born in Bethlehem)

_____ Joseph (who was given a coat of many colours)

_____ David (second king of the United Kingdom of Israel)

_____ Solomon (final king of the United Kingdom of Israel)

_____ Zedekiah (last king in Judah before deportation of Judeans to Babylon)

_____ Asa (reigned in Judah, also known as the Southern Kingdom)

_____ Abraham (travelled to Canaan)

_____ Moses (led the Hebrews out of captivity in Egypt)

_____ Saul (first king in the United Kingdom of Israel)

Chronology answer sheet

This is an answer sheet to use with the previous worksheet on Chronology. The Bible characters and events are numbered in chronological order.

1. Abraham (travelled to Canaan)

2. Isaac (son of Abraham and Sarah)

3. Jacob (son of Isaac who led his family to Egypt)

4. Joseph (who was given a coat of many colours)

5. Moses (led the Hebrews out of captivity in Egypt)

6. Joshua (led the Israelites into Canaan)

7. Saul (first king in the United Kingdom of Israel)

8. David (second king of the United Kingdom of Israel)

9. Solomon (final king of the United Kingdom of Israel)

10. Asa (reigned in Judah, also known as the Southern Kingdom)

11. Zedekiah (last king in Judah before deportation of Judeans to Babylon)

12. Nehemiah (probably returned to Jerusalem from exile in 445 BCE)

13. Christ Jesus (born in Bethlehem)

Noah and the Ark

Please read *Genesis 6:5 to 9:29; Hebrews 11:7*

1. Noah built an ark to protect his family and the animals from the flood. God told Noah how to build the ark. What kind of wood was Noah to use? *Genesis 6:13–16*

2. What did God tell Noah to take with him onto the ark? *Genesis 6:18–21*

3. What were the names of Noah's three sons? *Genesis 7:13*

4. While Noah and his family were safely inside the ark, "the rain was upon the earth forty days and forty nights." As the "waters returned from off the earth," the ark rested "upon the mountains of Ararat." What two birds did Noah send out the window? *Genesis 8:4–8*

5. What was God's "token of a covenant" between Himself "and the earth"? *Genesis 9:13*

6. How many years did Noah live after the flood? *Genesis 9:28*

7. In chapter 11 of Hebrews, the author lists "the elders" who "obtained a good report" by their faith. Some of the patriarchs listed include Abel, Enoch, Abraham, Isaac, and Jacob. Is Noah mentioned?

Abraham and Sarah

Please read the following citations and then answer the questions. *Genesis 11:27–32; 12:1–5; 16:1–3, 15; 17:1–9, 15–22; 21:1–5, 9–21; 24:1–28, 61, 66, 67. Nehemiah 9:7*

1. God chose Abram and brought him forth out of Ur of the Chaldees and gave him the name of Abraham. Abram's family also "came unto Haran, and dwelt there." Please name Abram's wife. *Genesis 17:15*

2. At the age of 75, Abram left Haran with his wife and Lot, his brother's son. Where did they go, according to the Lord's command? *Genesis 12:5*

3. Abraham had two sons: Ishmael and Isaac. Sarah was Isaac's mother. Who was Ishmael's mother? *Genesis 16:15*

4. What was Abraham's name before the Lord appeared unto him and said, "I will make my covenant between me and thee"? *Genesis 17:1–9*

5. When Abraham was ninety-nine years old, God said He would bless Sarah and give Abraham a son of her. Why did Abraham fall upon his face and laugh? *Genesis 17:17*

6. When Abraham was one hundred years old, he and Sarah had a baby son. What was this son's name? *Genesis 21:1–5*

7. What happened to Abraham's bondwoman, Hagar, and their child, Ishmael, after she and the boy "departed and wandered in the wilderness of Beer-sheba"? *Genesis 21:9–21*

8. When the time came for Isaac to marry, Abraham sent his servant back to Mesopotamia to find a wife for Isaac. Please name Isaac's wife. *Genesis 24:63–67*

Jacob

Genesis, chapters 25–36

1. Who was Jacob's father? *Genesis 25:21–28*

2. Who was Jacob's brother? *Genesis 25:21–28*

3. Who sold his birthright for some red pottage of lentils? *Genesis 25:27–34*

4. Who helped Jacob deceive his father, Isaac, and cheat Esau out of his father's blessing? *Genesis 27:1–44*

5. Why did Jacob leave his home and go to live with his mother's brother, Laban? *Genesis 27:1–45; 28:1–9*

6. What did Jacob call the place where he had a dream in which he saw angels going up and down a ladder? *Genesis 28:10–22*

7. Please name Jacob's two wives. *Genesis 29:9–30*

8. What is the new name given to Jacob at Peniel? *Genesis 32:24–30*

9. Did Esau ever forgive his brother, Jacob, for cheating him? *Genesis 33:1–10*

10. How many sons did Jacob have? *Genesis 35:22–26*

11. Of Jacob's sons, who were the two children of Rachel? *Genesis 30:25; 35:18*

Joseph

Genesis 30:22–24; chapters 37, 39 to 45

1. What did Israel (also called Jacob) make for his son Joseph to show his great love for him? *Genesis 37:3*

2. Why did Joseph's brothers hate him? *Genesis 37:2–11*

3. Joseph's brothers dipped the coat of many colours in goat's blood and brought it to their father. What did Israel think had become of his son, Joseph?
   Genesis 37:31–34

4. Please name the Egyptian, an officer of Pharaoh, who bought Joseph. *Genesis 37:36; 39:1*

5. Who "cast her eyes upon Joseph" and said to him, "lie with me"? *Genesis 39:7*

6. Why did Potiphar's wife lie to her husband about Joseph and cause Joseph to be put into prison? *Genesis 39:1–20*

7. What was Joseph's interpretation of the Egyptian Pharaoh's dream?
   Genesis 41:1–37

8. How did Pharaoh reward Joseph for his wisdom in interpreting his dream?
   Genesis 41:37–41

9. Joseph tested his brothers' love for young Benjamin when he had his steward hide a silver cup in Benjamin's sack. How did the older brothers react when this alleged crime was discovered? *Genesis 44:1–34*

10. Joseph was able to forgive his older brothers for throwing him into the pit. Joseph knew he had a special part in God's plan for the Hebrew people. What was Joseph's part in God's plan? *Genesis 45:5*

The Ten Commandments

Exodus 20:1–17

1. Who wrote down the commandments given to us by God?

2. Which commandment states: "Thou shalt have no other Gods before me"? *Exodus 20:3*

3. Which commandment tells us not to make any graven images? *Exodus 20:46*

4. Which commandment tells us not to kill? *Exodus 20:13*

5. Which commandment states: "Thou shalt not commit adultery"? *Exodus 20:14*

6. Which commandment states: "Thou shalt not steal"? *Exodus 20:15*

7. Which commandment tells us not to take the name of the Lord thy God in vain? *Exodus 20:7*

8. Which commandment reminds us to remember the Sabbath day to keep it holy? *Exodus 20:8–11*

9. Which commandment tells us to honour our father and mother? *Exodus 20:12*

10. Which commandment forbids us to bear false witness against our neighbour? *Exodus 20:16*

11. Which commandment teaches us not to covet any thing that is our neighbour's? *Exodus 20:17*

12. Please copy a dictionary definition of the word *covet*.

Ruth

Ruth is the eighth book of the Bible. Please read these passages and answer the following questions. *Ruth 1:1–6, 8, 16, 22; 2:2, 3, 5–8, 10–12, 15, 16; 4:13, 16, 17*

1. The book of Ruth is a wonderful short story about two women who were loved and protected by God. After the death of her husband, Ruth left her own country and went with her mother-in-law to Bethlehem. Please name the mother-in-law.

2. Why did Elimelech, Naomi, and their two sons leave Bethlehem-judah and go to sojourn in the country of Moab? *Ruth 1:1, 2*

3. Please name the country where Ruth grew up. *Ruth 1:1–5*

4. Who said this? "Entreat me not to leave thee, or to return from following after thee: for whither thou goest, I will go; and where thou lodgest, I will lodge: thy people shall be my people, and thy God my God...." *Ruth 1:16*

5. What was Ruth's plan for feeding herself and Naomi after they arrived in Bethlehem? *Ruth 2:1–3*

6. What was the name of Ruth's second husband? *Ruth 4:9, 10*

7. Ruth and Boaz had a son named Obed. What was the name of Obed's son, as recorded in Ruth? *Ruth 4:17*

8. David, who fought Goliath and later became king, was descended from Ruth. Please name David's father. *Ruth 4:17*

9. True or false? Ruth's name appears in Matthew's genealogy of Christ Jesus. *Matthew, ch 1*

10. What two books in the Old Testament are named for women?

David

1. The prophet Samuel came to Bethlehem to anoint one of Jesse's sons as the new king of Israel. Seven sons passed before Samuel, and the prophet said: "The Lord hath not chosen these." Where was David, the youngest son?   *I Samuel 16:1–13*

2. Who was refreshed and well after "David took an harp, and played with his hand"? *I Samuel 16:23*

3. What animals threatened David's flock as he cared for his sheep? *I Samuel 17:34–37*

4. How many smooth stones did David choose from the brook before fighting the nine-foot Philistine named Goliath? *I Samuel 17:40*

5. Although David was generally faithful to God, once he sinned terribly and "displeased the Lord." First he committed adultery with Bathsheba, then he arranged for her husband to be killed in battle. Please name Bathsheba's first husband. *II Samuel 11:3*

6. Which of the Ten Commandments did David break in the story about Bathsheba? *Exodus 20:1–17; II Samuel 11: 2–6, 14, 15, 26, 27*

7. Seventy-five of the hymns in the book of Psalms are attributed to David, including the well-known Psalm 51. Though David's authorship is debated, this psalm sheds light on the David and Bathsheba affair. What feelings does the author express in this psalm? *Psalm 51*

8. King David had eight wives and many children. Bathsheba's son became the next king of Israel after David. This son is credited with having said many proverbs. Please name him. *I Kings 2:12*

9. David's third son was beautiful, but he was guilty of many evil deeds. After conspiring for David's throne, he was killed while hanging by his long hair in an oak tree. David greatly mourned his death. Please name this son. *II Samuel 3:2,3; 14:25; 18:5–15, 32, 33*

Kings of Judah

At the end of Solomon's reign, the United Kingdom was divided into two parts: the northern area, known as Israel, and the southern portion, known as Judah. Both of these kingdoms were plagued with inadequate kings. Four exceptions in the kingdom of Judah were Asa, Jehoshaphat, Hezekiah, and Josiah. Important periods of reform occurred during their reigns in Judah.

1. Please name Asa's son, who reigned after Asa and became the fourth king in Judah.
   I Kings 15:24

2. Please name the king who "did that which was good and right in the eyes of the Lord his God: For he took away the alters of the strange gods, and the high places, and brake down the images, and cut down the groves: And commanded Judah to seek the Lord God of their fathers, and to do the law and the commandment." *II Chronicles 14:2–4*

3. Although Asa, the third king of Judah, was generally faithful to God, he had an "exceeding great" disease in his feet toward the end of his reign. What did Asa do as a result of this disease? *II Chronicles 16:12, 13*

4. Please name the king who was assured by God: "Be not afraid nor dismayed by reason of this great multitude; for the battle is not yours, but God's." *II Chronicles 20:2–15*

5. When this king became mortally ill, he turned to God (as King Asa had not), and was healed. His life was lengthened by fifteen years. Please name this thirteenth ruler of Judah. *II Kings 20:1–7*

6. "In the eighth year of his reign, while he was yet young, he began to seek after the God of David his father: and in the twelfth year he began to purge Judah and Jerusalem from the high places, and the groves, and the carved images, and the molten images." Please name this sixteenth ruler of Judah. *II Chronicles 34:1–3*

7. During the reign of the last king of Judah, Nebuchadnezzar's army captured Jerusalem in 586 BCE. After the siege, Judah became a part of Babylon. Please name the last king of Judah. *II Kings 24:17 to 25:7; Jeremiah 1:3; 27:1; 52:3–11*

Elijah

Elijah was the first great prophet of the Northern Kingdom of Israel. In the New Testament he is called Elias, the Greek form of the name.

1. During a time of drought and famine, what kind of birds fed Elijah at the brook Cherith? *I Kings 17:1–7*

2. Who was obedient to Elijah's directions and made him a little cake from her "handful of meal" and a little oil? *I Kings 17:8–16*

3. Whom did Elijah raise from the dead in Zarephath? *I Kings 17:17–24*

4. The Phoenician and Canaanite nations worshipped a heathen god. Even the Israelites were attracted to this worship until the prophet Elijah exposed this god's false power in a dramatic contest on Mt. Carmel. Please name this heathen god. *I Kings 18:17–40*

5. When Ahab and Jezebel, wicked rulers of Israel, threatened to kill Elijah, the prophet hid in the wilderness. Elijah was so discouraged that he sat down under a juniper tree and requested that he might die. Who touched Elijah as he slept under the tree and said, "Arise and eat"? *I Kings 19:1–8*

6. On Horeb, the mount of God, Elijah experienced wind, earthquake, and fire. What did Elijah hear after the fire? *I Kings 19:12*

7. Elijah was translated to heaven without dying. A chariot and horses of fire took him up in a whirlwind to heaven. Who was translated before Elijah? *Genesis 5:24; II Kings 2:11; Hebrews 11:5*

8. Moses, Elijah and Jesus each went without food for a period of time. For how long did each of them fast? *Exodus 34:28; I Kings 19:8; Matthew 4:2; Mark 1:13; Luke 4:2*

9. When Jesus was transfigured on "an high mountain", Moses and Elias talked with him. Who witnessed the transfiguration? *Matthew 17:1–1*

Elisha

1. In Exodus we read that Moses led the children of Israel across the Red Sea on dry ground because "the waters were divided" by the Lord. Elijah and Elisha had a similar experience in which they divided the waters and "went over on dry ground." What waters did the two prophets divide? *Exodus 14:21; II Kings 2:1–18*

2. Elisha saved the two sons of a widow from becoming bondmen to their creditor. How did the prophet accomplish this? *II Kings 4:1–7*

3. Elisha's servant told Elisha that the Shunammite woman "hath no child, and her husband is old." Please name Elisha's servant. *II Kings 4:8–17*

4. When the Shunammite woman's son died, she laid him on Elisha's bed, shut the door, and went to get "the man of God." How did she answer Gehazi's question: "Is it well with the child?" *II Kings 4:17–37*

5. Please name the Syrian captain healed of leprosy by Elisha. *I Kings 5:14, 915 (to second :)*

6. In what river did Elisha instruct the Syrian captain to wash seven times? *II Kings 5:1–4, 9–15 (to second :)*

7. Elisha and the sons of the prophets were too crowded where they were living, so they agreed to go to Jordan to make a better place to dwell. One man was using a borrowed axe when the axe head fell in the water. What happened to the axe head? *II Kings 6:1–7*

8. During the time of Elisha, "the king of Syria warred against Israel." Elisha's city was compassed with enemy horses and chariots. Yet, he told his servant to "fear not...." After Elisha prayed that the eyes of his servant might be opened, what did his servant see? *II Kings 6:8–17*

9. In the Gospel of Luke, Jesus refers to the works of both Elijah and Elisha. The Greek forms of the prophets' names are used in the New Testament. Please give the Greek form of Elisha's name. *Luke 4:25–27*

Nehemiah

Please read the book of Nehemiah in the Old Testament.

1. While the Hebrew people lived in captivity under the rule of foreign kings, their holy city, Jerusalem, was left in ruins by invading armies. Nehemiah helped his people rebuild Jerusalem's walls. Who was the Persian king whom Nehemiah served as cup-bearer? *Nehemiah 2:1*

2. Where was Nehemiah living when word was brought to him that the walls in Jerusalem were broken down? *Nehemiah 1:1–3*

3. Who taunted and mocked Nehemiah and the other Hebrews as they worked to rebuild the wall of Jerusalem? *Nehemiah 4:1–3*

4. Enemies tried to stop Nehemiah from rebuilding the wall around Jerusalem. Nehemiah didn't stop his work; he knew the work was wrought of God. How long did it take to complete the wall? *Nehemiah 6:15*

5. How was Nehemiah able to keep from being deceived by his enemies?

6. What spiritual qualities did Nehemiah exercise in this story?

7. Many years before Nehemiah lived, another Hebrew leader was concerned with the walls of a city. Please name the walled city which Joshua and the Israelites encircled once a day for six consecutive days. On the seventh day they compassed the city seven times. On the seventh time around, the host shouted, the walls fell, and the Israelites entered. *Joshua 5:13 to 6:26*

8. Please match the following people with the government under which they lived:
    1. Jesus   a. Israelites enjoy independent rule
    2. David   b. Israelites under Persian rule
    3. Nehemiah   c. Israelites under Roman rule

Book of Daniel

1. When Daniel was a child, he was taken captive with other Hebrews to Babylon. Daniel, as well as three of his companions, "purposed in his heart that he would not defile himself with the portion of the king's meat, nor with the wine which he drank." Who was the Babylonian king in this story? *Daniel 1:1–20*

2. Daniel, Hananiah, Mishael, and Azariah were able to prove to Melzar that their countenances were "fairer and fatter in flesh than all the children which did eat the portion of the king's meat." What did they eat and drink during the ten-day testing period? *Daniel 1:3–20*

3. What were the names of the three Hebrew boys cast into the fiery furnace? *Daniel 3:12–20*

4. How many times a day did Daniel pray to God? *Daniel 6:10*

5. In the story of Daniel in the lions' den, what is the name of the king? *Daniel 6:1–28*

6. Why was Daniel cast into the lions' den? *Daniel 6:1–28*

7. Is there any evidence that Daniel felt angry and resentful toward the princes and presidents? *Daniel 6:1–28*

8. What protected Daniel in the lions' den? *Daniel 6:22*

9. Babylon was the capital of the Babylonian Empire. It reached the height of its glory in the 6th century BCE, during the time of King Nebuchadnezzar. Who lived first: King David or King Nebuchadnezzar?

10. An unknown author wrote the Old Testament book of Daniel about 168 BCE. The stories and visions in this book "comprise a type of secret language" intended "to encourage the faithful to have hope in the eventual triumph of God in history." This type of writing is called "apocalyptic." Please name another book of the Bible that contains apocalyptic writing. *Young People's Bible Dictionary, Smith*, p. 50

Jonah

Please read the story of Jonah. It is a short book in the Old Testament.

1. Please name the city God told Jonah to visit. *Jonah 1:1, 2*

2. Why did God want Jonah to go to Nineveh?

3. What did Jonah do when God first told him to go to Nineveh and warn the people against their wickedness? *Jonah 1:3*

4. What had the Lord prepared to swallow up Jonah? *Jonah 1:17*

5. How long was Jonah in the belly of the great fish? *Jonah 1:17*

6. Jonah prayed while he was in the belly of the great fish. What was the result of this prayer? *Jonah 2:1, 10*

7. Once Jonah finally got to Nineveh to convert the people, did they turn from their evil ways? *Jonah 3:5*

8. After his successful mission in Nineveh, Jonah became angry with God. Why? *Jonah 3:10; Jonah 4:1–4*

9. Outside the city of Nineveh, a gourd vine sheltered Jonah. According to the allegory, God first caused the vine to spring up over-night and then let the vine wither and droop. How does this make Jonah feel? *Jonah 4:5–11*

10. What is the central message of the book of Jonah?

Prophets

Please read about each of the seven Hebrew prophets listed below in a Bible dictionary. Then match each prophet with the correct description.

1.   Active for over forty years, this prophet dictated his prophecies to Baruch, who wrote them in a scroll. Though often lonely and persecuted by his countrymen, he remained faithful to God and his prophetic work.

2.   This prophet lived in the Northern Kingdom and prophesied to the people of that kingdom. He was a contemporary of Isaiah, who laboured in Judah. His ministry likely extended over a period of forty years. He compares Israel's relationship to God with his own marriage to the unfaithful Gomer. *Hosea 1:1; Isaiah 1:1*

3.   He was a prophet from Tekoa, in the territory of Judah, about six miles south of Bethlehem. He was called to prophesy in the Northern Kingdom. His visions are written in one of the twelve books known as the minor prophets.

4.   He was an eloquent prophet of the Southern Kingdom during the reigns of Uzziah, Jotham, Ahaz, and Hezekiah, kings of Judah. He lived in Jerusalem, was married, and had two sons.

5.   Brought to Shiloh when he was still a boy, this prophet was the son of Elkanah and Hannah. As a boy, he was in the care of Eli, the high priest. This prophet anointed first Saul and later David to be kings.

6.   This prophet lived after the period of Babylonian exile. During the time of Zerubbabel, he helped rouse the people to proceed with the building of the second temple in Jerusalem. *Ezra 5:1, 2; 6:14*

7.   Naaman was healed of leprosy when he obeyed this prophet's command to wash in the Jordan river. *II Kings 5:1–19*

Hosea	Amos	Elisha	Isaiah
Samuel	Jeremiah	Haggai	

Old Testament Books

Please match each description below with the corresponding book of the Bible from the list at the bottom of the page.

1. This book of the Bible tells about the lives of the patriarchs, Abraham, Isaac, and Jacob. It also tells the stories of Adam and Eve, Noah's ark, the tower of Babel, and Joseph and his coat of many colours.

2. This book of the Bible is a short story about a young widow and her mother-in-law, Naomi. Both women were loved and protected by God as they left Moab and moved to Bethlehem.

3. This historical book was named for a Jewish woman who became the queen of Ahasuerus, also known as Xerxes, king of Persia.

4. This book contains many prophecies about the coming of Christ Jesus, such as this one: "For unto us a child is born, unto us a son is given: and the government shall be upon his shoulder: and his name shall be called Wonderful, Counsellor, The mighty God, The Everlasting Father, The Prince of Peace."

5. This historical book is about the Hebrew leader who returned to his homeland to help his people rebuild the wall around Jerusalem.

6. This book includes 150 poems, seventy-three of which are ascribed to David.
   An Outline of the Bible: Book by Book, Landis, p. 48

7. This book includes the well-known story of the Hebrew man cast into the lions' den. God, who sent an angel to shut the lions' mouths, saved him.

8. This eighteenth book of the Bible is named for the man whose life and words are recorded therein. He was a good man from "the land of Uz": who suffered many misfortunes until "the Lord blessed the latter end of his life."

Esther	Isaiah	Ruth	Psalms
Nehemiah	Genesis	Job	Daniel

Old Testament Husbands and Wives

Please identify the person described by choosing a name from the list at the bottom of this page.

1. Please name the Jewish king who had seven hundred wives, most of whom were foreign. *I Kings 11:1–4*

2. A resident of Sodom, this wife is remembered as the woman who was disobedient to an angel's command. She "looked back" at the city as it was being destroyed and "became a pillar of salt." *Genesis 19:15–26*

3. What husband served Laban a total of fourteen years for his wife, but "they seemed unto him but a few days, for the love he had to her"? *Genesis 29:18, 20*

4. Abigail gathered provisions, including bread, wine, raisins, and cakes of figs, for David and his men. To whom was Abigail married at that time? *I Samuel 25:14–20*

5. Abraham's servant travelled to the city of Nahor in Mesopotamia with the objective of finding a bride for Isaac. At a well near the city, Abraham's servant met a beautiful young woman with a pitcher who generously offered to draw water for his camels. Please name this damsel, a daughter of Bethuel, who became Isaac's wife. *Genesis 24:51–67*

6. Manoah's wife is one of a number of women in the Bible who bears no name of her own but is known as a certain man's wife. Her story is told in the book of Judges. An angel of the Lord appears unto her and says, "thou shalt conceive, and bear a son." Who is the son of Manoah and his wife? *Judges 13:2–24*

7. After the death of her first husband, Ruth and her mother-in-law, Naomi, moved to Bethlehem. Please name Ruth's second husband. *Ruth 4:13*

Nabal   Boaz   Lot's wife   Solomon   Rebekah   Jacob   Samson

Old Testament People

Please match the descriptions below with a name from the bottom of the page.

1. Although this king asked for "an understanding heart" early in his reign, his later life was marked by excessive indulgence. He "did evil in the sight of the Lord; and went not fully after the Lord, as did David his father." *I Kings 11:6*

2. Who was the leader of the Hebrew people when the walls of Jericho fell? *Joshua 6:1–20*

3. What prophet ascended into heaven by a whirlwind? *II Kings 2:11*

4. What was the new name given to Jacob at Peniel after he spent the night wrestling with "a man"? *Genesis 32:24–30*

5. Who was called out of prison to interpret a Pharaoh's dream? *Genesis 41:14–16*

6. Moses' older brother helped him lead the children of Israel out of Egypt. What was his name? *Exodus 7:1, 2, 7*

7. This king of Judah was the son of Asa. He did "that which was right in the sight of the Lord," and reigned twenty-five years. *II Chronicles 20:31–33*

8. This man of God was both a prophet and a judge. The son of Elkanah and Hannah, he "judged Israel all the days of his life." *I Samuel 7:15*

9. After Nebuchadnezzar, king of Babylon, besieged Jerusalem, he took certain Hebrews captive. One of the young people brought to the king's palace "purposed in his heart that he would not defile himself with the portion of the king's meat." Please name him. *Daniel 1:8*

| Elijah | Samuel | Joshua | Aaron | Joseph |
| Solomon | Israel | Daniel | Jehoshaphat | |

Old Testament Places

The list of places at the bottom of this page will help you answer the following questions. A Bible dictionary is also a helpful resource.

1. Please name the place where Moses prayed and made the bitter water sweet. *Exodus 15:22–26*

2. The walls of this city fell at the loud blast of trumpets. *Joshua 6:1, 20*

3. God commanded the prophet Jonah to preach in this great city. *Jonah 1:2*

4. Naaman was healed of leprosy after he washed seven times in this river. *II Kings 5:10–14*

5. On a plain in the land of Shinar, the people said, "let us build us a city and a tower, whose top may reach unto heaven...." Please name this ancient city. *Genesis 11:1–9*

6. Nehemiah helped rebuild the walls of which city? *Nehemiah 2:13; 6:15*

7. Please name "the mountain of God" where Moses saw a burning bush and heard God call him "out of the midst of the bush." *Exodus 3:1–4*

8. When Moses led the children of Israel out of Egypt, they walked on "dry ground" through the Red Sea. Please name the river Joshua and the children of Israel "passed over on dry ground." *Joshua 3:17*

9. A "great woman" and her husband lived in a town of Canaan. When Elisha came to town, she invited him to "eat bread." In return, Elisha prayed and she bore a son. Please name the town where this "great woman" lived. *II Kings 4:8*

10. This city of ancient Sumer (later known as Babylonia and still later occupied by the Chaldeans) was the birthplace of Abraham. *Genesis 11:28, 31; 15:7*

Babel	Jerusalem	Jericho	Horeb	Ur
Jordan	Nineveh	Marah	Shunem	

Old Testament Who's Who

Please match each description below with the correct Bible character listed at the bottom of the page.

1. Who built an ark to protect his family and the animals from the flood?
   Genesis 6:13, 14

2. What was Abraham's name before the Lord appeared unto him and said, "I will make my covenant between me and thee"? *Genesis 17:1–9*

3. Who was Jacob's father? *Genesis 25:21–28*

4. Who worked seven years for a wife and got her sister instead? *Genesis 29:16–30*

5. Who was the sister of Aaron and Moses who watched over the ark which contained baby Moses? *Exodus 2:1–10; 15:20–22*

6. What Bible character asked God this question: "Who am I, that I should go unto Pharaoh, and that I should bring forth the children of Israel out of Egypt"? *Exodus 3:11*

7. Who healed Naaman of leprosy? *II Kings 5:1–15*

8. Who said, "the Lord that delivered me out of the paw of the lion, and out of the paw of the bear, he will deliver me out of the hand of this Philistine"?
   I Samuel 17:37

9. What little boy in the Old Testament learned to listen to God after jumping out of bed and going to Eli, his teacher, three times? *I Samuel 3:1–10*

10. Jesus refers to a prophecy made by "Esaias" while in the synagogue at Nazareth. What Old Testament prophet is called Esaias in the New Testament? *Luke 4:16–21*

Isaac	Miriam	Jacob	Isaiah	David
Noah	Elisha	Samuel	Abram	Moses

The Christmas Story

Please read: *Matthew 1:18–25; 2:1–23* and *Luke 1:21–35, 37, 38; 2:1–20*

1. In what town was Jesus born? *Matthew 2:1–6; Micah 5:2*

2. Who was told by an angel that "with God nothing shall be impossible"? *Luke 1:37*

3. Why was Jesus born in a manger, rather than the inn? *Luke 2:7*

4. The angel of the Lord said: "Fear not: for, behold, I bring you good tidings of great joy, which shall be to all people. For unto you is born this day in the city of David a Saviour, which is Christ the Lord." To whom was the angel speaking? *Luke 2:8–11*

5. Who came to see the infant Jesus? *Matthew 2:7–11; Luke 2:15, 16*

6. What did the wise men bring Jesus? *Matthew 2:7–11*

7. How were the wise men from the east warned that they should not return to Herod after worshipping Christ Jesus in the manger? Matthew 2:12 (Herod the Great is the Herod mentioned in the Nativity stories. To distinguish among the Herods mentioned in the New Testament, see *The New Westminster Dictionary of the Bible*, pp. 379–384.)

8. Why did Joseph take Mary and the baby Jesus to Egypt? *Matthew 2:13, 14*

9. Please fill in the blanks: "Glory to _____ in the highest, and on earth _____, good will toward men." *Luke 2:14*

The Beatitudes

Please read Christ Jesus' Sermon on the Mount, chapters five through seven of Matthew. Then complete each of the following Beatitudes.

1. Blessed are the meek:

2. Blessed are the pure in heart:

3. Blessed are the poor in spirit:

4. Blessed are ye, when men shall revile you, and

5. Blessed are they which do hunger and

6. Blessed are they that mourn:

7. Blessed are the peacemakers:

8. Blessed are the merciful:

9. Blessed are they which are persecuted for righteousness' sake:

Christ Jesus' Healings

1. In the Gospel account of ten lepers healed by Christ Jesus, how many turned back to give thanks? *Luke 17:11–19*

2. The Gospels record our Saviour healing the following four people. What do they have in common besides being healed by Jesus?
    a. man with a withered hand *Matthew 12:1–13*
    b. man with an unclean spirit *Mark 1:21–28; Luke 4:31–37*
    c. woman bowed together for eighteen years *Luke 13:11–17*
    d. man with dropsy in Pharisee's house *Luke 14:1–6*

3. Did Jesus of Nazareth heal Zacchaeus of sickness or sin? *Luke 19:1–10*

4. The Gospels record the Nazarene healing the following four people. What do they have in common besides being healed by Jesus?
    a. Jairus's daughter *Matthew 9:18, 19, 23–26*
    b. Syrophenician woman's daughter *Mark 7:24–30*
    c. epileptic boy *Luke 9:38–4*
    d. nobleman's son *John 4:46–54*

5. Who wanted Christ Jesus to come to Capernaum to heal his son and said: "Sir, come down ere my child die"? *John 4:49*

6. Christ Jesus raised three people from the dead during his three-year ministry. Please name them. *Luke 7:11–16; Luke 8:40–42,49–56; John 11:1–44*

7. Jesus healed people with many different diseases. Please match the following maladies with the one who was healed. *Matthew 8:5–15; Mark 7:24–30;10:46–52*

1. Peter's wife's mother	a. blindness
2. centurion's servant	b. a fever
3. Syrophenician woman's daughter	c. palsy
4. Bartimaeus	d. an unclean spirit

Christ Jesus' Parables

1. In Jesus' parable of the sower and the seed, in what four places does the seed fall?
   Mark 4:3–8; 14–20

2. In the parable of the sower and the seed, what is Jesus' interpretation of the seed?
   Mark 4:3–8; 14–20

3. In the parable of the ten virgins, what do the five foolish virgins request from the five wise virgins?   *Matthew 25:1–13*

4. Please name at least three qualities the Good Samaritan expresses.   *Luke 10:25–37*

5. What three things does the woman who loses one of her ten pieces of silver do?
   Luke 15: 8,9

6. What happens to the prodigal son's inheritance?   *Luke 15: 11-32*

7. In the parable of the tares and wheat, an enemy sowed tares, or weeds, among the wheat "while men slept." Who said, "let both grow together until the harvest"?
   Matthew 13:24–30; 36–43

8. Jesus compares the kingdom of heaven to a merchant man, seeking goodly pearls. What does the merchant man do when he finds "one pearl of great price"?
   Matthew 13:45, 46

The Twelve Disciples

Please see the following citations in the Bible which list the names of the twelve disciples of Christ Jesus: *Matthew 10:2–4; Mark 3:16–19; Luke 6:13–16; Acts 1:13.* You will note that these lists are not identical. The books use different names for the same person. For example, Bartholomew is the same as Nathanael; Thaddaeus is another name for Judas the brother of James.

1. Please list Jesus' twelve disciples.

    a. ———————————————— g. ————————————————

    b. ———————————————— h. ————————————————

    c. ———————————————— i. ————————————————

    d. ———————————————— j. ————————————————

    e. ———————————————— k. ————————————————

    f. ———————————————— l. ————————————————

2. What did Jesus do all night before he chose his twelve disciples? *Luke 6:12, 13*

3. One of Jesus' twelve disciples was Nathanael. This name is used only in the Gospel of John, but it is believed to refer to the person called Bartholomew in the other three Gospels. Please read how Nathanael became a disciple in *John 1:44–50.* Who was the other disciple who came to Nathanael and said: "We have found him, of whom Moses in the law, and the prophets, did write, Jesus of Nazareth, the son of Joseph"?

4. Who worked at "the receipt of custom" (the tax office) when Jesus said, "Follow me"? *Matthew 9:9; Mark 2:14; Luke 5:27, 28*

5. Please name the two sons of Zebedee. *Matthew 4:18–22*

6. Three of the disciples were accorded the special privilege of being present at the following events: the healing of Jairus's daughter, the transfiguration, and in Gethsemane the evening of Jesus' betrayal. Please name these three disciples. *Luke 8:51; 9:28–36; Matthew 26:36, 37*

Easter Story People

Please match each description with a name from the bottom of the page.

1. On the day before he was crucified, Christ Jesus shared the passover feast with his twelve disciples. After eating, Jesus prepared to wash his disciples' feet. Who said, "Thou shalt never wash my feet"? *John 13:1–14*

2. In the garden of Gethsemane, Simon Peter cut off the right ear of the high priest's servant. Luke records that Jesus "touched his ear, and healed him." Please name the servant. *Luke 22:51; John 18:10*

3. After his arrest, Jesus faced two Jewish trials. Jesus appeared first before Annas. Then he was bound and sent to the council (later known as the Sanhedrin) and the high priest. Please name the high priest. *Matthew 26:57–68; John 18:13*

4. The Roman civil trial followed the Jewish trials. Only the Roman governor could lawfully put a man to death. The chief priests accused Jesus of treason, and this governor was forced to make a decision. Please name the Roman governor who pronounced Jesus' death sentence. *John 19:15, 16*

5. Who asked the Roman authority for the body of Jesus? *John 19:38, 41, 42*

6. In John's version of the resurrection, who first came to the sepulchre and "seeth the stone taken away"? *John 20:1*

7. After the resurrection, two of Jesus' followers saw him as they walked along the road to Emmaus, a town about seven miles from Jerusalem. Please give the name of one of these disciples. *Luke 24:13–35*

8. Of the twelve disciples, who said, "Except I shall see in his hands the print of the nails...I will not believe"? *John 20:24, 25*

Mary Magdalene	Malchus	Pilate	Caiaphas
Simon Peter	Thomas	Cleopas	Joseph of Arimathaea

Gospel People

Please use a Bible dictionary to help you identify the person described. A list of names is included at the bottom of this page.

1. He was a ruler of the synagogue and a Pharisee. He asked Jesus to heal his twelve-year-old daughter. *Mark 5:22–43*

2. He was a member of the governing council known as the Sanhedrin, who secretly followed Jesus. After the crucifixion, he put Jesus' body in his own new tomb. *Matthew 27:57–60*

3. He was the Roman governor who agreed to crucify Jesus after he "washed his hands" of the whole matter. *Matthew 27:1, 2, 24*

4. This Pharisee came to Jesus by night to ask questions. *John 3:1–7; John 19:38, 39*

5. This son of Zechariah and Elisabeth became a preacher who lived in the wilderness. He baptized people in preparation for the coming of the Messiah. *Matthew 3:1–6; Luke 1:5–44*

6. After his resurrection, Christ Jesus first appeared to this woman. *Mark 16:9; John 20:11–17*

7. After witnessing Jesus' transfiguration, this disciple suggested that they build three tabernacles. *Mark 9:2–10*

8. This king built major palaces throughout Israel. He wanted to kill the baby Jesus. *Matthew 2:16*

Peter	Jairus	Joseph of Arimathaea	Herod the Great
Nicodemus	Pilate	John the Baptist	Mary Magdalene

The Acts of the Apostles

Please answer these questions with a name from the bottom of this page.

1. There was a man of Ethiopia who had great authority under Candace, queen of the Ethiopians. He had charge of all her treasure and had come to Jerusalem to worship. Who baptized this man? *Acts 8:26–40*

2. Of the twelve disciples, who came down to Lydda and healed a man named Aeneas, who had kept his bed eight years, and was sick of the palsy? *Acts 9:32–35*

3. Who healed the crippled man at Lystra? *Acts 14:8–10*

4. What was the name of the woman in Joppa who was "full of good works" and who made "coats and garments"? Simon Peter raised her from the dead. *Acts 9:36–41*

5. Many members of the early Christian church were gathered together praying for Peter's release from prison. Please name the young damsel who excitedly informed them that their prayer was answered—Peter was at the gate! *Acts 12:5–11*

6. Please name the sorcerer in Samaria who long "bewitched the people" with sorceries, but was converted to Christianity by Philip the evangelist. *Acts 8:5–24*

7. "Paul was long preaching," and this young man fell into a deep sleep "and fell down from the third loft, and was taken up dead." Paul healed him. Please name the young man. *Acts 20:7–12*

8. Please name the Pharisee who said, "Refrain from these men, and let them alone: for if this counsel or this work be of men, it will come to nought: But if it be of God, ye cannot overthrow it: lest haply ye be found even to fight against God." *Acts 5:34–39*

Eutychus	Simon	Dorcas	Philip the evangelist
Rhoda	Peter	Gamaliel	Paul

Paul

1. According to the book of Acts, where was Paul born? *Acts 21:40–22:3*

2. Who was the disciple in Damascus who was obedient to God's command in a vision and healed Saul (later known as Paul) of his blindness? *Acts 9:10–18*

3. Some Jews plotted to kill Saul. The disciples helped Saul escape at night by lowering him down the city wall in a basket. Please name the city. *Acts 9:19–25 Then*

4. For his second missionary journey, "Paul chose Silas" to accompany him. In Philippi they met a woman who made her living by selling purple dyes or dyed goods. She listened to Paul and was baptized. Please name her. *Acts 15:40; 16:12–15*

5. In which city did Paul see an altar with the inscription, "TO THE UNKNOWN GOD"? *Acts 17:22, 23*

6. Paul was once long preaching when a man "being fallen into a deep sleep... fell down from the third loft, and was taken up dead." Paul healed him. Please name the man Paul healed. *Acts 20:9–12*

7. Who was the king who said to Paul, "Almost thou persuadest me to be a Christian"? *Acts 25:23–26:32*

8. Please name the centurion in charge of Paul and the other prisoners who were shipwrecked on their way to Italy. *Acts 27:1, 2, 20–24, 41–44*

9. What was the name of the island to which Paul and the other shipwrecked passengers escaped? *Acts 28:1*

10. Please name Paul's teacher in the law. This teacher was a member of the supreme governing council and a Pharisee highly respected by the Hebrew people. *Acts 22:3*

New Testament Husbands and Wives

Please match the following descriptions to the people listed below.

1. Married to the Roman governor of Judea and accompanying her husband to Jerusalem, this wife had a disturbing dream about Jesus. The book of Matthew relates her story: "his wife sent unto him, saying, have thou nothing to do with that just man: for I have suffered many things this day in a dream because of him." Please identify her. *Matthew 27:19*

2. Priscilla, also called Prisca, was "one of the most influential women in the New Testament Church." She and her husband lived first in Corinth, later in Ephesus, and finally in Rome. Originally a tentmaker, Priscilla hosted the apostle Paul, taught "the word of God" to others, and provided a meeting place for early Christians in her home. Please name Priscilla's husband. *Acts 18: 1–4, 18, 19, 24–26; Romans 16:1–5; I Corinthians 16:19; II Timothy 4:19; All of the Women of the Bible, pp. 227–230*

3. The author of Luke tells the story of Elisabeth, the mother of John the Baptist. While Elisabeth was expecting John, she hosted her cousin, Mary, who was expecting the baby Jesus. Please name Elisabeth's husband. *Luke 1:5–80*

4. John the Baptist condemned the marriage of Herodias to her second husband. John knew that the couple had indulged in an adulterous affair before their marriage, and that both had divorced their first spouse. Because John had the courage to speak out against this union, Herodias wanted him dead. Her evil influence caused John to be beheaded. Please name Herodias's second husband. *Matthew 14:3, 6; Mark 6:17, 19, 22; Luke 3:19; A Commentary on The Holy Bible, Dummelow, "The Dynasty of the Herods," p. lxxxvi*

5. This fisherman's wife and mother of two disciples, James and John, said to Jesus: "Grant that these my two sons may sit, the one on thy right hand, and the other on the left, in thy kingdom." Please name her. *Matthew 4:21, 22; 20:20–22*

Herod Antipas   Zebedee's wife   Zacharias   Pilate's wife   Aquila

New Testament Places

Please match the place names below with the following descriptions.

1. Where did Jesus live after Mary and Joseph returned with him from Egypt?
   Matthew 2:23

2. What city did Jesus visit at age twelve? *Luke 2:42*

3. Where was Jesus baptized? *Mark 1:9*

4. Where did Jesus attend a wedding and turn the water to wine? *John 2:1*

5. Where was Jesus when he raised from death the only son of a widow?
   Luke 7:11–15

6. What was the name of the town of Mary and Martha? Here Jesus raised their brother, Lazarus, from the dead. *John 11:1–44*

7. Where was the apostle Paul born? *Acts 9:11*

8. Where did Paul see an altar erected "TO THE UNKNOWN GOD"? *Acts 17:22,23*

9. Where was Paul when a poisonous snake bit him but he "felt no harm"? *Acts 28:1–5*

10. Where were the followers of Christ Jesus first called Christians? *Acts 11:19–26*

11. Where did John write the book of Revelation? *Revelation 1:9*

Antioch	Athens	Bethany	Cana of Galilee	Jerusalem	Nain
Jordan	Melita	Isle of Patmos	Nazareth	Tarsus	

New Testament Who's Who

Please match each description with a name from below.

1. This man at Lydda was bedridden for eight years with palsy. His restoration to health through prayer resulted in a large increase of the church in that region. *Acts 9:32–35*

2. This devout centurion lived in Caesarea and was baptized by Peter. His experience marked the beginning of the calling of Gentiles to Christianity and revealed that nationality was not a factor in the church. *Acts, ch. 10*

3. This robber and murderer was a notorious prisoner when Jesus was arrested. Pilate, anxious to release Jesus, offered the Jews the option of releasing this man or Jesus. They chose to release this man. *Matthew 27:16–26; Mark 15:7–15; Luke 23:18; John 18:28–40*

4. He was an early Christian who travelled with Paul on a missionary journey. They visited Cyprus, Perga, Pisidian Antioch, Iconium, Lystra, and Derbe. *Acts 13:4 to 14:28*

5. A just and devout man, he learned from the Holy Spirit "that he should not see death, before he had seen the Lord's Christ." Coming into the temple when Joseph and Mary had just brought in the infant Jesus, this man recognized him as the promised Messiah. *Luke 2:25–35*

6. He was a well-known companion and assistant to Paul. Paul refers to him as "my beloved son, and faithful in the Lord." *I Corinthians 4:17*

7. He was an early Christian martyr. *Acts 7:51 to 8:2*

8. One of the twelve disciples, he was probably the same person as Bartholomew. *John 1:45–51*

Timotheus	Barnabas	Aeneas	Barabbas
Stephen	Nathanael	Cornelius	Simeon

Biblical Vocabulary

Please match each vocabulary question with an answer from the bottom of this page. Please use a regular dictionary or a Bible dictionary to look up definitions.

1. Please give another word for "an authoritative teacher of God's will" or one who instructs men in God's ways, helping others deal with the present and the past. *The New Westminster Dictionary of the Bible*, p. 766.

2. This stringed instrument is mentioned twenty-eight times in the King James Version of the Bible.

3. The lame man shall "leap as an hart" writes Isaiah. What is an *hart*? *Isaiah 35:6*

4. This Jewish feast, also called the feast of unleavened bread, celebrates "the rescue of the Israelites from Egypt." *Young People's Bible Dictionary*, Smith, p. 112

5. People with this infectious skin disease "were forced to live apart from others and to warn anyone of their presence or approach so that people might avoid them." *Young People's Bible Dictionary*, Smith, p. 94

6. Who has been called the Prince of Peace, Saviour, and "the prince of the kings of the earth?" *Isaiah 9:6; Acts 5:31; Revelation 1:5*

7. What does *prodigal* mean? *Luke 15:11–32*

8. In New Testament times, these people were members of one of the major religious parties of the Jews. They emphasized strict and detailed conformity with the law and the traditions. *Young People's Bible Dictionary*, Smith, p. 114

passover	Christ Jesus	leprosy	Pharisees
prophet	psaltery	a male deer	reckless/extravagant

Vocabulary Match

Please match each question with an answer from the bottom of the page.

1. Paul writes: "Though I speak with the tongues of men and of angels, and have not charity, I am become as sounding brass, or a tinkling cymbal." What does *charity* mean?
   I Corinthians 13:1

2. What is an *epistle*?

3. During the time of Joseph, there was a famine "over all the face of the earth...." What is a *famine*? *Genesis 41:56*

4. Jesus said: "And other sheep I have, which are not of this fold: them also I must bring, and they shall hear my voice; and there shall be one fold and one shepherd." Please define a *fold*. *John 10:16*

5. Jonathan, King Saul's son, "had a son that was lame of his feet." What does *lame* mean?
   II Samuel 4:4

6. The Beatitudes say that the merciful are blessed. What does *merciful* mean? *Matthew 5:7*

7. Who were the *patriarchs*?

8. In Psalms we find this short prayer: "Preserve me, O God: for in thee do I put my trust." What does *preserve* mean? *Psalms 16:1*

A pen or enclosure for sheep.

Love and good will.

Founding fathers of the Hebrew nation: Abraham, Isaac, Jacob and Joseph.

An extreme scarcity of food.

A letter.

Compassionate.

Having a disabled limb.

Protect; save.

Prayer

1. Where in the Bible can you find the Lord's Prayer? Please tell the book, the chapter, and the verses.

2. Please tell at least two things we learn about how to pray from Christ Jesus' parable of the Pharisee and the publican? *Luke 18:9–14*

3. "Ye shall know the truth, and the truth shall make you free." Who said this? *John 8:32*

4. Please look up James 5:16 and write the sentence that begins: "The effectual fervent prayer...."

5. What prophetic words did Jesus say to his disciples about the future of healing? *John 14:12*

6. Psalm 42 is described as an "ardent prayer." It begins: "As the hart panteth after the water brooks, so panteth my soul after thee, O God." What is a *hart*? *An Outline of the Bible: Book by Book*, Landis, p. 50; see a dictionary, regular or Bible, for the definition.

7. "Now Hannah, she spake in her heart; only her lips moved, but her voice was not heard...." This passage is an example of silent prayer to God. What did Hannah desire? *I Samuel 1:13*

Kings

Please match the king described with a name from the list below.

1. The prophet Samuel anointed the first king of Israel. Please name him.
   I Samuel 9:1–3, 14–17; I Samuel 10:1, 24

2. Of the kings of Israel, who was once a young shepherd who slayed the Philistine, Goliath? *I Samuel 17:1–50*

3. When David's son became king of Israel, he asked for an understanding heart, that he might justly judge the people. Please name him. *I Kings 3:5–14*

4. For many years in Bible times, foreign kings ruled the Hebrew people. Who was the king of Babylon who cast Shadrach, Meshach and Abed-nego into a fiery furnace when they refused to worship idols? *Daniel 3:1–30*

5. Please name the Persian king who reigned when God protected Daniel in the lions' den. *Daniel 6:1–28*

6. Who was the king of Persia who allowed his cupbearer to return to Jerusalem to rebuild the walls? *Nehemiah 2:1–6*

7. An angel told Mary: "thou shalt...bring forth a son...and the Lord God shall give unto him the throne of his father David: And he shall reign over the house of Jacob for ever; and of his kingdom there shall be no end." Who was this king to be? *Luke 1:30–33*

8. Who was the English king who appointed forty-seven scholars to prepare a new English translation of the Bible in 1604?

| Nebuchadnezzar | David | Christ Jesus | Saul |
| Artaxerxes | Darius | Solomon | James I |

Mothers

Please match the mothers listed below with the correct description.

1. Samson's mother entertained an angel of the Lord. She was "reverent and silent and obedient" to the angel's voice. *Judges 13:2, 11, 19–23; All of the Women of the Bible,* Deen, p. 325

2. When this great woman's beloved son died suddenly, she went to Elisha, a man of God, for help. Elisha raised her son from death. *II Kings 4:8–37*

3. The mother of Samuel, the last of the judges, prayed fervently for a son. She consecrated Samuel to the Lord, and he went to live with the priest Eli in Shiloh. Each year she made Samuel a new coat. *I Samuel 1:2–22; 2:1, 21*

4. Married to Zacharias, this godly woman was the mother of John the Baptist and a cousin to Mary, Jesus' mother. *Luke 1:5, 6, 13, 24, 36, 40, 41, 57*

5. Abraham's servant chose this woman to be Isaac's wife. After twenty years of marriage, she gave birth to twins, Jacob and Esau. *Genesis 25:25, 26*

6. The mother of Solomon became King David's wife after her first husband, Uriah, was placed in the forefront of the hottest battle and died. She was "very beautiful to look upon." *II Samuel 11:3; 12:24; I Kings 1:11, 15, 16, 28, 31; 2:13, 18, 19*

7. The angel Gabriel said of the mother of Jesus: "Blessed art thou among women." *Luke 1:28, 42*

8. The mother of Isaac is listed with others of outstanding faith in chapter 11 of Hebrews. She "was delivered of a child when she was past age, because she judged him faithful who had promised." *Hebrews 11:1*

| the Shunammite | Elisabeth | Bathsheba | Manoah's wife |
| Rebekah | Mary | Hannah | Sarah |

Women of the Bible

Please match each description with a name from the list below.

1. Who was told by an angel that "with God nothing shall be impossible"? *Luke 1:37*

2. Please name the two sisters of Lazarus of Bethany. *John 11:1, 2*

3. To whom did Jesus first appear after the resurrection? *Mark 16:9; John 20:11–17*

4. Simon Peter raised a woman from death in Joppa. She made "coats and garments" and was "full of good works." Please name her. *Acts 9:36–41*

5. Who was tempted by a talking serpent to eat the forbidden fruit from the tree of knowledge of good and evil? *Genesis 3:1–6*

6. Who helped Jacob deceive his father, Isaac, and cheat Esau out of his father's blessing? *Genesis 27:1–44*

7. Please name Jacob's two wives. *Genesis 29:9–30*

8. Who left her own country and people to follow her mother-in-law to Bethlehem? *Ruth 1:11–22*

9. Please name the Hebrew woman whose daughter-in-law came from Moab. *Ruth 1:11–22*

10. Which Old Testament book, besides Ruth, is named for a woman?

Leah and Rachel	Esther	Rebekah	Mary Magdalene	Mary
Mary and Martha	Naomi	Eve	Dorcas	Ruth

Who Said This?

From the list below, choose the name of the person who said the following words.

1. "I am come a light into the world, that whosoever believeth on me should not abide in darkness." *John 12:46*

2. "I looked on all the works that my hands had wrought...and behold, all was vanity and vexation of spirit, and there was no profit under the sun." *Ecclesiastes 2:11*

3. "Silver and gold have I none; but such as I have give I thee...." *Acts 3:6*

4. "Fear ye not, stand still, and see the salvation of the Lord, which he will shew to you to day...." *Exodus 14:13*

5. "He that cometh after me is mightier than I, whose shoes I am not worthy to bear ... whose fan is in his hand...." *Matthew 3:11*

6. "Lord, now lettest thou thy servant depart in peace, according to thy word: for mine eyes have seen thy salvation, which thou hast prepared before the face of all people; a light to lighten the Gentiles, and the glory of thy people Israel." *Luke 2:29–32*

7. "Fear not: for they that be with us are more than they that be with them." *II Kings 6:16*

8. "Give therefore thy servant an understanding heart to judge thy people, that I may discern between good and bad...." *I Kings 3:9*

9. "Speak; for thy servant heareth." *I Samuel 3:10*

10. "What is truth?" *John 18:38*

| the Preacher | Simon Peter | Samuel | Solomon | Elisha |
| Christ Jesus | John the Baptist | Moses | Simeon | Pilate |

Z Words

Please choose an answer from the list below.

1. Please name a wealthy tax collector of Jericho who climbed a tree to see Jesus.
    Luke 19:1–10

2. Who was the father of John the Baptist and husband to Elisabeth?
    Luke 1:523, 57–80

3. At Leah's request, this maidservant became the secondary wife of Jacob. She is the mother of Jacob's sons, Gad and Asher. Please name her. *Genesis 30:913*

4. This fisherman was the husband of Salome, and the father of two disciples—James and John. *Matthew 4:21, 22*

5. These two books of the Bible are the ninth and eleventh books of the minor prophets in the Old Testament.

6. Please name one of the hills on which Jerusalem stood. This name is often used for the whole of Jerusalem. *Psalm 48:1, 2*

7. This woman, a daughter of Jethro, priest of Midian, became the wife of Moses.
    Exodus 2:21, 22

8. Who was the tenth son of Jacob, and the sixth by Leah? *Genesis 30:19, 20*

9. A widow from this town gave Elijah a home during a famine. As a reward for her faith, her oil and meal failed not, and her boy was brought back to life. *I Kings 17:8–24*

Zebulun	Zarephath	Zilpah	Zipporah	Zacchaeus
Zechariah	Zebedee	Zacharias	Zephaniah	Zion

VII. BIBLIOGRAPHY

Bibles:

Albright, William Foxwell, and David Noel Freedman, eds. *The Anchor Bible.*, 40 vols., Garden City: Doubleday, 1964–1970.

The Amplified Bible, Expanded Edition. Grand Rapids, Michigan: Zondervan, 1987.

Chamberlin, Roy B., and Herman Feldman. *The Dartmouth Bible: An Abridgment of the King James Version, with Aids to its Understanding as History and Literature, and as a Source of Religious Experience.* Boston, Massachusetts: Houghton Mifflin Co., 1961.

Good News for Modern Man (The New Testament in Today's English Version). New York: American Bible Society, 1966.

Hastings, Selina. *The Children's Illustrated Bible.* New York: Dorling Kindersley, 1994.

The Holy Bible, Authorized King James Version. England: Eyre & Spottiswoode Limited.

Interpreter's Bible (in 12 volumes). Nashville, Tennessee: Abingdon Press, 1952–1957.

Metzger, Bruce M., ed. *The Reader's Digest Bible: Condensed from the Revised Standard Version.* Pleasantville, New York: The Reader's Digest Association, 1982.

Moffatt, James. *The Bible: A New Translation.* New York: Harper and Brothers Publishers, 1954,

The New English Bible. New York: Oxford University Press, 1961.

The One Year Chronological Bible, New International Version. Wheaton, Illinois: Tyndale House Publishers, Inc., 1995.

Phillips, J. B. *The New Testament in Modern English, Revised Edition.* New York: Macmillan Publishing Co., 1972.

Other Sources:

Please note that some of the following sources are dated. Though all these books have been helpful to me, I would recommend that Sunday School teachers rely on books which take advantage of recent developments in Bible scholarship.

Anderson, Bernhard W. *Understanding the Old Testament,* Fourth Edition. Englewood Cliffs, New Jersey: Prentice-Hall, Inc., 1986.

Armstrong, Karen. *A History of God: The 4,000-Year Quest of Judaism, Christianity and Islam.* New York: Ballantine Books, 1993.

Becker, M. L., ed. *The Book of Bible Stories: Old and New Testaments.* The World Publishing Co., 1948.

Blair, Edward Payson. *Abingdon Bible Handbook.* Nashville, Tennessee: Abingdon Press, 1975.

Bowen, Barbara M. *Strange Scriptures that Perplex the Western Mind.* Grand Rapids, Michigan: William B. Eerdmans Publishing Co., 1944.

Carey, Elizabeth L. *The Commands of Jesus.* Etna, New Hampshire: Nebbadoon Press, 1997.

Carlinsky, Dan. *The Complete Bible Quiz Book.* New York: Gramercy, 1976.

Chase, Mary Ellen. *The Bible and the Common Reader.* New York: Macmillan, 1994.

Christian, Kristy L., and Kathryn L. Merrill. *Paul and Early Christianity.* 2 vols. Oklahoma: Infinite Discovery, 1996.

Christian, Kristy L., and Kathryn L. Merrill. *In Jesus' Times.* Oklahoma: Infinite Discovery, 1991.

Chute, Marchette. *The Search for God.* New York: E. P. Dutton, 1941.

Concord, A Study Package. Boston, Massachusetts: The First Church of Christ, Scientist, 1999.

Connolly, Peter. *Living in the Time of Jesus of Nazareth.* Israel: Steimatzky, 1983.

Cruden's Complete Concordance to the Bible. Grand Rapids: Zondervan, 1949.

Darling, Frank C. *Biblical Healing: Hebrew and Christian Roots.* Boulder, Colorado: Vista Publications, 1989.

Deen, Edith. *All the Women of the Bible.* New York: Harper, 1955.

Dodd, C. H. *The Bible Today.* Cambridge: Cambridge University Press, 1965.

Dore, Gustave. *The Dore Bible Illustrations.* New York: Dover Publications, Inc., 1974.

Dummelow, J. R., ed. A *Commentary on The Holy Bible.* New York: Macmillan Publishing Co., Inc., 1908, (Thirty-fifth printing, 1973.)

Eddy, Mary Baker. *Church Manual of The First Church of Christ, Scientist.* Boston: The First Church of Christ, Scientist, 1895, 1936. (Note, especially, Article XX Sunday School.)

Eddy, Mary Baker. *Science and Heath with Key to the Scriptures.* Boston: The First Church of Christ, Scientist, 1909, 1971.

Frank, Harry Thomas. *Discovering the Biblical World.* Maplewood, New Jersey: Hammond, 1975.

Forsee, Aylesa. *They Trusted God: Bible Stories Retold.* Boston, Massachusetts: The Christian Science Publishing Society, 1980.

Fosdick, Harry Emerson. *A Guide to Understanding the Bible.* New York: Harper and Row, 1938.

Friedman, Richard Elliott. *Who Wrote the Bible?* San Francisco: HarperSanFrancisco, 1987.

Gardner, Joseph L., ed. *Reader's Digest Atlas of the Bible.* Pleasantville, NY: Reader's Digest, 1981.

Garland, George Frederick. *The Power of God to Heal.* Harrington Park, New Jersey: Robert H. Sommer, Publisher, 1973.

Garland, George Frederick. *Subject Guide to Bible Stories.* Harrington Park, New Jersey: Robert H. Sommer, Publisher, 1969.

Gehman, Henry Snyder, ed. *The New Westminster Dictionary of the Bible.* Philadelphia: Westminster Press, 1970.

Goodspeed, Edgar J., *How Came the Bible.* Nashville: Abingdon, 1979.

Goodspeed, Edgar J., *Paul.* Philadelphia: John C. Winston Co., 1947.

Grosvenor, Melville Bell, and Frederick G. Vosburgh, eds. *Everyday Life in Bible Times.* Washington, DC: National Geographic Society, 1967.

Hoyt, Edyth Armstrong. *Studies in the Bible for the Modern Reader.* Ann Arbor: Edwards Brothers, Inc., 1963.

Kee, Howard Clark, Eric M. Meyers, John Rogerson, Anthony J. Saldarini. *The Cambridge Companion to the Bible.* Cambridge, United Kingdom: Cambridge University Press, 1997.

Landis, Benson Y., *An Outline of the Bible: Book by Book.* HarperCollins, 1994.

Lang, J. Stephen, *The Complete Book of Bible Trivia*. Wheaton, Illinois: Tyndale House Publishers, Inc., 1988.

Leishman, Thomas Linton. *Continuity of the Bible*. 5 vols. Boston, Massachusetts: Christian Science Publishing Society, 1966–77.

Levey , Judith S., and Agnes Greenhall, eds. *The Concise Columbia Encyclopedia*. New York: Columbia University Press, 1983.

Lockyer, Herbert. *All the Men of the Bible*. Grand Rapids, Michigan: Zondervan, 1958.

Miller, Madeleine S., and J. Lane Miller. *Harper's Bible Dictionary, Seventh Edition*. New York: Harper & Row, 1961.

Over 6,000 Bible Questions and Answers. Nashville, Tennessee: Thomas Nelson Publishers, 1987.

Putcamp, Ann. *Guide for Bible Teaching*. 3 vols. Boston, Massachusetts: Christian Science Publishing Society, 1971, 1973, 1975.

Robinson, Russell D. *Teaching the Scriptures, Sixth Edition*. Milwaukee, Wisconsin: Bible Study Press, 1993.

Shotwell, Berenice Myers. *Getting Better Acquainted with Your Bible*. Kennebunkport, Maine: Shadwold Press, 1972.

Smith, Barbara. *Young People's Bible Dictionary*. Philadelphia: Westminster Press, 1965.

Terrien, Samuel. *The Golden Bible Atlas*. New York: Golden Press, 1957.

Trammell, Mary Metzner, and William G. Dawley. *The Reforming Power of the Scriptures: A Biography of the English Bible*. Boston, Massachusetts: The Christian Science Publishing Society, 1996.

Trench, R. C. *Notes on the Parables of Our Lord*. Grand Rapids, Michigan: Baker, 1948.

Trench, R. C. *Notes on the Miracles of Our Lord*. Grand Rapids, Michigan: Baker, 1949.

Waggener, Florence E. *The Story of the Old Testament Simply Told*. Hicksville, New York: Exposition Press, 1979.

Wangerin, Walter, Jr. *The Book of God: The Bible as a Novel*. Grand Rapids, Michigan: Zondervan Publishing House, 1996.

Wright, G. Ernest. *Biblical Archaeology, Abridged Edition*. Philadelphia: The Westminster Press, 1960.

Ward, Kaari, ed. *Jesus and His Times*. Pleasantville, New York: Reader's Digest Association, 1987.

Willmington, H. L. *Willmington's Guide to the Bible*. Wheaton, Illinois: Tyndale House Publishers, 1981.

Notes

That Ye May Teach the Children

VIII. Index

N

O

P

Q

R

V

Vulgate 12, 13, 178

W

wedding 106, 124, 227

X

Xerxes 75, 76, 212

Y

Yahweh 92, 178, 179, 181

Z

This book was designed by Michael Höhne
with the types Palatino, ITC Eras, Myriad Tilt, and Cloister Black
using QuarkXPress on Macintosh equipment.

Ordering Information

That Ye May Teach the Children: A Bible outline with questions for parents and teachers and related products are available directly from the publishers, Bible Teaching Press. We appreciate your support.

How to contract Bible Teaching Press:
- telephone   304 - 876 - 1332
- email: snipes@principia.edu
- fax: 304 - 876 - 6685 (call first)

Contact us for information about *That Ye May Teach the Children:*
- to obtain descriptive flyers
- if you are interested in *That Ye May Teach the Children* in a flashcard format with questions and answers

For more information about *That Ye May Teach the Children* **see:**
- www.sbpbooks.com

For more information about the author, Joan Koelle Snipes, see:
- www.authorsden.com

For more information about the illustrator, Kristin Joy Pratt Serafini, see:
- www.serafinistudios.com

To order Bible Teaching Press products:

1. Please fill out your shipping address and contact information below:

Name: _____

Address: _____

City: _____ *State:* _____ *Zip:* _____

Phone: _____ *Email:* _____

2. Contact us for quantity discount information.

3. Send the above form along with a check payable to:

Bible Teaching Press
2016 Willowdale Drive
Shepherdstown, WV 25443

Ordering Information

That Ye May Teach the Children: A Bible outline with questions for parents and teachers and related products are available directly from the publishers, Bible Teaching Press. We appreciate your support.

How to contact Bible Teaching Press:
- telephone   304 - 876 - 1332
- email: snipes@principia.edu
- fax: 304 - 876 - 6685 (call first)

Contact us for information about *That Ye May Teach the Children:*
- to obtain descriptive flyers
- if you are interested in *That Ye May Teach the Children* in a flashcard format with questions and answers

For more information about *That Ye May Teach the Children* see:
- www.sbpbooks.com

For more information about the author, Joan Koelle Snipes, see:
www.authorsden.com

For more information about the illustrator, Kristin Joy Pratt Serafini, see:
www.serafinistudios.com

To order Bible Teaching Press products:

1. Please fill out your shipping address and contact information below:

Name: _____

Address: _____

City: _____ State: _____ Zip: _____

Phone: _____ Email: _____

2. Contact us for quantity discount information.

3. Send the above form along with a check payable to:

Bible Teaching Press
2016 Willowdale Drive
Shepherdstown, WV 25443

What others are saying about this book,

That We May Teach the Children

"What a treasure this book is — a real gift to parents and teach-ers. Above all, it's a boon to the children. You have devoted yourself — mind and heart — to something obviously dear to you. Your love for your subject fairly shines through each page. Bravo to you!"

Beverly Jean Scott, Sunday School teacher, Camden, Maine

"This book is a gold mine of ideas for teacher, parent, grand-parent, or anyone interested in ideas for teaching children about the Bible. It is 'reader friendly'. It inspires and encour-ages even the most reluctant teacher."

Penny D. Seay, Sunday School teacher, St. Louis, Missouri

"Your new book is marvelous! Thank you for the time and love that went into the preparation of this."

Barbara Wallace, Sunday School teacher, Arlington, Virginia

"For any parent seeking to school their own children or anyone who teaches in a Christian Sunday school, this excellent new book should be at the top of your list to read and use."

Alan Caruba, Editor, October 2000 issue of Bookviews, on the Internet at http://www.bookviews.com